Hardcover Edition
ISBN-13: 979-8-9890130-7-4
© 2024 Andreas Johansson

Published by Harker Press
http://HarkerPress.com
Book Design by Dustin McNeill

ESCAPE ARTISTS VOL. 2

ESCAPE FROM L.A. INTERVIEWS

ANDREAS JOHANSSON

TABLE OF CONTENTS

* This is a vintage interview / article.

INTRODUCTION

Who am I? Just a nut/loner from Sweden. I first saw the *Escape* movies back in 1997 and they immediately became a part of my DNA. Since 2002, I've become the biggest online authority on these films. (Should I seek help?)

Why do I like John Carpenter's *Escape* movies so much? The hero is much darker and cynical than usual, but is also a man of honor because he's incorruptible. Additionally, he's played by a guy named Kurt Russell, who made an unredeemable and disillusioned asshole named Snake Plissken an intriguing and sympathetic character. Furthermore, the director is a stylistic, prescient, and subversive guy named John Carpenter. He's dark and cynical as well, but doesn't take himself too seriously. I enjoy that he had fun with the sequel and basically remade his own movie, exaggerated it, and forced his hero to go through another similar mission that won't change things much. I find *Escape From L.A.* to be a very funny and rebellious movie with interesting themes about freedom.

Why did I do these books? When I did my first interview in 2011 for myself and fellow fans online, I never expected this to be the end result. Therefore, I want to sincerely thank all 113 interviewees for making these books possible. Hearing your stories, getting to know you a little bit, and preserving movie history is a BIG honor. John Carpenter rightfully puts his name above the title, but many people brought these cult classics to life and contributed to their legacy. I dedicate these books to you and your kindness.

Who else would I like to thank? Alexander Büttner, Brad Mathis, Carol Allen, Dana Ross, Daniel Schweiger, David Williams at *American Cinematographer*, Denise Davis, Erica Pearce, Ian Walker, Joe Diaz, Joseph B. Mauceri, Nigel Watson at *Talking Pictures*, Roger Romage, Tara Ansley at *Fangoria*, and everyone who helped me with contact information.

/Andreas

Author's Note: Some questions will be repetitive and scaled down for consistency and simplicity. Some interviews will also be a bit more personal than others.

Top: The Swedish logo for *Escape From L.A.*
Bottom: The author.

ENJOY!

Joseph B. Mauceri Makes His Escape From L.A. with Director John Carpenter

by Joseph B. Mauceri

1998: Forces hostile to the United States grow strong in the late 20th Century. A great moral crisis grips the nation as social revolution and a breakdown of the criminal justice system threaten society. To protect and defend its citizens, the United States Police Force is formed.

1999: The population of Los Angeles grows to forty million. The city is ravaged by crime and immorality. A Presidential candidate predicts a millennium earthquake will destroy the city in divine retribution.

2000: An earthquake measuring 9.6 on the Richter scale hits at 12:59 PM, August 23rd, in the year 2000. After the devastation, the constitution is amended, and the newly elected President accepts a lifetime term of office. Fearing a massive terrorist invasion from South America, the United States prepares for war. The Great Wall is built along the southern border, cutting off the flow of illegal aliens.

Street gangs, South American terrorists, and the criminally insane capture Los Angeles, the once great City of Angels. Now an island on the border of civilization, L.A. is a no-man's land of chaos, anarchy, and darkness. The United States Police Force, like an army, is encamped in the San Gabriel Mountains. The President's first act as Permanent Commander in Chief is Directive 17: protect the United States from this island of the damned, Hell on Earth.

2013: NOW!

- From the screenplay *Escape From L.A.*

8

Enemy forces are threatening the borders of the United States and the President's daughter has disappeared with the prototype of a secret weapon into the island of Los Angeles. The clock is ticking and their only hope resides in Snake Plissken, the cult antihero of *Escape From New York*. The stakes have been raised as Snake has been infected with a fatal virus, the antidote of which is his when he returns with the prototype. From John Carpenter, Debra Hill, and Kurt Russell comes John Carpenter's *Escape From L.A.* The film reunites the trio who worked on *Escape From New York*. The film is written by Carpenter, Hill and Russell, and is produced by Hill and Russell.

Kurt Russell reprises his role as Snake Plissken. As Snake searches for the prototype, he encounters many of L.A.'s unique inhabitants, including Pipeline played by Peter Fonda, Steve Buscemi as "Map to the Stars Eddie," the grizzly Surgeon General of Beverly Hills played by Bruce Campbell, and Pam Grier is Hershe, a.k.a. Carjack Malone. Also joining the cast are Stacy Keach and Cliff Robertson.

Escape From L.A. marks the eighteenth feature directed by John Carpenter. Screenwriter for both motion pictures and television, composer, television director, and producer, Carpenter is responsible for some of the most memorable cinematic nightmares ever to grace the screen, such as *The Thing*, *Halloween,* and *The Fog*. An alchemist of the cinema, he is able to take meager budgets and produce films that look as if they cost more. His first directorial sequel, *Escape From L.A.*, is the best sequel to explode onto the screen since *Terminator 2: Judgment Day*. So strap yourself in for an over the top, out of control, peddle to the metal, futuristic action adventure, as we talk with John Carpenter.

With more than ten years between *Escape From New York* and *Escape From L.A.*, were you worried about returning to this material? Also, it's been a while since you've done a real action-adventure film?

We actually wrote *Escape From New York* in 1974, and didn't start shooting it until 1981. So that makes it more like twenty years for me. A week or two before we began principle photography I was sitting around the house agonizing over the style of this film. *Escape From New York* was made with the vision of a young man's ideas. I'm an old veteran now and I see things differently. I worried that I won't be able to get back in the saddle again. On the first day, the first shoot, I looked around and realized, "What am I worrying about?" It was like riding a bicycle, you just climb on and off you go.

In the past we've talked about the fact that you don't like to do sequels. Why *Escape From L.A.*?

Hell, it's fun working with Kurt. He said that, of all the characters he has ever played, Snake Plissken is the only one he would like to play again. Snake is a classic character that you don't need to change. No one knows exactly who he is or where he comes from, but you know he's the baddest man in a bad world and he definitely takes care of business. This movie is basically what I call cowboy noir. It's a dark western placed in the future.

There was also a story with a little subversive message to it. The good old U.S. of A has become a theocracy that deports the morally guilty to L.A. They send atheists, teenage runaways, abortion doctors, etc, removing them from the new "moral" America. In addition, L.A. has just been through riots, mudslides, fires, and earthquakes. I think it was after the earthquake in Los Angeles when Kurt came to me and said, "I think it's time for us to do to L.A. what we did to New York." Kurt had this great idea that all these disasters happen and we're all sitting around in denial, not wanting to leave. That was the germ of it. So it was a combination of a good plot with a little subversive juice. Also, I thought we'd have some fun.

Escape From L.A. reunites you with Debra Hill, producer and co-writer, and Kurt Russell, who plays Snake Plissken and also did some work on the script.

Kurt is an amazing character. His work is almost invisible, and I enjoy that. He's extremely funny and doesn't show off. I think we all brought a greater ambition to this project, and you're going to see that, especially in terms of what you'll see on the screen.

A major reason for that is I had more toys at my disposal because this is a bigger budget film with a bigger studio. When we did *Escape From New York*, we were working for Avco Embassy, an independent film company, with a seven million dollar budget. Things were so tight on that on the first day of shooting that we had to use a sound cart as a dolly when our Panaglide broke down. We didn't have to worry about things like that on this film, and the budget allowed us more time to get the shots we wanted. After all, movie making is a question about time. How much coverage can you get in a scene, and how many setups do you get? Back in those days, I would've been forced into doing a big master scene in one shot, I get a couple of takes, and then have to move onto the next because we just didn't have the time.

L-R/BG: Unknown [Extra], John Carpenter [Director/Co-Writer/Co-Composer], Unknown [Extra]/FG: Johnny Torres [Extra] (Photo courtesy Johnny Torres)

I had the chance to read the June 23 draft of the script. There were some stylistic changes between that and the finished film, and some scenes were deleted. How many drafts did you Debra and Kurt do?

Many, many drafts. Kurt, Debra, and I did a lot of writing on this, and I think I worked harder on this script than any other I've written. Writing is not my favorite part of filmmaking. It's hard work, you're lonely, and there's not a lot of perks to it. You've just got to crank out the pages, and that's tough when you're a pre-computer writer. I take a little more time on a script because I'm a little ancient in my abilities. I have an electric typewriter with a little memory. I write, and rewrite and it's painful, but somebody's got to do it.

However, I know you enjoy composing the music for your films, and the opportunity to work with other musicians.

Indeed. I have a little studio set up in my home and I do most of the melodic "sketches." As a composer, I'm a carpet guy. I'm the guy who comes in and you say, "Hey, I've got a scene here." I stare at it and say, "It needs some help," so I carpet it to help you get through the scene and emphasize it. It's like laying down carpet in your home so that you have a pleasant time.

Do you generate those melodic "sketches" like storyboards, or do you get any inspirations while you're shooting the film?

I've tried that before, but it doesn't work. I revisited the theme for *Escape From New York* in this film, but Shirley Walker and I have brought it into the 90s.

What was the most challenging aspect of *Escape From L.A.*?

It was very physically and emotionally challenging. The entire story takes place at night. You really can't get through seventy days of mostly night shoots on just adrenaline and coffee. You need a strong will, and some good shoes.

There seems to be this underlying theme in your films, which I think really began with *Prince of Darkness* and carries through in *Escape From L.A.*, where the good guys don't seem to trust each other or get along, while the evil guys are able to get together to achieve their end. A good example of that is the alien children in *Village of the Damned*.

It's an observation of life. True evil really gets organized and dedicated. All you have to do is look at the Nazis. Before we entered the war, there were people who were Nazi sympathizers, and we were arguing and bickering with each other. It took the bombing of Pearl Harbor for us to say, "That's enough." Just look at our country today. We've got these Christian identity folks who want to start a race war. They say they need to get rid of all the Jews and blacks. They're white, Christian, right-winged racists called Freemen and Militiamen. They're organized without a leader. I take the side of the guys who try and maintain order. You know, none of us get along. We're not as organized as they are because we're not as crazy and evil.

A lot of us who grew up with Saturday Matinees and late night horror hosts have been greatly disappointed by the majority of the horror films being made these days. I was wondering what your thoughts are on the lack of good horror movies?

I hear that question all the time. I attended a French film festival recently and that was all anyone talked about. I was talking with Tobe Hooper, Charles Russell, Frank Darabont, and we all wondered why the ideas for horror movies are either so bad or not supported by the audience?

I think the problem is a lack of support by the fans and audience alike. The market for horror has dropped forty percent over the last three years. Horror movies go direct to video now. So people blame it on the demise of the drive-in theaters, but I don't believe that. They go direct to video because of small budgets. Now, maybe that's because the ideas aren't original. The critics are complaining that what we're doing is recycling old ideas and old themes over and over again.

Look at Francis Coppola's *Dracula*. It's also a movie about Vlad the Impaler. It wasn't a brilliant film, but people went to see it. *Interview with the Vampire* succeeded because of its stars and because it was based on a very popular series of novels. It wasn't an original idea, but it was popular.

Last summer there was *Species*, an *Alien* kind of picture. The actress, a model, took her clothes off a lot, which was fun to watch. She was supposed to be lurking around, but there wasn't anything scary about it. It was a hit. I think that's the level audiences can tolerate now. The popularity of the old-fashioned horror movie, where you're screaming and jumping, is gone.

The problem is that original ideas in horror films are not supported. You, the fans and audience, are not going to see them. You're not curious anymore, and that's the problem for all of us. If you love horror, or science fiction, or westerns, if you want to see something different on the screen, you have to get out there and support it by seeing it.

Speaking of supporting good horror, I've had the pleasure of enjoying the recent LaserDisc releases of *The Fog, Escape From New York, Halloween, Assault on Precinct 13*, and *In the Mouth of Madness*, which feature your commentary. I was wondering if there was any talks about doing a special LaserDisc release of *The Thing*?

Yes, there is. Universal is coming out with a Signature Series LaserDisc version. Kurt and I narrate the second audio track. We got all the cast and crew speaking on camera about *The Thing*. It's funny that, while it has this gigantic video afterlife, some people still think of it as being slightly above pornography. It was a very strong film for its time. Audiences had never seen a monster like that before. Even *Alien* wasn't as vicious as *The Thing*. I don't think American audiences were ready or were particularly interested in an invader from outer space like this. I was seeing the movie as a parable of our times. I was seeing a whole different film. The AIDS virus was just a little blurb.

The Thing was a virus that got into your blood. It's also a lot like the world we live in right now. Not only can we not trust that we don't have diseases or that we're not some kind of killer inside, but we also don't trust each other because of skin color or ideology.

[*This article first appeared in* World of Fandom *(Vol 2, Issue 27, Summer, 1996) and appears here courtesy Joseph B. Mauceri.*]

John Carpenter [Director/Co-Writer/Co-Composer]
at *Escape From L.A.*'s German premiere.
(Photo Courtesy Alamy)

Seeing with Snake Eyes: An Interview with Kurt Russell [Extended]

by Carol Allen

[September 11, 1996: Kurt Russell lights up a cigarette.]

I don't want my kids to do it. I didn't want to smoke, but there are some pleasures of life I think are worth that, at least at this age. Hopefully, I may get to ninety and I may say, "God I wish I hadn't done that," but I hope I don't, I hope I have the courage to stand there and say, "You know, I had a lot of fun."

If you live your whole life in fear, you're never going to get round to living.

One of the things that I've talked about when I've been talking about this movie [*Escape From L.A.*] is, I really do think we need a minister of fun, as much as we need a minister of safety. The country is swamped in living more safely, living longer, the quality of life - the quality of the individual's desire seems it's just not at the moment what the world's about to a lot of people in America. I'd rather do what I wanna do. I mean, I thought that's what that place was about [laughs].

Let's come back to that. When did the film open in America and how's it done?

It opened up August 9th after the Olympics. It's gone down interestingly, it's doing ok. It's doing better than the original [*Escape From New York*] did in its initial release. I think it's going to go down exactly as the original did. It's a picture we made because, over fifteen years, the audience for the other one grew. We meant to make a picture that would feel the same. That is to say that it would not be totally accepted at the time it comes out because it's not a picture that is made that way. I do think that the sensibility of the picture and the way the picture's made and the character in the piece are fairly unique and, as time goes by, I think that once again it will gain an audience. We were talking earlier about political correctness and stuff as in the movie. Though the main character does not concern himself with that, the background is sort of all about that. So the movie came out at an interesting period in time. It couldn't have picked a more

L-R/FG: Unknown [Extra], Unknown [Extra], Johnny Torres [Extra], Kurt Russell [Snake Plissken/Producer/Co-Writer], Unknown [Extra], Unknown [Extra]
(Photo courtesy Johnny Torres)

politically incorrect time as it came out immediately following the Olympics, which was nicely enough, you know, in Atlanta in an American city. For all the reasons concerned, it became kind of patriotic in a certain way, a good feeling of America winning gold medals and overcoming adversity, whatever, and our picture is seen by many as somewhat subversive. You either have a sense of humor or you don't - sometimes you need a little time to sit back and have a laugh.

It's the subversiveness actually I love about it. Coming hard on the heels of _Independence Day_, it's one of the few American action movies I've seen where the American way of life is not worth saving.

The movie is typically American in that it - I think it's a great arena, the science fiction arena, it allows you to look at subject matter in a very, very broad manner, and so this examines a concept, the concept being, I think, that what the left fears most is the right and what the right fears most is the left. What the left fears about the right is there'll be total control, what the right fears about the left is there'll be total anarchy, so I said let's just divide the two up, take them to their extremes and throw this guy down in the middle who doesn't care about either side, either one of them equally, and I think that character is truly American. That guy is singularly American. Don't tread on me and I won't tread on you.

Is this why you wanted to play Snake again?

I suppose part of the reason, but I'm just an actor. I did co-write this with John, but I've worked as a writer on lots of things I've worked on and I just always work to try to get the best movie and the best screenplay we can get to make the best movie. So I like the character, due to certain aspects of playing him, but it wasn't to espouse any political view that I wanted to play the character, it wasn't any of that stuff. I like the feeling of that world, the *Escape From New York/Escape From L.A.* world and I think it's unique and I think the character's ultimately unique. He's a socially unredeemed guy who just wants to survive another sixty seconds - that's how far the world has taken him. I think he's fun to be in a scene playing. I enjoy it as an actor.

It's been suggested there's some of you in him and some of John Carpenter in him?

I think that's true. John is, by nature I think, anti-authoritarian. I am, by nature, libertarian and I don't understand not being able to accept somebody's point of view just in conversation, any more than John can accept being told what to do when he doesn't want to do something. I don't have that much of a problem with that, the character is a combination of some thoughts. Ultimately, he's all of those things - he can't stand authority, he has no regard for it, but he has no regard for it because of a simple incorruptible belief, which is exactly as I said earlier, don't tread on me, just leave me alone, that's all. If you just leave me alone, you don't have any problem from me, but if you're gonna fuck with me, you're dead, and that's the feeling that I have.

How did Snake lose his eye?

That's something John and I have talked about. We reserve some things to ourselves, we always hold that one to ourselves. We've always felt there's many possibilities, one of them being that his other eye's fine [laugh] - he just decided to put an eye patch on one day! We had lots of fan letters as to what happened to Snake's eye and one guy felt that, earlier in World War III in Siberia or somewhere, I forget, he had some gas warfare or something. John and I have some thoughts on that, but some things we keep to ourselves about Snake's personality and statistics.

Can we talk about the America, the L.A. you've created for the film. It does go back to this anti-political correctness idea. It sounds like L.A.'s going to be a load of fun because nobody outside is having any fun.

That's the idea. The incorrect take on the president is that he's a right wing president, Christian coalition guy. I preferred my original thought, which was that he was politically correct - it's a strange mix of political bedfellows. If you take a just left of center president who happens to be politically smart enough to hook up with the Christian coalition, he would have a pretty broad political base. Now let's just take that guy. First of all, it's science fiction, so you're allowed to do, as far as I'm concerned, anything you want. I think your challenge should be that you should take what's possible and take it to the improbably. Let's take that guy and let's give him a vision of a catastrophe in Los Angeles, a religious vision, which he really has. He has that vision and it comes true, bang. Not only does he think he's right, everybody in the United States thinks he's right, so they make him king for a day, bang.

Well, in his dictatorship, which that statement is a right wing type statement but he's not a right wing guy, it's a guy who says, "I'm gonna do what's good for you. Smoking's not good for you, so you're not gonna do that. I'm gonna do what's good for you. Wearing fur is not appreciated by a lot of people, so we're not gonna allow that. Red meat is eventually going to get you, so I'm gonna help you out." So he takes it from the left side of the scale. The biggest fear that person has is he's tired of the crime and fed up with that, so he just takes control of the place to try to clean it up, which he does, probably very successfully. But it's a very boring place now because of all the control and off breaks L.A. in the earthquake. The gangs take it over and he says, "Fine, to hell with it, wall it off and anyone here who's found guilty of a moral crime, cos we're gonna keep this place clean, boom, we'll throw over there."

L.A. is not a prison, as the character Taslima [Valeria Golino] says. This is the only free zone left. The world, that's the prison. So L.A. now is this anarchistic state, which is the exact opposite. It's just out of control, but if you want action, it's going on there. I always felt like it was, what if we're in America in this movie in 2013, if you lived in Phoenix and you wanted to peek over that wall and see what's happening on the other side of the Berlin Wall? You say, "God, sounds like they've having a big party over there, I'd like to see it," and then the president's daughter, you notice, can't stand that she's a teenager, she wants to see the party, so boom, she goes. She's been told all her life it's hell on earth, but when she gets over there it's way worse than she thought, so it's like the existence is so bad in either place. Into the middle of that walks the man who just doesn't care.

There is some lovely dark satire on America today. Beverly Hills as a slum with Map to the Stars Eddie, but he ain't got an air-conditioned coach anymore.

Yeah, he shows you how to get around. And the guy who runs Beverly Hills now is the Surgeon General. Now that, for me, is possible and improbable!

All those face lifts gone wrong.

He discovered this new way, which was fabulous for about ten years, and then things started to fall apart and he realized the only way to keep it going was fresh body parts and hey, you gotta do what you can to survive.

I don't know where the guys here get their food from and I didn't see much sign of booze, cigarettes or drugs or rock and roll.

In the movie, you mean? It's a free zone, so they get it from anywhere they want. Again, it's not a prison. One of the misconceptions of this movie is that L.A.'s a prison [like New York was]. It's not, it's Hotel California. There's a big difference between a prison and Hotel California. Hotel California, you can check out any time you want but you can never leave. Why is that? That was my thinking when I was talking to John. I said, when we dealt with New York, the concept of New York as a prison is one that people totally understand because many people feel that way. But the way people feel about Los Angeles is that you go there and you talk to people and you say, you talk about not liking it, why don't you leave? And it got me to thinking about Pompei because the natural catastrophe that took place in Pompei always fascinated me. 20,000 buried in the rubble there. They all knew that volcano was going off, every one of them knew, and I always used to say to myself, why didn't they leave? So here I am living in

Los Angeles and years ago, went to Rome with the family and I said, hey look Pompei's just down the road, I'm going to see Pompei. Went down to Pompei and looked at it. There's that man, you know, and his wife, they're running away and you can see them looking back and they're frozen in ash. I looked at these quite beautiful homes that were there. You look up on the top of the walls in the homes and you see this pornographic art, really interesting and beautiful and pornographic, and I said, "Oh, there was a party going on. They're having fun, that's why they didn't leave, they went into denial." Obviously, the guy turned to his wife and said, "Honey, don't worry about that volcano, it won't be going off today and, if it does, we may be in Rome shopping that day. Don't worry about it, it's not gonna happen. Whoa. Here it comes!" And I think that in Los Angeles we have to do the same thing. We have these mud slides, riots, fires, we have the earthquake. Eventually, we are all going to have live with and die with this monstrous occurrence that's gonna take place. The only way you can deal with that is, as with cigarette smokers do, jumping on the other side of the scale. I'm not gonna get cancer from smoking cigarettes - you are. So I live in Los Angeles, just like every other Los Angelino and it's the only way you can survive there. But it is fun.

Getting the film off the ground came out of the earthquake of 1994?

In a way. Debra [Hill] said that and that's partially true, partially not. We talked about this back in 1983. I had an idea, *Escape From L.A.*, the earthquake had happened, broken it off, so I had this concept a long time ago. I had that idea for a story that I ran past John, he liked it, we continued the process. We didn't really have time to commit to it, so we gave it to a writer. The writer came back a year or so later. It was ok what he wrote, but it didn't have the same - the character wasn't quite, that guy, the story didn't quite work, didn't really turn us on and we had other things that we were doing so it just didn't happen. Then years went by, we approached it a couple of times, and then in '94, I was doing publicity in Europe and for the umpteenth time people kept asking me, "Do you think you'll ever play that character again, do you think you'll ever do another *Escape*?" And actually, exactly at that time, the Northridge earthquake happened. In the meantime, the Rodney King riots had taken - the rise out of the Rodney King verdict takes place, mud slides were just happening yearly, Santa Ana winds blow, the fires burn the city, all that drive by shooting, it became a city that was being increasingly defined by its violence and natural catastrophes and I came back and told John that, "More than ever, this place is perfect to escape from and put Snake into. I think we should commit ourselves to doing this and John, I think you and I should sit down and write it. If you guys want to do it, I'm interested and we'll go to a point where we look at the script and say, do we want to continue this or not." That was what we did.

You and John wrote it together. Was that a real co-writing thing, both of you contributing dialogue, action, story?

Equally.

You said you'd done this before on other films?

I've written on the last ten years I've worked. Not as much as on this because I didn't do it from scratch. I always took a project that already existed and worked with the writer and the director, but on this one we started from page one.

Do you usually get credited as a writer?

No, I never cared about it. People ask why - as far as I'm concerned, the only thing that matters is what's on the screen. I don't care how it got there. I don't care if the craft serviceman took over the role from leading lady who died the day before shooting. It doesn't make any difference. What matters is what's on screen. I've been involved with many productions, one in particular where I had to wear different caps. I had a lot of pressure from a lot of people to take credit for that. It didn't matter to me. I'm an actor for hire, that's what I am. As long as my input can help the movie, whether that be in a producing effort, a directing effort, whether that be in a writing effort, it doesn't matter who does it. I am experienced at it and, if I can sit down with each scene with the director and the writer and the actors, be part of making the scene better, however I can do that to help the picture, that's what I do.

In this instance, because we were starting from scratch, we felt it was important that my involvement and the commitment be displayed for the studios that were going to become involved. We just started out as the three of us together. This was our project, this was who was directing it, who was writing it, who was producing it, here's the screenplay, we'll walk in the door, who wants to do it, who wants to buy it, is anyone going to be interested? That was the only reason I took credit on this.

How about the producing element? Have you been involved in that before?

Very much.

Is this the first time officially?

First time I've had a credit, yeah. You see, people are fascinated by that. You guys make people like me want to take credit because it puts some sort of importance on it. It doesn't matter that I didn't get credit for producing *Tombstone*.

No, but it does matter that you had some power and input?

I did. So did the craft serviceman. So did the wardrobe man. My makeup man helps me come up with lines. I don't know how to explain that, except that all that matters is the movie. The individual effort should be thrown out the window in terms of ego so you can combine as a team on a movie. Cos everybody on a movie is equally involved and I don't care how small or large your job is in terms of what the media wants to know about what you did. Sometimes the finest moments of the movie can come from the set photographer - one simple idea that suddenly becomes the defining moment of the movie, it doesn't matter who does it, it matters that it got done. So yeah, I've spent a lot of time producing, I've spent a lot of time directing, I've spent a lot of time writing and, on this picture, because I started from the beginning with John and Debra, I decided to do that. I worked hard on *Breakdown* in terms of writing with the director, in terms of helping the producer get the movie produced. I don't care to take a credit, it doesn't matter. What matters is whether the movie works or not for an audience thirty years from now.

I guess what I'm getting at and why we're so fascinated by it, is there have been stars in the past, certainly in the old studio days, who were just pushed around?

Well, there's also been stars who just can't get enough. It just ain't enough to star in a movie, now they've gotta write it. It's not enough to write and star, now they've gotta direct it. I don't criticize - I criticize to the point where I say, "How much do you want? How much do you have to let the world know what you did?" I don't get it. It's just not a part of what makes me interested in the process. The only thing that makes me interested is just down at the end - because it's all - all we do on the set is just gather garbage to throw in the mill to be edited - that's where you make the movie and we're just out there putting stuff that's going to be put together and I dunno. I've a real personal problem with the need for lots of recognition. I also think it's pointless - it's pointless to me. I understand it, I guess everyone wants to be Orson Welles and no one is Orson Welles. You can be as effective as you want to be on a movie and, by either way if you get to the point, I understand, if you get to the point where you're disappointed in the outcome of the movies, you get to that point, you know what? Absolutely. Hopefully, your knowledge will be strong enough, it's time for you to direct, because it's a director's medium. That medium is a director's medium. He or she is responsible ultimately for the outcome of the movie.

Is that coming next - do you have a desire to direct a movie?

No, the input I have on them right now is fine.

In the opening scenes of the film, you're wearing the same costume that you wore fifteen years ago when you were only thirty and now you're forty-five, that seems to imply you ain't put no weight on?

I had it because I helped design the first costume and I just had a special affinity for the character and I thought, "You know, I'd like to know where it started." I put it on, I was able to get into it. I've been fortunate, I guess, that I haven't altered that much. Probably next week things will start to change drastically. [laugh]

Do you work out and all that stuff?

I don't work out that much or take care of myself to the degree that workout people do, but I don't indulge. I don't get more than five or six pounds overweight. I do get in shape when I have to do certain roles and then other roles, I don't do that. For *Escape,* I knew we were going to do seventy nights in a row and I knew it was going to be long and I knew I'd do a lot of physical stuff in the movie, so I said, yeah the character's supposed to be - he's a tough guy, he's physically tough and he's got to be in shape, so I worked out for about three months before we started.

As a European, I get the impression a lot of Americans are obsessed with working out, diet, exercise, the whole healthy lifestyle. It doesn't sound like it's quite your thing?

Again, I know a lot of people who like to feel as good as they can feel. I find the media is obsessed with writing about it. [GETS PASSIONATE] The media's obsessed with it. I don't find the people I know who work out obsessed about it. But the media's obsessed with pinpointing. They must know what that is, they must know how to write about that, they must know how to write about that person, and all they can do is pigeonhole that person as an idiot who works out, a blockhead who works out. I know people who are in relatively good shape, they feel good, they're fit, but intelligent people they seem to me. It's a far cry from photo ops with President Clinton running and then dropping into a McDonalds for three or four Big Macs. That's not what it's about, no. I think that it's not a phase or a fad or a craze. I think that it stems from fear and America, my generation being this big fat number of people, is obsessed with fear of death now and they're gonna stave it off as best they can. I'd assume that's normal behavior, except that they're doing it in larger numbers now and those people who were ten years old and wanted to be writers are now forty-five and they are writers and those people who started working out twenty-five years ago got a leg up on them.

You had a Hollywood childhood, didn't you? Your dad was a baseball player turned actor and you were a young [child] actor.

I didn't grow up in Hollywood. I grew up in Thousand Oaks, California and then I moved to outside of the valley and then I moved to Colorado. I started playing ball when I was nine. I started playing semi pro ball when I was thirteen. I grew up in the world of baseball, not the world of Hollywood. I don't know what town we could call baseball to be able to pinpoint that, but the motion picture industry is centered in Hollywood. Baseball is centered in Southern California. So I grew up in Southern California with those guys in that world, that mindset, and I was fortunate enough to be able to act from the age of nine and make money. Then when I got injured out of baseball, I joined my career and I began to pay attention to my career and to pay attention more to what Hollywood was about. Three years later, I moved out of Hollywood and moved to Colorado.

So, through your childhood, acting was a nice way of earning pocket money?

Well, for a nine-year-old kid to be able to earn $110 in one day compared to $10 for a paper round, the economics were obvious even to a nine-year-old. I forfeited a lot of money in my teens and early twenties to play baseball, cos I was making $600 a month playing ball, but I was hoping for the big league, which by the way it still runs in the family. My nephew just got called up to the Mets the day before yesterday, he's there. That means a lot in our family. I can think of no other job that is as much fun and pays you that much money as that business and that, as they say, is great work if you can get it. I've been fortunate enough to get it.

How did you get into movies? Through your father?

I got into movies because of my dad, because he was an actor. He went on an interview for a job with Micky Mennel and Roger Meris, two very famous New York Yankees in 1961 and he came home and told me there was a part for a ten-year-old kid in it and I said, "You mean the kid who gets that part gets to be with Micky Mennel and Roger Merris all day?" They were legendary ball players, and he said, "Yeah." I said, "Boy, I'd love to meet them," so I called his agent and I went to his agent and I got an interview and I was able to get a reading. They'd already cast the movie, but they felt bad for this ten year old kid, so they let me read and I said to my dad, "Is that what you do," and he said, "Yeah, that's all there is to it." And I said, "Boy I see why you like doing this." So I called his agent and I said, "Look, I wanna do this, I want to get a commercial or small parts or something," and you understand, in those days it took three days to shoot a half hour show, it took six days to shoot an hour's show, so if I did three or four shows during a year, I was not in my normal element as it were for a grand total of three or four weeks a year, so that was the offshoot.

Of course, that's the only thing people can visualize about my past is that I was working when I was nine, so obviously, I must have been living the life of Shirley Temple. I didn't really have much to do with it, except that I got the script, I'd learn my lines, go on the set, have a good time for three days and make more money than I could possibly imagine. That continued to expand and grow, but never really to my detriment. I never became involved in Hollywood or any of what the Hollywood perception of life is. It just wasn't part of my life.

So you were more interested in baseball?

I was only interested in baseball at that time. But as I got to acting, I did get an increasing appreciation of what was fun about it - I always liked making a show, that was fun, and I got an increasing appreciation for the fun I could have as an actor, so when I was twenty-three and I was injured out of baseball,

I in a short period of time did consciously transfer my feelings of desire about doing something to acting. In that regard, I do love watching and recreating life and people and I became very interested in acting. For the last twenty years now, I've involved myself with that world and learned about it and became very appreciative of the fact that you can do some great things in entertainment.

After you had that baseball injury, your first major role was playing Elvis for John Carpenter, wasn't it?

Actually yes, it was my first major role, but there was a role before that - it was a TV movie called *Deadly Tower* that was really more affective on my career. I played the role of Charles Whitman, who shot forty-six people from a tower in Texas, he just went nuts, and I got cast in that role. That really was truly casting against type and it opened up Hollywood's eyes to me. They said "Whoa, we really didn't see him in that role." A couple of years after that was when *Elvis* came along and that was an opportunity to do an acting job that was very splashy and colorful and could have been disastrous. They like that, when you could be disastrous and it worked and then they said, "Jeez, that was quite a surprise."

And then I did *Used Cars* after that, which was, again, extremely different from anything like *Elvis* and they were honestly confused. I remember my agent talking to me at the time saying, "This town really doesn't know where to put you anymore." And John had *Escape From New York* and the studio really did not want me for that, John fought for me and I did it. And when that came out, then, as my agent again said, "They've just thrown their arms up, they don't know what you are, they're realizing they had you all wrong, they just don't know where to put you. This is a very dangerous place to be because in this town they like to be able to know what you are," and I said, "I'll tell you what I am. I'm an actor." I'm going to make my living for however long I make it in this business playing different people. There will be times when I hopefully will play the kind of person that they're able to put their finger on and call for instance, a "leading man" or call for instance an "action actor" or call for instance a "dramatic actor" or "comedic actor," and so it's been throughout my career, whatever job I did last, that's the next twenty-five scripts I get.

Isn't that so with everyone though?

No, it's certainly not true for Schwarzenegger, Stallone, Bruce Willis. Do you see Tom Hanks in *Escape From L.A.*?

Well, it would be a very different interpretation.

You're not answering the question. They like to find specifically what you do, then they can promote it. They're able then to say, "Okay, we know how to promote this person as well as the movie to the audience." It's more difficult for them to take an actor who is basically, at heart, a character actor. There's no persona they can promote. In the last three years, they've been far more comfortable in trying to promote me as an action actor, when in fact what I did in *Executive Decision* was play the guy who was not the action man. I don't care, it doesn't make any difference to me because I'm still fortunate enough just to keep on going and enjoying myself and getting paid lots of money and all that, so I've no complaints. I've been completely satisfied.

Have you and John been friends since *Elvis*?

Yeah, we struck up, I think, a unique friendship at that time and it has remained.

This is only your fourth film together, one gets the impression you've made lots but it is only four?

Five [*Elvis, Escape From NY, The Thing, Big Trouble in Little China, Escape From LA*].

Here you are in this rather anarchic film playing this guy who doesn't give a shit either way and yet, in many ways, going to your private life, apart from the fact that you haven't married - an unconventional thing - you have about one of the most stable partnerships in Hollywood [with Goldie Hawn] - the epitome of family values. That's how it appears.

Well, my particular view of family values and Goldie's particular view, that's the thing doesn't make sense there. We've been together for almost fourteen years, we're extremely happy together. We do not live our lives like any other married couple that I know. We are very happy [lots of laughter] for one. I don't pretend to think I have any magic potion or any corner on the market on how to do that. I'm just as capable of blowing it off as she is. We're aware of that, maybe that helps us. But we don't - I just think it's sometimes there's people who meet who really are destined to love each other forever and be together regardless of how good or bad things are. I feel that's kinda the way Goldie and I are. I've no explanation for it except that I think she's a great, great time.

L-R: Goldie Hawn, Kurt Russell [Snake Plissken/Producer/Co-Writer],
and Pam Grier [Hershe] at the sequel's L.A. premiere.
(Photo courtesy Alamy)

You also have what could have been a difficult family situation mixing your kids, her kids, the kid you have together, there was also I believe Goldie's mum until she died a couple of years ago. That could have been a tricky situation. A lot of people have fallen foul of that one. How did you manage it?

Day to day. Again, it always depends who the people are, that's all that matters. And I think, ultimately, if you love each other, that's all that matters too. There's things about me Goldie doesn't like, vice versa, not enough so I would ever at any moment want to be without her. That's the way we look at life. I don't pretend to speak for next week, neither does she, so I take it for right now and right now has suddenly been thirteen and a half years. It doesn't seem like any time's gone by. I wish I had an answer. Maybe it's good that I don't, I don't know.

Looking for the secrets of these things is actually a load of bullshit, because...

Yeah, that's all there is. It's who the two people are and there's everything that goes into that. Are you still attracted to each other? Do you care to still be attracted? Do you still make each other laugh? Do you still deeply care about the other person's feelings? Then you've got your children and do they matter to you, is it your responsibility, is it what you want to do in life. There's a million things and all - it comes down to what kind of person are you and how do you do it?

Goldie had this image of being a pretty powerful lady. I seem to remember was one of the first women who started producing her own pictures and, since her mother died, she's been very quiet, I believe. But she's got a couple of pictures coming out now, hasn't she?

Yes, she did, for about three years I think she took some stock. Part of it was her mother dying, part of it was the age of our youngest child, part of it was her own desires to not do what she was being offered, part of it was not being offered what she wanted to do, so again, it was a million different things. As fortune would have it, time went by and she got into a frame of mind slowly, I think, of wanting to work for other reasons that she wanted to work for before and so now she's got *First Wives Club* that she did with Bette Midler and Diane Keaton. I think that comes out in America in a couple of weeks. I've got a feeling that's going to be a pretty big number. And she did a picture with Woody Allen, actually before that, an ensemble piece that - he's an interesting director, an interesting writer, very well respected by the critics of America, so therefore someone who an actor likes to work for. Yeah, these two things have come together for Goldie and so boom, she's gonna jump back out there again, which I'm really happy about because I know that she wanted to work when she did work.

You've mentioned you live in L.A.

We live in L.A. most of the time. We have a place in Colorado and I just built a place in Canada recently.

When you say in L.A., in the middle, suburb?

Suburb. There is no L.A., no center, it's one of the pieces of L.A., over by the ocean. Waiting to fall. One of the first to go!

Have you got another movie coming up?

I finished a movie right after *Escape*. I started one about three weeks later, a picture called *Breakdown*, which is about a man and his wife - she's kidnapped. He's a man at the beginning of the movie who very much, I think in a realistic fashion, questions his own courage and remains that character throughout the picture as he very impotently tries to somehow prevent this awful terrorist act from reaching its inevitable conclusion. I finished that a couple of months ago.

Directed by?

Written and directed by a man named Jonathan Mostow. He's a young guy from Harvard, very smart, and I think he's done a good job. I think it's a very good suspense picture.

[*A shorter version of this article first appeared in* Talking Pictures *(Issue 18, Summer, 1996). This expanded version appears here courtesy Carol Allen.*]

COLEMAN LUCK
Commissioned Script Writer

How did you end up being a writer and producer for film and television?

My interest in screenwriting started while I was at university after the Army. I had done advertising writing for years, but had never considered writing for screen. Taking a history of film course sparked the beginning.

How did you get the job of writer for an *Escape From L.A.* script in 1987?

The story behind the script is pretty simple. At the time, I was a writer/producer at Universal working on *The Equalizer* for CBS. I think Carpenter made contact with me through my agency. This was a long time ago. I don't know why he chose me, except that I was known for hard-edged fantasy material. We met at a local restaurant in the San Fernando Valley and talked briefly. He gave me no thoughts about the script at all. There was only one thing that he insisted on: the script had to be a prequel. That was it. I don't know why he made that choice. As far as Carpenter and Russell are concerned, I never had a single conversation about the script with them after it was turned in. What I wrote never got beyond first draft because the day I turned it in, the DeLaurentis Studio went bankrupt. The project became part of the bankruptcy, but I did get paid, which was a miracle. As you know, it stayed in limbo for years and years. When Carpenter finally got it back, it didn't surprise me at all that he tossed my version. I doubt that he even read it again. Truth is, I expected my version to be tossed when I first turned it in.

What got you interested in it?

I was interested in the project because I loved *Escape From New York*. Carpenter sent me off to write whatever came into my mind. I think I did do a treatment before I started the script, which he read but had no comment about. For me, the strength of *Escape From New York* was the dark comedy of it all married to action with a strong clock. The first film took a lot of pokes at New York and I think that's one of the reasons it worked. I wanted to do the same thing with Los Angeles and, of course, the darkest comedy should revolve around Plissken himself.

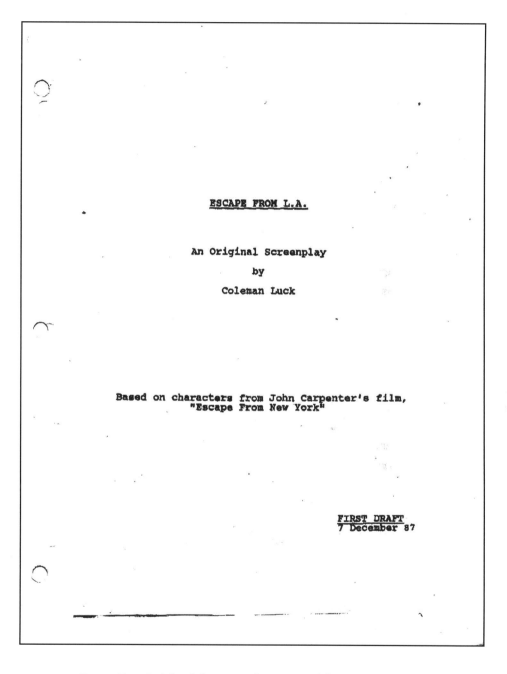

ESCAPE FROM L.A.

An Original Screenplay

by

Coleman Luck

Based on characters from John Carpenter's film,
"Escape From New York"

FIRST DRAFT
7 December 87

Escape From L.A. by Coleman Luck, First Draft [December 7, 1987]
(Courtesy Coleman Luck)

In your script's ending, Snake Plissken turned out to be a clone. Why did you decide to go with that approach?

I liked the idea. It turns the whole *Escape From New York* on its head, which I thought then and still think is great. People would have argued about it forever. You're talking about it and it was never even shot. Plissken freaks would have been shrieking about the clone ending, but I believe they would have bought it the way I wrote it. To say he was a clone is too easy. There was a lot more to it than that. The cloning revelation was really eerie, not just a science fiction cliché.

What material in your script do you like the most and is there anything about that material you'd like to discuss?

The strange thing about writing is that, after you have written it, the thing takes on a life of its own quite apart from you. People come into contact with it and there is an immediacy about it for them that is long past for the writer. I haven't read my version of *Escape From L.A.* in almost twenty-five years and I don't own a copy now. I remember the end and a few scenes such as the traffic jam frozen in place forever with crazy people living in their cars and the insane parade with deadly float wars. I remember the beginning sequence set in Las Vegas By the Sea where Snake participates in an awful game of chance called Bet Your Body Part, etcetera but I couldn't focus on any aspect at this late date and call it my favorite. It was full of things that had never been seen before and were as dark comedy as you can get. And there was plenty of action throughout culminating at Rodent Park, all that was left of Disneyland.

Did you draw any inspiration from being a Vietnam veteran while writing the script? Also, did your experiences as a former soldier somehow affected your interest in Snake Plissken?

I have drawn inspiration throughout my writing career from being a combat soldier and leader when I was young. That and the fact that I have been a Christian for many, many years have created the themes for all of my writing. Combat is not a video game. Killing people, even when it is justified, is a terrible thing and it does not leave you. All of us need the forgiveness of God for our sins. We need His redemption. The situation in the world is so awful that sometimes the only way to deal with it is through dark comedy and over-the-top characters like Snake Plissken. In the script, my view of Los Angeles, a city I love, was a dark parody based on reality.

Why did you sell your only copy of it?

I had no more interest in it and felt that someone else might enjoy it. Having someone pay for it guaranteed that it would go to a person who really wanted it.

What do you think of the final version of *Escape From L.A.* and in what ways do you think your version would've been better?

Everyone who has read it has told me so. They have been incredulous that Carpenter didn't make it, but beyond my script almost any script would have been better than the bucket of warm vomit that he threw at the audience. The truth is, I really don't care what he did or didn't do. It's ancient history.

What are you currently doing and what do you enjoy doing in your spare time?

I'm getting ready to start a new screenwriting project in the new year. Can't talk much about it at this point. I teach a monthly Bible study in Hollywood geared to people in the entertainment industry. The recordings of these are also on my website. Also, I live in beautiful mountains near Yosemite National Park. My wife and I enjoy photography and travel.

Author's Note: Several ideas and dialogue from Coleman Luck's draft were carried over to later drafts/scripts and some even in the final movie such as Snake Plissken being captured in New Las Vegas [early draft], Plissken firing blanks unknowingly with the submachine gun [in movie], Plissken meeting a hooker with a polypropylene condom attached to the inside of her lips [deleted scene], Plissken being chased by man with a metal jaw and fighting with him [early draft], Plissken being warned about bald cats and one dropping on his head [early drafts], Plissken's female companion being shot and killed at a freeway [in movie], a truck with a machine gun firing at a freeway [early draft], Plissken being shot from a dashboard and passing out [in movie], Plissken being driven in a golf cart to an underground control center [early draft], Plissken passing the twin towers of Century City and seeing vagrants clustering around the edge [omitted scene], Plissken passing another building and seeing people having dinner [omitted scene] and seeing a beautiful woman dancing on a narrow girder [deleted scene], the final confrontation taking place at Disneyland [Happy Kingdom by the Sea] [in movie] etcetera. Additional note: The draft was read after interview was conducted.

PETER BRIGGS
Speculative Script Writer

How did you end up being a screenwriter?

Maybe that should be, "How'd you START off being a screenwriter?" But no, you're right. I ended up a screenwriter, but that wasn't the intent. From the outset, I optimistically intended to direct. I'd started in the 80s as an assistant cameraman. Got my union card with the ACTT [The Association of Cinematograph, Television and Allied Technicians] [as the British Film Union was named then] just in time for the British film industry with Goldcrest and Cannon and a bunch of other companies imploding. I'd hoped to chase a directing path from being a cinematographer as a number of leading cameramen were becoming directors at that time and I naively thought I could follow. Candidly, I've a great eye for composition, but I wasn't technically, mathematically a good enough cinematographer. So that could never have happened, even though there were people like director Hugh Hudson and *Indiana Jones* producer Robert Watts who'd seen some sort of something in me and very kindly pushed me forward.

By way of strategizing another path, I'd been writing screenplays for myself for a couple of years and around 1990 thought I'd see if I could get a literary agent to represent me. These were scripts I'd written on a manual ribbon typewriter and I spent a lot of time photocopying and pounding shoe-leather delivering them to agencies. Long story short, I signed with the William Morris Agency and one of the first jobs I got from that was speculatively developing science fiction material for Paramount Pictures, who'd opened a branch in the U.K. to create contingency material in the wake of a then-recent Writers Guild of America strike. Britain, I think still to this day, doesn't have its "Film Head" screwed-on properly in developing commercial material and the process at Paramount was very frustrating. That peaked when I suggested to the head of the London office we develop Robert Heinlein's book *Starship Troopers*. She was scornful and a few weeks later in a big synchronicity Tri-Star Pictures bought those rights for themselves. I realized I was on a hiding to nothing so decided to write on-spec an *Alien vs. Predator* screenplay. It turned out to be a good move as my agent sold it overnight to 20th Century Fox. That lead to me writing on various movies, mostly uncredited, over the next decade. *Freddy vs Jason, War of the Worlds.* That kind of thing. Plus various other "development hell" projects that never saw the light of day but I was the credited co-writer in 2004 with Guillermo Del Toro on the movie *Hellboy.*

How come you wrote an *Escape From L.A.* script in 1994?

It came about in a fairly straightforward way. Back in 1992 or 1993, I'd had my first "baptism-by-fire" when I was hired as a writer on the *Judge Dredd* movie. It'd eventually star Sylvester Stallone and be directed by Danny Cannon, but when I was on it was Arnold Schwarzenegger and Tony Scott. I was one of a wake of casualties of writers on that project and it left me with a resolve to again spec something out in the vein of *Alien vs. Predator.* Something I controlled the writing on from beginning to end instead of being a dancing monkey for a bunch of organ grinders. I loved *Escape From New York* when it was released, and I remembered an interview with John Carpenter [it was either in *Starlog* magazine or the British publication *Starburst.* I forget which] in which Carpenter had mentioned specifically that he was mulling over a sequel, which would be called *Escape From L.A.* So that seemed a natural to have a go at.

To go off on a weird Carpenter connection tangent for a moment, which'll make sense later. Even before I'd gone out to get my first agent, I had in my early pile of sample scripts an adaptation of Robert Mason's memoir *Chickenhawk*, a book about helicopter pilots in Vietnam. The premise had fascinated me and on a whim I decided to write it as an exercise. At that same time, Carpenter had just made *Starman* for which he personally supplied the helicopters to the production from his own company I understand and said in an interview about *Starman* that he'd love to make Mason's *Chickenhawk!* The accumulation of coincidence was too much for me, so I blindly sent that finished [unrepresented] script off in a plain brown envelope to Carpenter's agent at the Gersh Agency in Los Angeles. I never got a response back, so that was that. I figured it'd ended up in a bin somewhere. So flash-forward almost ten years to the early 90s again and me sitting down and deciding to try do an *Escape From L.A. Escape From New York* was one of the first movies I had a VHS copy of in the 80s and it got played a lot. And when CD hit the market late 80s [as a big soundtrack buff], I remember being thrilled at finding a copy of *Die Klapperschlange* as the German CD release of *Escape From New York* was known at Tower Records in Piccadilly Circus. That disc also got a lot of rotation. So *Escape From New York* was sort of a minor obsession for me.

What did you want to accomplish with your *Escape From L.A.* script story-wise?

Well, at the end of *Escape From New York* it's clear Snake has screwed things up and the world's likely gone to war as a result of Donald Pleasence's [President] peace conference failing. So an "L.A." story by extension would have to cope with that aftermath. I was fascinated by Fresno Bob mentioned briefly in that exchange between Harold "Brain" Hellman [Harry Dean Stanton] and Snake. "You know what they did to Bob?" asked Snake about that botched job they'd all pulled years before. Well, something horrible you might think. What if Bob were still alive and Snake didn't know? And Bob being possibly Special Forces Black Light as well as Snake, I imagined they'd have some common history. Bob's specialist military talents might be put to some use somewhere by somebody similarly nefarious.

The story came together surprisingly quickly. This was the 80s and Cyberpunk literature was exploding and William Gibson was its king and kinda my own personal writing hero. If you flip through Gibson's *Burning Chrome* anthology of short stories, that particular story itself featured ex-military cyber cowboys who flew into Leningrad during some future war-that-never-was. I'd read some interviews with Gibson where he talked about how much he loved *Escape From New York* and this aspect of Gibson's *Burning Chrome* was clearly influenced by Carpenter's movie and Snake's own history with Black Light in it. And in turn my *Escape From L.A.* plot had its influence based in Gibson. I pieced the story together using index cards. At some point, my brother Andy came to stay with me in London and I used him as a sounding board for thrashing the story out.

What material in your script do you like the most and is there anything about that material you'd like to discuss?

Well, my story followed on from the ramifications of *Escape From New York*. The peace conference failed. The world went to war. All America's armed forces got hurriedly deployed abroad, so the Homeland [Security] was pretty much unguarded. And the South American drug barons had basically rolled in to America with a massive military invasion force and taken key cities. It wasn't until America's military began to withdraw for home that the pitched battle against the drug lords to retake the cities began. It's mentioned at one point they had to nuke Miami. Poor Miami! And the last city to resist being fully retaken

"ESCAPE FROM L.A."

By

Peter Briggs

FIRST DRAFT, 1994

Please return to:

Stephen M Kenis,
The William Morris Agency,
20th Century Fox House,
31-32 Soho Square London W1D 3HH

Escape From L.A. by Peter Briggs, First Draft [1994]
(Courtesy Peter Briggs)

was Los Angeles. The military had encircled large portions slowly closing in block-by-block, but the cartels had brought with them all kinds of sophisticated military hardware to fight back.

When a U.S. senator who is responsible for steering an upcoming key house land reclamation bill is snatched by the bad guys, Snake [now a freelance bounty hunter] is grabbed from one of his own gigs and brought back. In my story, it was Tommy Atkins' character Rehme from *Escape From New York* who brings Snake in as Lee Van Cleef [Hauk] had died in 1989 and I wanted to keep some continuity in the series. Snake doesn't want any part of Rehme's deal until it's revealed to him that Fresno Bob is alive and well and working with the bad guys. Snake refuses to believe that Bob, ex-special forces, would go work for the scumbags and agrees to fly into L.A. with a pair of B-2 stealth bombers accompanying a team of commandos in powered fighting armor.

As they say, "things go wrong" and Snake and his now depleted team have to trek across tribalized Los Angeles to extract the senator. That was the bare bones. There's a lot looking back on it that I really like about the script. There's a hooker that's locked up in the mansion that had been looking after the senator that reminded me a little bit of the Catwoman/Senator subplot in *The Dark Knight Rises* reading it recently. There's some really nice set pieces. There's a massive hardware-heavy pyrotechnic third act that has what starts off as a sneak infiltration on this drug lord's compound by what's left of the Marines and then escalates into a massive firefight culminating in Snake armed with a hunting knife taking on Bob in a powered fighting suit. Twenty years after I wrote this script, there was something similar in a little movie you might have seen called *Avatar*. I was very much into Japanese Manga comic books with powered armor, so I guess that's where that came from. Bob's a pretty big character throughout the story.

What happened to the script after you had finished it and is it true that John Carpenter, Debra Hill [Producer/Co-Writer] and Kurt Russell never got to read it?

Well, with the script finished, I took it to my agent Steve Kenis, who was then head of William Morris in London. A few years earlier when I'd brought him my *Alien vs. Predator* spec and shoved it across the table towards him, he'd groaned good-naturedly and then we'd gone out and sold the thing in less than a week. I optimistically hoped this might be the same story with *Escape From L.A.*

I sat in his office and he opened the front page and almost immediately gave me a very firm and dismissive "No." I was a little taken aback. In his view, it was an impossible sale. His logic was sound, but it wasn't anything I didn't already know. Avco Embassy had gone bust. The rights were all over the place. His take was, there was nobody to sell the project to and it was a flat-out waste of time. There had to be a solution. I reasoned starting with getting it to Carpenter, but Steve wasn't having it.

I can't remember how many months passed. Maybe almost a year. One day I got a call from the British journalist Alan Jones, a friend of mine who was organizing a fantasy/horror festival at the National Film Theatre on London's South Bank. Although Alan didn't know I'd gone through this demoralizing process with the "L.A." script, he knew how much I loved Carpenter and they'd managed to get Carpenter's new movie *In the Mouth of Madness* for a festival exclusive world premiere the 29th July, 1994. Not only did they have Carpenter for an onstage Q&A following the movie, but Alan said there was a VIP reception party afterwards for the festival in general and would I like to go.

I immediately got back onto Steve Kenis to formulate a plan. I had his assistant at William Morris coordinate a copy messengered over from the L.A. office to arrive at Debra Hill's production company in California at the precise same time I'd be meeting or hoped I'd be meeting Carpenter at the after-party in London. So that L.A. copy was officially and properly Agency-sent and represented legally as it ought to be. On the "showmanship" side of this heist, I also got the London office to make me a copy of the script with the regular blue William Morris covers to take with me to the NFT [National Film Theatre]. I don't think I've ever been as anxious watching a movie as I was that night watching *In the Mouth of Madness* sitting in the audience and willing time to speed up. Afterwards, Carpenter gave his Q&A. I was so focused on the task of getting to him I honestly don't recall a single reply he gave.

Afterwards, I bolted up to the reception party. Carpenter was milling around introduced to all and sundry. I circled nervously waiting for a right moment until Alan saw me and waved me over. I've since read an interview with Carpenter where somebody mentioned to him, him meeting him at the party. John's reported version of event. Well, I wouldn't say it was entirely factually accurate. He was in pretty high spirits from the occasion. It was the world premiere of his movie to be fair and his attention was fairly distracted let's say, but I'll gloss over that. Regardless, Alan introduced me. Carpenter knew or seemed to have heard about me working on *Alien vs. Predator* and *Dredd*. Then I happened to mention the *Chickenhawk* draft I'd sent to his agent at Gersh almost a decade before and he surprised the hell out of me. Turned out he'd actually read it and said he enjoyed it a lot. He enthused a little while and we talked about helicopters and the script and the book itself until I finally summoned up the moxie to make my move. "Well, I have something else for you to read." I remarked cagily. "I actually had my agent at William Morris send it over to your office in L.A. today, but I brought a copy with me." He looked bemused as I handed over that blue-and-white Morris bound script. Then he flipped the page and read the title and pretty much froze just like my agent had and snapped the cover closed with an immediate, "Aw, man. Oh, oh. No!" I'm sure he's had kids over the years press scripts on him at various occasions, but I started to reassure him and tell him it had already gone to Debra Hill's company properly through the Morris L.A. office. "No, no, that's all great. That's fine." he said. "If you'd brought this to me six months ago, I'd have loved to have read this, but Kurt and I literally just made the deal a couple days ago to write this thing! It isn't even in the trades yet. We managed to put the rights together. I can't read this now even if it's the most amazing script in the world! If you'd have only got it to me a little earlier. Sorry, kid."

I was floored because my instincts about writing this thing had been right as I'd insisted to my agent earlier in the year. If it had gone to Carpenter back then, who knows, but that was that. Carpenter's announcement made the trades just a short while later and that was the version that got made. Not the hundred-some pages of dead tree I was left holding. But to go back to your question about whether anyone on that team had read it. I don't know. It's entirely possible. I know given the circumstances in their shoes, I might have been tempted to take a peek. But I can tell you that their finished movie and my story pretty much had zero in common, so there's certainly no case of anything being sneakily taken from my draft at all. Not a thing.

Are you interested in sharing your script?

No! Sorry. It's a script I'm still very fond of. Obviously, it's never going to be an existing series sequel. Maybe it could be a reboot story for that notion that's been floating about for a few years now. But for myself I thought the story was strong enough that I've done a couple of reworkings of it to make it a standalone action movie that has nothing to do with the world of Snake Plissken.

How much do your reworks of the script differ?

Well, there was only ever one *Escape From L.A.* Snake Plissken draft. When I reworked it after that, the character that was Snake doesn't speak like that anymore, even though Snake is basically Joe Manko/The Man with No Name from the Sergio Leone spaghetti westerns! You know, there was that lawsuit recently between Carpenter and [Luc] Besson over Besson's movie *Lockout.* That story was so clearly obviously a thinly veiled version of an *Escape From New York* story. Maybe Besson originally even wrote it with the intention of partnering with Carpenter to do an actual "Escape From Space" story. Who can say?

What do you think of the final version of *Escape From L.A.* and in what ways do you think your version would've been better?

Well, my feelings about the filmed version of *Escape From L.A.* and my draft partially go some way towards explaining why my newer non-*Escape* reworked draft of my script still works pretty well as an entirely different movie. If you look at *Alien* and *Aliens,* they're two different films. One's a haunted house thriller. The other is a war movie. They just happen to have certain shared trappings and that's why partially I think the filmed version of *Escape From L.A.* failed. It's a remake rather than an attempt to tell another Snake Plissken story. It's got another guarded penitentiary island. It's got people ejecting in escape pods. It's got Snake again being injected with something that's going to kill him. There's a MacGuffin in there that has to be retrieved. It's a retread. The great thing about *Escape From New York* was you believed it. Dean Cundey's cinematography was gritty and raw and the look of the movie. You can almost smell it. The story drives along and you care about Snake and that's interesting because he's a character without much to recommend him plus he has no character arc! And I love that about him. And Carpenter's at the top of his game with his direction and his own music score absolutely zings.

Escape From L.A.'s the polar opposite. The cinematography in "L.A." is honestly horrible. The movie looks cheap, like a made-for-cable TV spin-off. The story is just a lesser version of the first one. Snake is kind of an asshole this time and none of the action sequences are particularly well done. I'll be honest. I don't much care for the *Escape From L.A.* that got made. That's not sour grapes but rather I was expecting more from that story. I saw it at the cinema and I've tried and failed to watch it a second time on video. It's a missed opportunity. All around. Where I think Carpenter did succeed in the film beyond what I did in my draft was in conveying the crazy essence of L.A. The plastic surgery, the Maps to the Stars, the surf culture. All that stuff. I was a kid living in London and, even though I'd a pair of studio scripts under my belt at that point, I'd really not spent any time in L.A. and I think you need to have lived in L.A. to understand L.A. I've spent years and years there now and if I were to begin from scratch and do that story again, it'd be very different. I got the geography accurate in my script, but I think Carpenter's local character crazies were more interesting than mine. Although saying that, I really like the marines in my story and Fresno Bob. And my overall story and action scenes had more depth. It's a shame Carpenter had signed that agreement and we never worked together because I think grafting on his quirky "local" characters on top of my story would have created something more in line with what I think the fans were expecting from that sequel.

What are you currently doing and what do you enjoy doing in your spare time?

I had a stint of family life since *Hellboy* came out. Dabbled in TV. The past few years I've been working with Gary Kurtz who produced *Star Wars* and *The Empire Strikes Back* and Ivor Powell who produced *Alien* and *Blade Runner* on putting together an independent movie called *Panzer 88*. A supernatural World War II action thriller about a German tank crew being chased by a creature. I'm directing this from a script by Aaron Mason, James Cowan and myself. Being an indie it's taken longer to put the financing together than we'd anticipated. Richard Taylor's Weta Workshop are doing the creature and some other elements. Peter Jackson was very supportive and helpful to us early on. What else do I enjoy? Movies. It's all about movies. Every day and twice on Sunday!

STACY KEACH
Malloy

How did you end up being an actor?

I think I've always wanted to be an actor ever since I was cast as Old King Cole in my kindergarten pageant. Growing up in a theatrical family, I took great pleasure in re-enacting scenes from movies that I had recently seen playing all the parts with my pals.

How did you get cast as Malloy in *Escape From L.A.*?

I had worked with John Carpenter on a short film, *Hair*, part of a trilogy of short horror films [*Body Bags*]. We had a great time together.

How did you prepare for the role and what kind of discussions with John Carpenter did you have about it? How was it to step into Lee Van Cleef's [Hauk] shoes so to speak?

Naturally, before I stepped into Malloy's shoes I wanted to peruse *Escape From New York* and glean whatever clues I could gather from the nature of Van Cleef-Kurt Russell relationship. Ultimately, my objective was to make Malloy a unique individual, totally avoiding any semblance of the Van Cleef character. However, I did have an oblique connection to Van Cleef in that I lived in the same house he had lived in during a movie shot in Spain in my early career, *Doc*.

What's your favorite scene or scenes and which were the most challenging, problematic, memorable, and fun to work on?

My favorite scene was with Kurt Russell in the first part of the film when Snake disappears behind a manhole cover.

How come you brought a cactus to the set?

I wanted to have something alive in the bunker that wouldn't require a lot of water given the fact that life on earth and specifically in L.A. was in danger of extinction.

How was your experience working with the cast and crew?

I loved working with the entire cast and it's always a pleasure to work with a master like John Carpenter. It was a genuine honor to work with Cliff Robertson [President], an actor I had long admired.

What's your favorite memory or memories of working on the movie?

My favorite memory of the movie was the helicopter landing scene. I was having trouble with my knee as I was directed to move quickly through the open spaces. One of the crew saw this, approached me, and gave me the name of a knee surgeon whom I later hired to give me new knee.

What do you think of the movie personally?

Personally, I love the film but then, I'm prejudiced!

What are you currently doing and what do you enjoy doing in your spare time?

I'm currently playing Matt LeBlanc's dad on the CBS sitcom *Man with a Plan*, Scott Bakula's dad on *NCIS: New Orleans*, The Archbishop of New York with Tom Selleck's *Blue Bloods* and am the voice of CNBC's *American Greed*. I recently starred as Ernest Hemingway in Jim McGrath's *Pamplona* directed by Robert Falls at Chicago's Goodman Theater. We are in the process of planning future productions in Los Angeles, Washington, DC, New York and London.

VALERIA GOLINO
Taslima

How did you end up being an actress and director?

I started very, very early. I did my first movie when I was sixteen, seventeen, something like that, so it almost happened without my permission. You know what I'm saying, circumstances. I did my first movie when I was still in high school. I was planning to do other things after when I finished high school, to go to university, etcetera. So, the first movie that I did changed my plans. I met Lina Wertmüller by chance. She asked me to do a screen test and she offered me the movie and that's how I became an actress. She was preparing her next movie and she needed a very, very young girl to be the daughter of Ugo Tognazzi, who was a great Italian actor, big movie star at the time. When I finished school, I kept doing meetings and working. I didn't do any acting school, theater school. The job came to me instead of me going to it. After that I kept working and working and when I was twenty-one, I went to America to do one movie. Then I was supposed to come back and then I did many movies in the United States. I became a director much later in life. Few years ago, eight years ago. Much too late I think now. I should have started earlier because I always wanted to do it, but I was too busy.

How did you get cast as Taslima in *Escape From L.A.*?

I met him in a very conventional way. They were looking for the girl and I went to do a screen test. I met John [Carpenter] and they offered me the role. We got along right away. I knew who he was. I had seen his movies. I was very interested. I was extremely happy to be cast in it, even if it was not a big role.

How did you prepare for the role and what kind of discussions with John Carpenter did you have about it?

If we did have discussions, which I'm sure we did, I don't remember them. A lot of discussions happened during the costume meeting because the costume was very representative of her. How she was gonna look, her hair. During those moments we were talking about her.

What's your favorite scene or scenes and which were the most challenging, problematic, memorable, and fun to work on?

I fell during a scene and hurt my ankle quite badly, so I couldn't finish the movie. There were like three or four scenes that I was not able to change because there was running all the time, you know. It was like an *Escape From L.A.* situation. I couldn't run anymore, so I didn't finish the movie. I remember when I went home from the hospital, John sent me flowers with such an amazing, beautiful little message for me of affection and respect. I was moved by it.

I remember a moment when I had to come out underground. It was one of the hardest moments. I had to be on my knees. There were moments where it was like, "Damn it's so hard." I mean, I haven't done many action movies, so it was also that. I remember I was so surprised. The set of the movie was humungous. It was huge. Even working in Hollywood, I was surprised how many means, how many people, how many you know.

How was your experience filming the Surgeon General of Beverly Hills [Bruce Campbell] scenes?

If you think how prophetic it was. It was already happening, all that. Particularly in Hollywood. It was a niche already. When the movie was being made, plastic surgery was a niche. Even the fear of that, what is gonna happen. There was a philosophical question. Now it's a normality. Even before Carpenter, there was a movie coming out many years before *Escape From L.A.* that was *Brazil.* In *Brazil,* it was a little bit of the same grotesque excruciating with people being older, you know. Existential fear. Prophetic? Yes, in a way, but also I think of the time it was much more talked about because it was like a phenomenon.

How long were you and Kurt Russell tied up?

I think it was done in a few moments. I'm not sure, but we were tied up for a while. They treated us fine, but it was a heavy movie. It was all at night and outside and you had to run. It was not an easy movie physically. We were tied up and Kurt is very kind of like, makes funny jokes. He's very playfully insolent.

How was your experience working with Bruce Campbell and were you ok with him groping you?

Such a good actor. I don't remember how much I was playing with him. I remember looking at him. Very, very good actor. Of course, that's my job. That was his job as well. This is part of the work. Actors very often do what they wouldn't do in life, of course.

How was your experience working with the cast and crew?

I really, really got along with John very much. He's a different kind of person even for Hollywood, kind of an outsider in the way that he behaved and dressed, his way of talking. He was very different than other directors I've worked with. Very free. Kind of cheapish. I don't know if he was bitter about Hollywood. In a better word, he wanted to be an outsider. He didn't like the system, I think. This is my perception. I don't want to talk for John Carpenter. He knows. My impression was that he didn't like the Hollywood system, the way the industry worked. I remember him being very critical. He was very good at being a leader in his own way. I thought it was very interesting to see his way of being the head, being the boss.

I remember Steve Buscemi [Map to the Stars Eddie]. I knew Steve a little bit and I remember the night we worked together being very, very joyful and funny.

I remember vaguely some moments with Kurt Russell. For me, he was Snake Plissken. He was not even Kurt Russell. So when I went to Snake Plissken, it was quite an experience working with Snake. Kurt? I don't know him. I only know Snake. I had seen the first movie when I was much, much younger. A kid. I remember thinking when he starts talking like Snake with that voice, that kind of thing that he put on. I thought it was awkward when I was there in real life and he was playing Snake. It was awkward. Very often with good actors because he's a good actor, no doubt. While you're playing with them and you think, "That's not very good. That's awkward," you know and then you see the movie finished and they're great and maybe you're the one who's awkward.

What are you currently doing and what do you enjoy doing in your spare time?

This week I'm in recreation but like in ten days it is all over because the festival of Venice starts again. I have three movies there, so I have to be in Venice for a week. One of them with Costa-Gavras. He's a very, very interesting director. I'm writing right now as well. Possibly my next movie. I'm writing with my co-writers. I'm working, working. I like to travel, go to the movies. I love movies. I love cinema. I'm a cinefile. I like the sea so I rent a house on the beach. That's the one luxury I have.

GEORGES CORRAFACE
Cuervo Jones

How did you end up being an actor?

That is a very long story. There's so many angles to that. I guess it was just luck. I had other plans. I wanted to be an artist. I wanted to be a writer and travel. I admired Henry Miller very much and wanted to be sort of a Henry Miller of South America. I wanted to study international law so that I could have a job to sustain myself while I was living in South American countries. The actual process of being in a law school was pretty grim. At some point, a friend of mine who was also in law school said, "Why don't we check out the local drama conservatory?" and we just went in the middle of the year. I think it was the end of December and they said, "Look. We're doing a middle of the year exam. The exam could be your entrance exam if you want? We have a lot of girls and not too many boys. You're welcome to do that exam." During the Christmas break, we just worked on some scenes and auditioned and I was taken directly in the superior class, which was flattering. There were three levels. I was immediately accepted in the top level and, from then on, I was given the opportunity to work in the local theater. We were both going to law school in Paris, but we were living in the neighboring city of Versailles, so we went to the conservatory on their side. Our teacher was the director of the Versailles theater. We would also start making some money because we would be stagehands and play silhouettes and change the sets between scenes and learn the trade from the bottom up.

It was a beautiful, beautiful Louis the 14th theater, very well preserved, all with old machinery. The ropes all in wood. Beautiful seats. Beautiful stage. It was very, very charming. I fell in love with the theater at that point. I started taking this very seriously and, after six months, the teacher announced to me that I was going to play Bassanio in the *Merchant of Venice* with a great cast, the famous Claude Dauphin playing Shylock and Geneviève Grad playing Portia. Anyway, it was all totally unexpected and I realized that immediately we started going on tours before the play settled in a Parisian theater. So here I had an artistic expression and traveling. I saw that I could travel the world being an actor. Then, of course, I auditioned for the big national schools. There were two

L-R/FG: William Luduena [Mescalito], George Corraface [Cuervo Jones]
(Photo Courtesy William Luduena)

of them and I was accepted into both. First in one and then the other in Paris. At the same time, I also continued making a living by playing in plays at night. Immediately I became professional and started making money as an actor. That's the story. There's a lot more to say but that's enough for this question.

How did you get cast as Cuervo Jones in *Escape From L.A.*?

I had an agent in America, which I got when we played in New York and Los Angeles. We played the *Mahabharata*. That play was directed by Peter Brook and was a big success, a big event and that attracted a lot of attention. It got me an agent at William Morris. The agent would send me scripts and say, "Are you interested and do you want to audition for this?" I was a fan of *Escape From New York* and when I got the script I said, "Yes, of course I want to audition for that," and all I had to do was pay my plane ticket. The agent arranged for an audition with John Carpenter and Debra Hill [Producer/Co-Writer]. It was at Paramount and at the audition was Kurt Russell also. The three of them were core producers in that adventure. So I got myself to L.A. two days before to not be completely jetlagged for the audition and also to create my character. I went along Hollywood Boulevard where they were selling all sorts of secondhand clothes and weird stuff flea market style. I don't know if it's still the case today, but at the time there was a lot of little stores with a lot of clothes, bags, belts, and various hand bracelets, you name it. I just created a character and I went to the audition dressed like that. The whole Che Guevara kind of guerrillero look was coming from Hollywood Boulevard. That's how I imagined the character. That really hit the spot. They liked it. We talked first. They could all see that I was really appreciating *Escape From New York* and that I liked very much the script that they had come up with for the sequel.

When I first got the script, it really was a sequel. It was not a sequel/ remake as it ended up being. I remember at Paramount, all the offices were behind where the office where I was gonna audition, so I just said, "There's gonna be some screaming! Don't be afraid! It's only me! It's only Cuervo Jones!" I slammed the door and went directly into the scene with the energy of that screaming to all the secretaries who were going, "What the fuck is this? What the hell is going on?" We did a couple of scenes and that was it. I could see that they all enjoyed the meeting. Kurt Russell was playing his role and I was playing Cuervo. It was a good chemistry. That's how it all happened. I went back to Paris. Only months later I got the new script and I was a little surprised.

How did you prepare for the role and what kind of discussions did you have with John Carpenter about it? Did you draw any inspiration from Isaac Hayes' performance as the Duke in *Escape From New York* for instance?

In the new script, there was a parallel structure but still Cuervo Jones was Cuervo Jones. Isaac Hayes' character was perfect and very distinct, so I just continued researching along the lines of the Shining Path [The Peruvian revolutionary group]. I investigated lots of books about the guerillas of South America and learned a lot of very interesting things about the political and religious syncretism. I don't think we had that many discussions before we started shooting. Actually, the first day of shooting... when I say day I mean night because all the shooting schedule was nighttime, so for about two months we were living upside down.

It was quite exciting. They had already started shooting like two days before my first day, so I was there in advance. I went into John's trailer and said, "Look, I got some ideas. I've written some dialogue for two scenes." I just played it for him. One scene was the first scene where Cuervo goes through the crowd on the car and he's talking to them. There was no dialogue written there and I thought since I was supposed to be talking to the crowd, I should be saying something. I drew from that research that I had made about the Shining Path and the syncretism. I had found a very interesting metaphor, which was that there is a legend saying that the last Incan king was beheaded and his head and body were buried miles apart. There's a legend among the descendants of the Incas that underneath the Earth his body crawls to find its head and the day it does will be a day when the Incan nation lives again and rules the world. I was saying to the crowd that they were my body and I was the head and together we're going to kick ass. Of course, I was doing all this with a language that was a street language. John loved that and said, "Ok. We can do that."

I said, "I also have something for the first scene we're gonna do tonight." It was the scene where Snake is tied to the treadmill and I'm talking to the President of the United States [Cliff Robertson] and I'm saying something very threatening. I had really made that very, very aggressive and very political. John said, "That's interesting. Why don't you try that? We'll see." When we got to that point, it was like two o'clock in the morning just before we broke for lunch. John said, "Ok. Let's make a rehearsal of that moment." He said, "Go ahead, George. Do what you did before." So I did the scene and I did it very convincing because all the people around it knew of the other scene. My people in Cuervo Jones' entourage, they looked surprised and Steve Buscemi [Map to the Stars Eddie] just looked at me and gave me thumbs up and then we broke for lunch.

At the end of lunch, an assistant comes and says, "We need to talk to you," so we went into Kurt's trailer. Kurt was kind of, "What is this shit? This is not a political movie. It has to be like a comic book. It's an adventure film. It has to have that quality." I said, "Alright, I guess you're right," and he was right. My take there had gone too far. I had gone too far. I went too serious and political instead of keeping that kind of ironic and sarcastic quality. My sarcasm was becoming too political. I was ending up also with stuff that was not political. I was saying stuff like, "Get ready, we're coming and we're hungry." I don't know exactly what I was negotiating there in that scene. My wife hears this and says it's because I'm French. My input was French. Possibly, possibly, possibly. Anyway,

I do think Kurt was right and everybody else was agreeing with him. John was agreeing with him, "Yes, yes, yes," so we went back to the original thing and we did it the way it was written. Whenever there was a little suggestion, John was completely open to it as long as it was in the spirit of the film. We went on and, scene after scene, I collaborated with John and with Kurt in great complicité we say in France. We were on the same wavelength. It was a great collaboration.

Was the Che Guevara connection something that you discussed?

This whole Che Guevara, guerrillero approach was meant to say beware of the costume of people. Beware of what image they project because behind that there is a thug. I have the greatest respect for Che Guevara, but I used him to show someone who walks in the room projecting an image and is not at all Che Guevara. He's not even a guerrillero, a revolutionary. He's just someone who is trying to grab the power and grab the money and grab the girls. He's a villain. He's a total villain and that is also something which I loved in that series of films. Everybody is pretty dark. Even the hero is an antihero, a hero not driven by the need to save America or save the world like the film that did a lot better when it came out the same year, *Independence Day*. It came out at the same time we did and, of course, *Independence Day* just had all the right ingredients to make a killing. It had a hero from every category of American society and the message was, we can save the world.

After *Escape,* I started getting offers to play villains in stupid films. Even if they were million dollar films, dozens of million of dollars, I turned them down. I chose to go back to Europe and do independent films and art films and theater. I just could not bear to cross that line.

Were you disappointed to see certain scenes go during rewrites of the script?

Yes, no matter what the scenes were. When you read a version and you like it and then it changes, you are always a bit disappointed. You always get attached to some scenes because you start to imagine them. You work them into the system and then, all of a sudden, they're gone. In this particular case, I was slightly disappointed that they decided to go for a remake format because I didn't think it was necessary. Obviously, it was not Kurt, John, or even Debra's input. The original script that they came up with was structured differently and it was a great script. They were able to keep the punch of the first script, but they did it within a structure that mimics *Escape From New York*. I think that is something that came from the executives of Paramount. I imagine that. It smells of studio mingling. They're thinking, *Escape From New York* was fifteen years ago and it's not the same generation. Let's do the same thing. It has its good side at the same time because having these two parallel structures, you can really see the evolution of American pop culture, of American culture period. The parallel becomes more eloquent than if it was just a totally new adventure of Snake Plissken. In the end, I'm very happy with it, what we have there.

If I was an historian of the cinema, I would say that it's very interesting that they decided to do that. It really makes the two very significant metaphors of America fourteen or fifteen years of difference.

How was your experience filming at the Los Angeles Memorial Coliseum and doing that epic speech?

That was great. That scene was like a dream. You dream something totally unbelievable. Some dreams you go, "Where did I get that? Where did that come from?" It was like that. A coliseum and those bikers, guerrilleros, hoodlums in the crowd and the basketball in the middle. It was surreal. It was very exciting and satisfying. It was a great speech. Beautifully written. It was really a lot of fun to do.

How was your experience working with the cast and crew?

I had the luxury of being in a private trailer with a fridge full of all sorts of beers and cheeses and stuff. It was completely luxurious. Next to me was my friend Steve Buscemi who was also very often there. We were paid by the week, so we had so many weeks. Therefore, we were called every day and we were never sure if we were gonna shoot or not. Sometimes we would arrive at seven o'clock in the evening and then shoot at five in the morning. Maybe just one moment or sometimes we were shooting all night. We were just going with the flow. They had rented the studios of Universal [Happy Kingdom by the Sea]. We were shooting in Universal Studios [Lot] even though it was a Paramount film. We were using the decor that is like a square [Courthouse Square] where they filmed *Back to the Future*. Since we were there for long hours and not knowing when we were gonna be called, we decided to run a sort of a festival. We would each choose films from the video store. There was a video store that had a lot of European films called Vidiots. It was not too far from where I lived, so we stopped by and chose films that Steve hadn't seen and Steve would also show me some of his films. We would watch all sorts of films during those nights. Of course, there was a screen and a VCR in the trailers. It was great. I loved working with him and I loved working with Kurt. It was fun being in the trailer with all the other actors, even those Cuervo doesn't run into. Since I was there all the time, we would spend a lot of time waiting, talking, and bonding.

I love John Carpenter. This guy kills me. I love his humor. He's so laid-back. He's so cool. He doesn't take himself seriously. He's really all that I like in a man. There are directors which are very, very different and I like other kinds of directors too, but he's so perfect in his style and with his humor and his irony and his sarcasm. I think he is a lot more subversive the way he is than if he was really making films with big political messages. I love him for that. He's understood it all and him occupying the realm of B movies is the genius decision to stay in that category and to have done all these very subversive films. He's got a great sense of humor. I remember one day we were shooting that little moment. It's something that Utopia [A.J. Langer] sees in her computer or something and I'm sending her a white dove. I'm trying to attract her with my false ideology with my hypocritical ways. I was supposed to send the white dove towards the camera, but the dove wouldn't fly. It would just bump, fall. We did it once then I tried to toss it a little further. You could see they had clipped the wings so the dove wouldn't get lost, so he was not really flying off and John says to me, "That was the five-dollar dove. We didn't have enough money to get the fifteen-dollar one, so we got the five-dollar one. It doesn't fly."

How long did you and Kurt Russell rehearse for the fight at Happy Kingdom by the Sea and how long did the scene take to film?

I think we rehearsed it at least two days before. We did the first rehearsal and then a really good rehearsal with stuntmen that decided all the moves. Then we did it again the day of the shoot. I don't know if it was a whole night, but we did it many, many times and it was lots and lots of parts. We were not holding back in any scene. We were really giving it our best. It was exhausting.

What's your favorite scene or scenes and which were the most challenging, problematic, memorable, and fun to work on?

Maybe that fight was "problematic" because it always had to be timed. It was not really problematic. It was just something more complex than others. As I was saying, the scene in the coliseum was unforgettable. The first scene in the movie where I'm on the car and going through the crowds telling my legend story with all the noises of the cars and so on. You can't really hear much of it. At least I had something to keep me happy and focused. I was happy to have the green light from John to do that. All the scenes with Steve Buscemi were great.

What's your favorite memory or memories of working on the movie?

I guess the Los Angeles Memorial Coliseum scene was my best moment. There was a lot of great moments. It was a lot of fun. Every sequence was a lot of fun.

How was your experience promoting the movie and do you have any fond memories with John Carpenter, Kurt Russell, and Debra Hill [Producer/ Writer]? You went to the Deauville Film Festival in France for instance.

I don't think I went to any opening in the states. I must have been working somewhere and I couldn't do it. Otherwise, I'm sure they had invited me. I remember going to Deauville. I was available and they were all there, the usual suspects, John, Kurt, and Debra and that was fun. It was fun promoting it because Kurt also has a great sense of humor. Kurt and John in the same room is a lot of laughs. We enjoyed talking to the press, the four of us together. Debra was more reserved and not as expansive like the rest of us but she did the work.

What do you think of the movie personally?

It's a great memory and I'm very proud of the film. I think it's an honor to have been in Carpenter's world.

What are you currently doing and what do you enjoy doing in your spare time?

What spare time? There's no spare time. I have projects that I'm promoting, financing. I have a project for the theater. I have a project for a documentary which has already been half done, half filmed. There's no spare time. I wished that every day was forty-eight hours instead of twenty-four and I had the energy to work forty-five of them. At least I'm not bored at all. I'm having a very exciting time.

LELAND ORSER
Test Tube

How did you end up being an actor?

Always was an actor since the third grade.

How did you get cast as Test Tube in *Escape From L.A.*?

Auditioned for John Carpenter. Got called into the room early with a mouth full of red vines. Had to chew and swallow for way too long before I could speak.

How did you prepare for the role and what kind of discussions did you have with John Carpenter about it?

Preparation was memorizing my lines, choosing the glasses and wardrobe, then just going for it.

What's your favorite scene or scenes and which were the most challenging, problematic, memorable, and fun to work on?

Los Angeles [Memorial] Coliseum. Lot of night shoots. Lots and lots of extras.

How was your experience working with the cast and crew?

Great cast. Had my first fitting at the same time as Peter Fonda [Pipeline]. Am a big *Easy Rider* fan. Joked around with makeup and hair who dressed me up as Snake Plissken's little brother Squirrel Plissken. When we weren't shooting, we would have an *Escape From L.A.* film festival in our trailers. One of us would supply the movie, another the beverages and another cigars.

What's your favorite memory or memories of working on the movie?

Favorite memory was shooting in the Los Angeles Coliseum.

What do you think of the movie personally?

I love the movie. I loved the original too.

What are you currently doing and what do you enjoy doing in your spare time?

I'm currently appearing on Season 3 of *Ray Donovan*. Had a movie, *Faults* come out this year. Available on Netflix and iTunes.

EDWARD A. WARSCHILKA
Editor

How did you end up being an editor as well as the editor for six John Carpenter movies?

I had been working for a number of years as Mark Warner's first assistant. That was my role again on *Big Trouble in Little China* in addition to being the liaison between editorial and the VFX house. Back then in the days of celluloid, the VFX would come in dribbles and scenes needed to be constantly updated with new versions of the VFX shots and that would cause picture edit changes. It was like having two jobs at the same time and I drove back and forth a lot. I'm not even sure we had fax machines at that time. After filming was over John wanted to come in and work on the end battle sequence and Mark Warner and Steve Mirkovich had their hands full with other scenes. I was promoted to editor and worked with John exclusively for that huge sequence and then after that moved on to other scenes. I had really enjoyed my time with John and learned a lot from him then and through the following years. After *Big Trouble,* I had gotten a call from John and Sandy [King] to come work on *They Live,* which if I remember correctly was already underway. I was on another project that I didn't feel I could abandon, so it wasn't until *Body Bags* that we got together again.

How did you and John Carpenter prepare/collaborate for this project?

You would think that would be the situation before starting a bigger studio production. The truth, however, was that right up until before that I was finishing another show. Even though John and I had done a couple shows together at that point, the studio wanted a very well-known and respected editor to cut the show. By the way, someone I too respected and admired. I didn't think I was going to get a chance on it, but I remember saying that I'd love to help out in any capacity I could, maybe as a second editor if one was needed. John never told me how it all worked out, but the other editor ended up being otherwise occupied and John endorsed me. John also was knee-deep in the thousands of production decisions leading up to the beginning of photography. This was the first show the two of us worked together using the Avid digital editing system, although I had used it before for someone else. Back then, we still had film dailies that we would conform to match the digital edit so we could take it to theaters to run for testing. Another benefit of the Avid is that, with our tight schedule, I could go out to set with VHS copies of cut scenes for John to give feedback and notes. The show was for the most part shot at night and so I would occasionally go out to set during their lunch hour and run cut scenes with John as we went. The Avid made that possible so much quicker and easier. I remember one time going out because I wanted to try something different with the basketball scene. The Avid allowed me to do an alternate version unlike if I had been editing on celluloid and a KEM [Keller Elektro Mechanik]. The alternate version didn't make it, but John allowed me to try. After that, sometimes when he'd talk about a scene during dailies/rushes, he'd finish by teasing me in good fun, "Oh, that's right. You're going to go off and do what you want anyways." There weren't any disagreements.

What kind of challenges did this project provide and which scenes or sequences were the most challenging, problematic, memorable, and fun to work on?

The schedule was definitely the most challenging aspect. It made it so much harder getting the time devoted to the visual effects teams. At one point, we had to bring in another editor, David Finfer, for an insurance claim. When the night battle at the end of the show was shot, they couldn't use charges in the guns because of complaints from the neighbors of the studio it was filmed at [Universal Studios Lot, Courthouse Square]. No, that scene wasn't filmed at Paramount. David put together the first pass of the battle for me so that they could start to process the claim that would pay for all the gunfire to be added later by a VFX company. I always regret that David didn't get credit for that, but he and I became the best of friends and worked on a couple of more shows together. The end battle in Anaheim [Happy Kingdom by the Sea] took a lot of time and the poor actors had to pantomime shooting guns with no charges in them.

How long did it take to edit the movie?

Started shouting December 11, 1995 and sent it to the negative cutters June 12, 1996. Then came mixing, color timing, and print mastering ending about July 16 and had a press screening July 19.

Were there any significant changes or different cuts done and were there any scenes or material that you and John Carpenter wanted to keep but had to drop at the very last second so to speak?

Not that I can still recall.

John Carpenter has said that he would have liked to have more than only nine weeks of post-production time to work on the movie. He only had one day to look at his rough cut before it had to be sent in to Paramount for release as well. Do you feel the same way or are you satisfied with the final cut? If not, what would you have liked to have done differently?

It was a shame about the schedule. Projects like this, especially with fantasy and VFX, need more time to develop and polish. Story and structure have their demands and then as VFX roll in adjustments have to be made to accommodate it. I remember the tidal wave surf scene, which had been discussed one way and the VFX just wasn't working out and we were already on the mixing stage before I recut the action to work with what they were able to accomplish. As an avid surfer back then, I was unhappy with it. They could have used more time. Back then Paramount was known for their short editing schedules. I had worked on *48 Hours* and *Staying Alive* and both had similarly tight schedules WITHOUT the VFX.

What's your favorite memory or memories of working on the movie?

My favorite time on all of John's shows was when the shooting ended and he came into the cutting room to work. We'd open the belly of the beast and then had fun discovering where it took us. I enjoyed working with John. I have a lot of love and respect for the man. He along with a few others have been wonderful mentors. I learned a lot from John and have always been thankful for the time I got to spend with him.

What do you think of the movie personally?

It's fun, it's campy and a statement of living here in L.A. Nowadays it's prophetic with the pandemic virus hanging over our heads. Of course, our virus had a different name but just as deadly!

What are you currently doing and what do you enjoy doing in your spare time?

I just finished working on Season 2 of *The Twilight Zone* and, like so many others, waiting for the day we can go outside and continue our lives. I've been trying to play the guitar for the last forty-seven years. Still do every morning. Still suck. I've always been a water rat. Scuba diver, surfer, sailor, and ocean kayaker. I was a competitive swimmer and still get in the pool for workouts. I'm slower now and less energetic so more time for roasting coffee for me and the missus [who I met on *In the Mouth of Madness*].

ROBIN MICHEL BUSH
Costume Designer

How did you end up being a costume designer?

I began my career as a costumer at Western Costume Company in 1976. My stepfather was Broderick Crawford and he agreed to open a door for me to work there as long as I gave it my all. In those days, it was a training ground for costumers as well as the largest costume company in the world. You were required to work there a minimum of two years so in essence it was an AA [Associate of Arts] degree in costuming. I had the opportunity to work with and train under the best. William Travilla, Dorothy Jeakins, and Edith Head to name a few. I learned period clothing, military, fabric, construction, etcetera and progressed to doing shows on the floor. A wonderful supervisor, Agnes Henry took me out of Western [Costume Company] and I became a set costumer on a TV miniseries called *Moviola.*

Through the years, I learned more, became a key, and eventually a costume supervisor. Although I had a great eye, I never considered myself a designer of the caliber of the above mentioned from the golden days of Hollywood. However, times changed and studios began to phase out costume designers in favor of supervisors setting the look of TV shows and costume designers were only hired for large films. When I did my first show with John Carpenter, which was *Starman,* there wasn't a designer. Although not titled, that was one of my first "design" jobs. John was very loyal to his crew and continued to hire me for his independent films.

How did you get the job of costume designer on *Escape From L.A.*?

When *Escape From L.A.* was first brought up, he asked me to do it and I studied and broke down the script months before official prep started. The studio required John to hire a costume designer who was in the Guild, Local 892. Not just an IATSE [The International Alliance of Theatrical Stage Employees], Local 705 member who is a costumer. I was asked to do four preliminary sketches which Debra Hill [Producer/Co-Writer] and John presented to Sherry

L-R: Jason Roberts [Second Second Assistant Director], Robin Michel Bush
[Costume Designer], Robert L. Bush [Costume Supervisor]
(Photo Courtesy Jason Roberts)

Lansing [Former Chief Executive Officer of Paramount] and the studio heads at
Paramount and I was hired and joined the Costume Designer's Guild.

**How did you, Robert L. Bush [Costume Supervisor] and Landys Williams
[Costume Supervisor] as well as Lawrence G. Paull [Production Designer]
and John Carpenter prepare for this project and how did you collaborate?**

Working with John and Larry Paull to come up with the overall look of the film
was a huge collaboration with lots of ideas flying. I was honored to work with
Larry and admired his vision. Often in futuristic films, I go back to the past to
find the future. The Mescalitos were an example of that. Drawing from years of
Mexican culture and looks. I had to envision the materials that would be at hand
following a quake of that magnitude.

How were some of the costumes created and is it true that the fabric of Snake Plissken's suit was custom made to make it reflect in sunlight and go black in other light to make him undetectable for instance?

John, Larry, Kurt, and myself had discussed making the suit somewhat like a stealth bomber where it was visible or not as much depending on the light. I actually don't recall if it was John or Larry's suggestion but we all melded together often. We made forty-five in total. For stunts, to age, for movement, for wet, and of course the multiple Hero looks. His leather coat was a throwback to German WWII as well as his boots.

Cuervo Jones [George Corraface] original helmet was an Aztec design made of crushed glass from car headlights and his coat was a faded out doorman coat from the Hotel Bel-Air with the sleeves cut off.

The Saigon Shadows costumes were made from old furniture blankets we thought they might have found on the Queen Mary and the net shirts were reminiscent of the fishing nets in Saigon.

Pam Grier's [Hershe] one costume was supposed to be the gold curtains torn down from the QM [Queen Mary] and she always had a sock stuffed you know where cause she was a transvestite. She grew hair under her arms for the part!!!

What kind of challenges did this project provide and which scenes or locations were the most challenging, problematic, memorable, and fun to work on?

Kurt's stealth costume was probably the hardest because we had to invent the material and resources available today, were not then. Shooting as many nights as we did was also difficult because we were continuing to have costume fitting during the day as well as building thousands of costumes.

What's your favorite memory or memories of working on the movie?

I loved the street scenes. I was able to get VERY creative. There were so many strange and surreal looks. The polypropylene hooker, rat man, condom man. We did one scene laughingly called one hundred hookers, one hundred fantasies. The layers of Larry Paull's design, Gary Kibbe's lighting, John's direction and the costumes to me as well as the amazing cast we had remain a symphony to this day in the street scenes and through the movie.

I will say that *Escape* was one of my favorite films I've ever done costume wise and I believe spirit played into the design ideas. That may sound strange but I honestly don't know how we came up with so many different and complex costumes. I had an amazing costume department. Steven Loomis [Costume Manufacturing Supervisor], the costume designer on *Escape From New York* came out of retirement to run the workroom. I had at least a half dozen costumers with me who were also costume designers, but agreed to work as costumers for the film. My crew was truly the best there was from the aging, dying, construction to the set. Top Notch. The amount of costumes that had to be custom made was huge in the short time frame we had but somehow it happened.

What are you currently doing and what do enjoy doing in your spare time?

I mentor young costume designers today, play piano, guitar, hike, travel, and spend a lot of time with family and friends. Enjoying life to the fullest. I also am involved in the spiritual arts.

PETER JASON
Duty Sergeant

How did you end up being an actor?

That's a good question. Everybody is an actor, aren't they? We're all born actors. Just some of us are better than others. I guess growing up and lying and getting away with it. I can get away with lying? I might just as well be an actor. How did I start off? Well, I was gonna be a professional athlete. My dad was a physical education teacher, so I was probably the best kid in school in all the sports because he played with me when I was young. Then I got up to eighteen, nineteen and they started getting really big. It kind of faded out and girls came into the picture, so that was another thing. One girl I had a crush on brought me in to audition for a high school play. It was a play called *The Man Who Came to Dinner* and I got the lead. When I went up for my curtain call and it exploded into applause, I went, "Oohh, I like this." That was pretty much the way it began. I was bit by the bug and I was eighteen. Now I am seventy-three, so for the past fifty years I've been pursuing this career as an actor. I've never had to work for a living, so things have went exactly the way I had planned.

How come you and John Carpenter have worked together so much and what do you like about each other?

Nothing. Just kidding. His wife Sandy King, I worked with her on *The Long Riders*, a Walter Hill movie and she liked what I was doing. She introduced me to her husband and he put me in *Prince of Darkness*. The thing I like about John is that he creates a family when he makes a movie. Every player on both sides of the camera are all part of a family and we all help each other. It makes it a lot easier and a lot more fun to get through whatever you're trying to make. When everyone is working for the thing, it seems to be a lot more fun than when a couple of egotistical individuals start saying, "Look at me." instead of look at us. John insists of creating a family every time he makes a movie and that's why I like working with him. I don't know why he likes working with me, except that I usually show up knowing my lines.

How did you get cast as Duty Sergeant in *Escape From L.A.*?

I think he likes using me in his movies and at that point there might not have been a part available for me. He knew that Stacy Keach [Malloy] was a friend of mine and we'd worked together in many, many different shows, so I think he took Lee Van Cleef's [Hauk] role and divided it into two parts. I got the beginning when I arrest Kurt and bring him in and then Stacy takes over from there.

How did you prepare for the role and how was your experience filming?

Well, I didn't drive around in a police car or anything to prepare for it. I've played many, many police and I've ridden in police cars and it's no fun. I'm the kind of actor that just does what the director says. I'm not a guy who likes to invent my own process. I like to be told what to do and then I like to do it. I like a director who tells you how to do it and leaves you open to do it your own way. My first movie I ever did was *Rio Lobo* with Howard Hawks. I never even saw a script. He just told me exactly what to do. He said in the opening scene, "Have your men pick up that box of gold. Kind of let them know there's gold in there. One of them will drop it. You say, 'Pick up your feet there private,' and he'll say, 'It sure is heavy, sir.' And you say, 'Gold usually is.' Then you have him take it over to the train and put it all up. You'll be the last one looking around nervously. You are the last one jumping on the train and you close the door to make sure no one is looking at you." You know exactly what to do and he leaves it totally open for you to do it your own way. I love that kind of direction.

"Call me Snake." You knew when he was saying it that it was an iconic line. That's what he says. That's what his character does. You want to be paying attention as much as you can on moments like that. John always has a few of those. He had a couple of them in *They Live* I remember for me too. He wants it to be tongue-in-cheek when you're saying those lines, but you also want to be as real as possible. John likes you to be as real as possible. His stories are usually larger than life and to make it palatable and believable to the audience your performance has to be real, so it's a challenge but that's why we get the big bucks.

One interesting story about making that movie involved Kurt Russell's younger son [Wyatt Russell]. He brought him to the set one day. We were both walking from our cars to go to the shoot where we're walking down the hall. He was one of the producers and he's walking with his kid and he says, "You think I can get my kid to be an extra in this?" and I looked at him and I went, "Well, I don't know. Do you know the producer?" He says, "Yeah." He was the producer. I said, "Just give him to me. I'll take over." and I took him into wardrobe and got him mixed-up like all the extras kids. There were all kinds of people in the thing. Homeless looking people and I walked to the AD [Assistant Director] and told him, "This is Kurt's son. I want him to be seen," and so on. We did the first rehearsal where we walked down the hall and turn to the left. The Steadicam is in front of us and I knew when we turned the Steadicam would follow us. I said, "You stand right here," and stuck him there. On the first take, I came down and when we got there around the corner, I smashed him up back against the wall with my hand like, "Get out of my way," you know, and his expression on his face was such shock. For every take after that, I didn't have to touch him. He was just terrified when I turned in the corner and the camera moves in right on him. That was a really fun moment on that show that day. It's called a play you know. It should be fun. Everybody should be having a good time and I usually do.

How was your experience working with the cast and crew?

John is a guy who doesn't yell. He likes everything calm. I find it to be very conducive for an artistic atmosphere if there is a calmness. People who scream and yell on the set tend to make people tense. They tend to drop things and break stuff and takes are ruined and it takes more time and more money. When you create a family of people with respect for each other, there's no need to yell. The first thing you notice on a John Carpenter set is how calm it is, how calm he is. I remember one time, there was some commotion going on the side with a couple of members of the cast and crew. They were raising their voices, arguing about something. He walked over and said, "What seems to be the problem here?" and they said, "Well, argh." He said, "You know what? Have you ever been in a video store? Have you ever looked up on the wall seeing all those videos? It's been done before. It can't be that difficult." I always loved that image of him walking into a video store and looking up on the wall. "Yeah, yeah. It's been done before." He keeps a very calm set and it's really easy to work with John Carpenter.

Forty years ago on a TV series called *Daniel Boone,* Kurt played my little brother. I forget what the story was. That was a long time ago. Daniel Boone came into our house and he was seeking help in the American revolution period there. I forget what we were doing. We were trying to help him out in some way and Kurt played my younger brother. He was a feisty little kid. I remember having to hit Daniel Boone. Fess Parker played Daniel Boone. I had to hit him over his head with a frying pan and he was like six foot six and I was like five, ten. Probably smaller because I was like twenty years old and I had to hit him over his head with a frying pan. They gave me this fake frying pan that looked real and I had to make it look like it was heavy but it was made out of fiberglass. When I swung on him the first time, he wasn't sitting down in a chair. I said, "I can never reach his head." When I swung the frying pan at him the first time, I pulled my swing so I wouldn't hurt him you know, and kind of looked like I swung it hard. He looked at me and said, "No. Hit me harder." I said, "Ok," and the next take I did it again and I kind of hit him a little harder, but I still pulled it. He said, "No, no, no. Hit me, hit me with that thing," and the third time I hit him so hard and he went, "Something between those two." Kurt was great to work with. Always amiable. Always in a good mood. Always easy to be around. Always fun.

What's your favorite memory or memories of working on the movie or other John Carpenter movies?

I've told you several already. I have lots of memories of working on John Carpenter movies. One of my favorite things. I made another movie with John Carpenter called *Village of the Damned* and he gave me a lot more responsibility on that movie to help all the departments. I think he did it for several reasons. One to bring the cast and crew closer together and one because I told him I wanted to produce, so he wanted me to find out little bit about every aspect of making a picture. The cast was sent home and we were doing beauty shots of the area with a really stealth crew. Just like six of us. We're going around the city of Inverness and Point Reyes up in the San Francisco area getting beautiful shots on the cliffs where the action was and I kept telling them, "We got to get a shot of a sunset. It's the most beautiful shot of all of California." They kept saying, "We don't have time."

I kept telling them and telling them. Finally at the end of the day, they say, "The sun is going down, so we can't get it. Just take us to the airport." I turned around and I drove to the top of a mountain. "What are you doing? We're missing the plane." "No, we are not," and I drove them to the top and as soon as we ended up on the top of the mountain the camera men looked at me and went, "Oh my God. You can see everything from here. Look at that sunset. Set the camera right here." It was a beautiful sunset shot that he took. When he got ready to go to the car I said, "No, no, no, no, no. We can't leave yet." "We have to go now." I said, "No, no. We have to wait five more minutes." "Why?" "Because an explosion is gonna happen. Just watch. Wait five minutes. Have a cigarette. Relax. Just five minutes," and they were very unhappy with me, but they waited five minutes. Sure enough, the sun went down and five minutes later an explosion of orange light happen over the ocean that was magnificent and it's in the movie twice. I think it opens the movie and I think it's later in the movie again. It's moments like that that you love.

What do you think of the movie personally?

Escape From L.A. or *Village of the Damned*? Both of them I like. It was so inventive, so new, so fun. It's kind of away what John's usual movies are. They are sometimes darker. I mean, it's dark and everything because all of his characters have a little bit of that, but this had a lot more zany qualities to it and it was a lot more fun. There's so many wonderful characters in it. Everybody is really great in that movie.

What are you currently doing and what do you enjoy doing in your spare time?

I like to work with wood. It's Christmas now. Everybody has a Christmas tree and when they throw them away, I usually drive by with my convertible and cut all the branches off and keep the stocks and I dry them out. Those are my arms and legs in chairs and tables that I make in my shop. I don't use nails. I only use dough. I like working with wood. It's something I've picked up over the years that I love doing. In the movie business, we just wrapped yesterday a series called *Baskets* which is on FX with Louie Anderson and Zack Galifianakis and I play Louie Anderson's older brother uncle Jim. It's a dark comedy and the Baskets family are just crazy as you can get. We just ended shooting our third season and it will coming out shortly. I just stepped back last June from England where we shot the new *Jurassic World* movie where I play a congressman with Jeff Goldblum and that was fantastic.

JORDAN BAKER
Police Anchor

How did you end up being an actress?

I was a ballet dancer since three years of age. Socially, I was very shy and dancers don't talk. We move. After high school, my mother sent me to an acting summer session at the Pasadena Playhouse being taught by the American Academy of Dramatic Arts. A teacher there said I had talent as an actor. I was fairly without direction after high school. I got into college but didn't go. My parents were divorcing and I was not top focus at the time. I found myself in New York with my mother. I remembered what the AADA [American Academy of Dramatic Arts] had said and I sought out the school in New York two years later. They said I had no talent and was too shy. I ended up in general studies at Marymount Manhattan College. While there, a great teacher, Bill Bordeaux, saw my talent and recommended I transfer. I went to Smith College. Turns out I was smart. Who knew? There I really found teachers who pushed me through my shyness. I won URTA [University/Resident Theatre Association] competitions, was an Irene Ryan contender at the [Kennedy Center] American College Theatre Festival, and finally earned a full scholarship to Rutgers University/Mason Gross School of the Arts where I had the privilege of earning my MFA [Master of Fine Arts] with William Esper. Our final year we did a showcase in New York and I signed with the J. Michael Bloom agency and went to work.

How did you get cast as Police Anchor in *Escape From L.A.*?

Originally, the role was written for a man, but I'm tall. My agent at the time was clever. He talked casting into taking a look at a strong woman. John Carpenter loved my work and while on set kept writing more and more. I'd learn it quick and we filmed.

How did you prepare for the role and how was your experience filming?

The role is very close to who I am so the most prep I needed was delivering the news quickly and adding to the building urgency of the scene it underlays. Much of that was designed by Carpenter.

How was your experience working with the cast and crew?

The night I shot there were hundreds of extras, military helicopters, tanks, etcetera. I didn't work with another actor. I was the only principal actor with lines for the night. We shot at the reclamation center [Donald C. Tillman Water Reclamation Plant] [Firebase 7 Exterior/Access Tunnel] in the San Fernando Valley at 3 AM. It was daunting! So much action. The lighting was so dramatic. So were all the trucks and aircraft when "action" was called. Very exciting.

What's your favorite memory or memories of working on the movie?

Kurt Russell showed up on the set, said hello in the makeup trailer, and stood with Carpenter watching all the action when he would cue me up. I have always been a fan of both men. They were incredibly generous. True gentlemen.

What do you think of the movie personally?

It's fun. It's escapist. There are days I look at the world and think it's possible.

What are you currently doing and what do you enjoy doing in your spare time?

I just finished *American Secretary* [premiere], *The Americans* [premiere, season 3], *The Good Wife* [final season] and two features. *5 Flights Up* [Diane Keaton and Morgan Freeman] and *5 Doctors* [what's with the number 5!], a wonderful comedy that has not released yet. I was on stage in Rebecca Gilman's new play *Luna Gale* at the Goodman in Chicago and the Kirk Douglas in Los Angeles. [We just won two Drama Critic Circle Awards for the Los Angeles production]. I am now on *The Morning Show with Steve & Jordan* WRCR 1700 AM 6-10 AM EST [Eastern Standard Time] Monday-Friday. If you want to listen, get the app WRCR or if you live in the tri-state area you can listen on 1700 AM. We do weather, traffic, local news and live unscripted talk! I love it! Funny that someone so shy and incapable of talking would grow up to be a talk radio host. Don't let anyone box you in!

ROBERT CARRADINE
Skinhead

How did you end up being an actor?

Are you familiar with my family? My father John [Carradine], my brother David [Carradine], my brother Keith [Carradine]? They're all actors so the trap was laid and I got caught in it.

How did you get cast as Skinhead in *Escape From L.A.*?

I worked for John Carpenter on a film called *Body Bags* and when I heard he was doing *Escape From L.A.*, I wanted to be in it. I talked to him about it and he said, "Well, it's pretty much cast." The bigger parts all went to Mexican Americans. He said, "There's a part as Skinhead. Do you want to shave your head?" "No, I don't want to shave my head." He said, "Well, that's what it got to take." I said, "Why don't you just put a skull cap on me?" He said, "Because they always look fake." and I said, "Ok. Why don't I come down to the set and have the makeup guys do a skull cap for me and see what you think?" So I went down to the set and two hours later I had the skull cap out on and I went over to John and I said, "What do you think?" He said, "Well, you shaved your head. Thank you." I said, "No, John. This is a skull cap." That's how I wound up in *Escape From L.A.*

How did you prepare for the role and how was your experience filming?

It was not really anything to discuss. I mean, the Skinhead was an asshole and a violent person and I just tapped into that. I just made myself available and I was on the set and kind of absorbing the vibe of the location which was a practical location. It was really an old movie house [Los Angeles Theatre] that we took over and yeah just, I paid attention, you know. I just tried to emulate what I was feeling.

Is it true that the rigging didn't work properly when Snake Plissken blew you away with his Coreburner and the effect had to be toned down?

I don't remember that. I think it was a one take deal and it worked perfect.

FG: Robert Carradine [Skinhead]
(Photo Courtesy Robert Carradine)

That's what I recall. I'm happy to be wrong. I know that the scene where I take a knife and flip it in the air and catch it by the blade and I want to throw it at Kurt Russell. I think that was one take.

How was your experience working with the cast and crew?

They were great. Everybody was great. It's one of my favorite movie sets. Kurt is a real sweetheart on the set and very accessible. He doesn't have any airs about him. He's a great guy. As for John, the night that I went down to the location to try out the skull cap, I was on the set with him. It was the scene where they had to drive the Cadillac towards camera and they're blowing things up with near misses and it goes roaring pass camera. It was a big setup to do it and it went off perfect and John says, "Let's go again." and I said, "John. Why are you going again? That was perfect!" He said, "Well, I like it."

What's your favorite memory or memories of working on the movie?

There's nothing that really jumps out. It was just the experience of being on the set for a night in a film with an iconic title. That in and of itself was kind of exciting.

What do you think of the movie personally?

There's aspects of it that I really like but, you know, nothing can follow *Escape From New York*.

What are you currently doing and what do you enjoy doing in your spare time?

I'm a guitar player and I play out whenever I can. I'm also a motorcyclist and I ride my motorcycles often.

SHELLY DESAI
Cloaked Figure

How did you end up being an actor?

Well, I was working in a company as an engineer. My first job. I met some people, my neighbors and stuff. They were involved in the theater and they took me around and showed me some plays and stuff. Somehow, I got the bug to try acting, so I took some classes and eventually I think I got pretty good. People started casting me. That's how it happened. It wasn't planned.

How did you get cast as Cloaked Figure in *Escape From L.A.*?

I never had much to do with John Carpenter. Indirectly I did, yeah. I think he'd seen me in something. Some other movie that I can't recall now. Not a huge part but he saw something so I was asked.

How did you prepare for the role and how was your experience filming?

Former Cal Compact Landfill [Beverly Hills Hotel Exterior]: There was quite of bit of physical stuff, running around and escaping and things like that. It was a crazy area. Kind of dangerous, kind of industrial. A lot of water and stuff like that. So to get me from the dressing room to the set, there was no way to get a car there. You had to walk. It was rough. We had to go through part of the water and mud and things like that and they were afraid to get the fashion dirty or wet. They usually have one or two people with you when you walk from your dressing room to your set. I was there at least two or three nights.

Pacific Electric Building [Beverly Hills Hotel Interior]: There was no mud there. It was a different setup. From what I remember on the set, they had a reclining thing on it [Camera]. I had to deal with that. That was a little tricky because it was a movable thing that they built so they could use different angles. Sometimes, it was difficult. The contraption they had didn't have much of a floor, so he had to kind of stand on beams and stuff. It was somewhat risky, but no one got hurt fortunately. We got through. That scene took a couple of nights,

I think. A lot of the shooting was at night. I don't know why but they wanted some darkness and feeling of darkness.

Were you disappointed that they cut you out saying your line, "It was a slow night, Surgeon General?"

Yeah, I was. But you know, movies are like that. Sometimes you shoot a lot and not much is left in the movie. Sometimes you shoot a smaller amount, but it fits in the movie well so it stands out.

How was your experience working with the cast and crew?

There was a lot of down time. I used to just rest and stuff. I would either read or take naps between the time they called me. There was one other actor next door to me in the next dressing room in the trailer. I don't remember his name. Nice guy. He seemed to be kind of impressed with what I was doing. That's all I remember. Overall, they were courteous and they were aware that we were working in difficult circumstances. I guess you could say by the design there. They didn't want anybody to be too comfortable. They wanted a sort of edginess because when you walk through water and mud and stuff you're not the happiest person in the world.

What do you think of the movie personally?

I liked it. I liked it. I liked it. I liked a lot of the shots along the freeway and the water on the side. I like that stuff.

What are you currently doing and what do you enjoy doing in your spare time?

I'm a football fan. American football. I like going to movies. I read books. I love working. I enjoy what I do. It's almost like they don't have to pay me. Sometimes, I do help out some people like young filmmakers who can't pull a lot of money. Recently I did a thing with a guy, I think he was just out of college. Film program. It was a good part and I liked it. It was an interesting part. Lot of violence and stuff. I like physical stuff.

WILLIAM LUDUENA
Mescalito

How did you end up being an actor?

An old girlfriend showed me a flyer looking for movie extras for the film *The Doors*. I needed a job, so I called the number, set up an appointment, met with casting director Bill Dance, and he gave me my first movie job as an extra on Oliver Stone's *The Doors* and I loved it! It was so exciting for me to see how the process was done. From there, I just kept at it and eventually joined SAG and started getting union extra work, then stand-in jobs, photo double jobs, and then speaking parts.

How did you get cast as Mescalito in *Escape From L.A.*?

Jennifer Bender, who is now VP at Central Casting, sent me to an interview/audition. I was first sent to the set to be the Jacket Mescalito, but my friend William Pêna was there and they picked him over me. I believe they liked his look better, but they liked me and they kept me as one of Cuervo's [Jones] [George Corraface] henchmen.

How did you prepare for the role and how was your experience filming?

I am in a ton of scenes since I worked on the film for a month. You know how things work, especially in big budget films. They cut a lot of things out. I worked mainly in the L.A. Memorial Coliseum basketball court scenes, the treadmill scene and at the Universal [Studios] backlot [Courthouse Square] [Happy Kingdom by the Sea]. Right after the "Bangkok Rules" when Kurt Russell throws the can up, I get out of a taxi and yell out a few lines.

First day of shooting was in a warehouse in downtown L.A. at an abandoned building [Morell Meats Building] [Los Angeles Memorial Coliseum Locker Room]. I don't know if you can see me in that scene, but that was the first day of shooting. I got there and immediately saw super cool dude Christian Della Penna, 1st AD [Assistant Director], who I had just worked with on a previous film, so I know we were in for a great time. It was a fun time plus I love

William Luduena [Mescalito]
(Photo Courtesy William Luduena)

working at night and this movie was all shot at night. It was 5 PM till sun up. I loved it. Best movie experience of my life.

How was your experience working with the cast and crew?

John Carpenter has a particular way of shooting or at least he did on this film. It was all very organized and structured. One, let crew do their job setting up shot. Two, rehearse on the spot a few times and get everything right then shoot scene two or three takes and that's it. It's all in the setup and the work before the shot. They had it all figured out. He rarely shot more than a few takes on every scene as I recall. It really stood out as a very efficient workflow and most of the time it's not done this way. Usually they do several takes until it looks good. Since I got to work on the film for so long, I was able to get a good look at the way this movie was made and the personalities behind it. Observing is a great way to learn about the biz. Everybody has a different personality. For example, John Carpenter is a very serious guy. He doesn't smile much. Even when you see pictures of him with fans, he always looks serious, but he always seemed to be happy and in a great mood when he and Kurt were talking. Kurt Russell's presence seemed to really delight him.

Kurt Russell is just a super cool dude beyond the movie star/actor thing. He's a real man's man. He was always friendly to anybody who might approach him. One day a bunch of extras came up to him and asked for pictures and he said, "Sure, no problem." Can you imagine? A picture with Snake Plissken. How cool would that be?

George Corraface was also just a sweet human being. Pleasant and well-mannered. One day at lunch he came over and sat with me. We talked about his background in acting and he told me he was more of a comic actor in France. We continued talking and Steve Buscemi [Map to the Stars Eddie] came and sat across from myself and George. Unlike George, Steve Buscemi was very serious and not very engaging. He didn't say much at all through the whole lunch.

I recall everybody being exceptionally professional. Especially Chris Della Penna, 1st AD and Jason Roberts, 2nd AD. I kept in touch with Jason for a while. I even worked on a short he directed, but I haven't seen or talked to him in years. He goes and gives talks about the industry at Central Castings and on visiting days one day I will go and say hello to him. Overall, everybody on the set was very excited to be part of such a cool movie. There was a feeling you were part of something special.

What's your favorite memory or memories of working on the movie?

Maybe the big days on the Universal back lot. Seemed like a thousand extras and hundreds of crew people. The shots of the hang gliders flying down on everybody were so great and so exciting. It felt like I was in a different world. Also the L.A. Memorial Coliseum. As I recall, it was the exact middle of the shooting days and at lunch they had a party. There was a band and an incredible feast. Just amazing. I've never seen anything like it. I can't remember if it was that same day, but basically shooting just stopped and they turn on the jumbo screen in the Coliseum to watch a Lakers playoff game. Imagine hundreds of people just stop working and sit down to watch a basketball game. John Carpenter and Kurt Russell were big Laker fans and I heard it cost Carpenter $5,000 to have the jumbo screen turned on. CRAZY HOLLYWOOD MOVIE STUFF. So glad I was a part of it.

What do you think of the movie personally?

I love the movie. As John Carpenter has said, "*Escape From L.A.* is better than the first movie. Ten times better," but unfortunately it didn't do so well at the box office. You never know why some movies have success and others don't. The CG was a bit cheesy in some parts, but I like that kind of thing. Anyhow, personally I think it has a great message and the concept is ahead of its time. A lot of people just didn't get it. On the other hand, a lot of people really like the film. I believe it has achieved "cult status" and that's the highest honor a movie can have in my book. John Carpenter has a very 70s, 80s filmmaking style, which I personally love, but *Escape From L.A.* came out at a time when people wanted to see super CGI special effects like *Jurassic Park*. Possibly Carpenter's style was not that. Funny, now people want to see more practical effects.

What are you currently doing and what do you enjoy doing in your spare time?

A lot of my spare time has been going into a new show I am producing tentatively called *Deconstruction TV*. I've been working on it for a couple years now and it should be done very soon. I also play guitar and record music.

MARK THOMPSON
Guard [Uncredited]

How did radio personalities Mark Thompson and Brian Phelps from *The Mark & Brian Show* end up having minor roles in about forty movies and TV shows?

We were invited to be a part of *A Very Brady Christmas*. We had Florence Henderson on the show and they were just about to shoot that movie and she said, "You guys should come and be in it," and we thought, "Sure." So we did it. We were standing right beside Florence in a role and our listeners just loved it. In that particular show, in the script our part was called Concerned Onlookers so that was what that series became. The series of Concerned Onlookers.

How did you and Brian Phelps get cast as guards in the submarine launch area? The final shooting script doesn't feature these guards.

No, I don't think it was in the script. Kurt Russell was a friend of the show and he knew about the thing that we do with Concerned Onlookers. He was about to shoot *Escape From L.A.* He said, "Why don't you guys come down and be in it?" We said, "Great," and so we went down and I think they just created a part for us when Kurt was coming down the ladder in the submarine. We're playing guards with guns and we're making sure he's behaving himself as he comes down. We did it because we love Kurt and we were happy to be in the film.

How did you prepare for the role and how was your experience filming? Was your line, "Nice and easy now," written, improvised, or dubbed?

Well, there wasn't really much to prepare for. We got there and they gave us our wardrobe and we put it on and we hung out with Kurt for a little while. When it was time to shoot it, they just said, "Ok. Kurt's gonna come down the ladder and, when he does, point your gun at him and make sure that he is a good boy and continues to go where he's supposed to go." That was kind of it. There wasn't much preparation for it. It was a set, a set that was built to look like a submarine. We were on a sound stage. Line? I don't remember, but I think we had the freedom to say a little something. It wasn't in the script. I do think that somebody just said, "Feel free to say a little something to him as he comes down." and that came out. The actual filming was maybe two hours total but we spent the entire day there with Kurt. We ate on the set with him. Takes? I don't remember but probably three or four, just to make sure because we did it from different angles.

How was your experience working with the cast and crew?

Well, I mean obviously working with Kurt was great because he's a buddy and we love being around him. It was a great honor for me to meet John Carpenter, who directed two of my favorite movies of all time, which is the first *Halloween* and, of course, *The Thing* with Kurt. So to meet him and speak with him was a great honor.

What's your favorite memory or memories of working on the movie?

Hanging out with Kurt. After we shot our scene with him, he asked us to hang around, but didn't say why. So, we hung in Kurt's trailer watching old baseball games. At that time, he was addicted to watching old baseball games from the 1950s and we sat around while he watched that and we watched him watch old baseball. I went to take off my soldier uniform and Kurt asked me to keep it on, but not saying why. Kurt kept looking at the sky and when the moment was right he said, "Let's go." We walked to the top of a nearby hill. Me, Brian, Kurt, and a photographer. Kurt had been waiting for dusk for what they call "magic hour" where the sun has set but it's not yet dark. There the three of us stood. Us in our soldier uniforms and Kurt dressed as Snake Plissken. The photographer took a ton of pictures and told us, "These will turn out great." We hugged Kurt goodbye, changed, and left. What I hate is that I never saw the pictures. I'm sure they look awesome and I will never know.

What do you think of the movie personally?

I thought it was good. I liked *Escape From New York* better, but you know it's still Snake Plissken. It's still Kurt. I enjoyed it thoroughly.

What are you currently doing and what do you enjoy doing in your spare time?

Well, these days I've been painting a lot. When I'm not doing anything constructive, I just put a bunch of paint on the canvas and see what happens.

MICHAEL DAWSON
Extra

How did you end up being a stunt man, fight coordinator and martial art/ fight trainer?

I had been involved with Chinese martial arts for many years. I really credit my primary teacher with giving me the skills to work in stunts and David Carradine for giving me my start in the business. My primary teacher, Grandmaster Liang Kam Yuen, was also the kung-fu technical advisor for the old 70s *Kung Fu* TV series. He also taught and worked with David for years beginning with his involvement on that show. Through my teacher, I worked on a couple of David's kung-fu and tai chi workout videos back in the mid-1980s as a martial arts trainer. Sometime later in 1993, David himself hired me to be his stunt double on the *Kung Fu: The Legend Continues* TV show, which was shot in Canada. That was my start.

How did you get cast as an extra in *Escape From L.A.*?

It was over a pool game. I was still working on the *Kung Fu: The Legend Continues* show with Al Leong [Stunt Player] [Saigon Shadow] [Uncredited] when he got word he'd be working on *Escape From L.A.* I have always been a major fan of John Carpenter and *Escape From New York* was one of my favorite movies. I just had to work on that show. You could say that working with John Carpenter was something on my "bucket list." Anyway, Al and I were on the tail end of *Kung Fu* and I lobbied him pretty hard to try and get me on *Escape*. After pestering poor Al for a few weeks, he finally broke down and said he could talk to *Escape* stunt coordinator Jeff Imada to get me on, but I had to win him in a game of pool. One of our favorite pastimes was playing pool at this diner in Toronto, which was co-owned by a good mutual friend and stunt guy we worked with. We would often play for money and I would usually lose. Among Al's myriad of talents, he was also a pool shark. This time around, to my surprise, I ended up winning. A week or so after we got back from Toronto, I went to work on *Escape*. Al had later told me that he was going to get me on that show in any case, but he was clearly bemused by the idea of a pool game over it.

How did you prepare for the role and how was your experience filming?

I worked towards the end of the movie in the Happy Kingdom [by the Sea] melee. I started out as a skinhead during the scene where Cuervo Jones [George Corraface] is assembling all the gangs. A little later, I was re-dressed as a sort of non-descriptive gang member during the big battle sequence. I was one of so very many. There were a lot of people on that set and a lot of guns! I worked about two or three weeks, I think.

How was your experience working with the cast and crew?

I had one of the best times I've ever had on a film set. I was getting to work on a John Carpenter film. I was working with Kurt Russell as Snake Plissken. I couldn't really ask for a better gig. Al and I hung out quite a bit when either of us weren't working. He let me crash in his trailer, which is where all of the other Saigon Shadows' dressing rooms were located. I more or less hung out with them. Jeff Imada [Saigon Shadow/Stunt Coordinator], James Lew [Stunt Player] [Saigon Shadow] [Uncredited], John Koyama [Koy] [Stunt Player] [Saigon Shadow] [Uncredited], Stuart Quan [Stunt Player] [Stunt Player] [Uncredited], Leo Lee [Stunt Player] [Saigon Shadow] [Uncredited] and the rest. We passed the time either standing by on set and watching or hanging back at the trailers and chatting. On long breaks, some took naps in their respective trailers [these were all night shoots!].

Is it true that each group that was similarly dressed started to hang out together and really got into their characters?

Yeah, it is true. Most of the gangs all stuck together. Their dressing rooms were generally cloistered together too, so that was certainly a factor. I think everyone got into their characters, but everyone got along exceptionally off-camera. Everyone was excited to be there on an *Escape* movie. The energy was always high and everyone wanted to do a good job.

What's your favorite memory or memories of working on the movie?

I have a lot of great memories from that set. I had an opportunity to chat with John Carpenter a little bit. That was pretty unforgettable. Rushing the chopper with hundreds of guns was quite a thrill. Getting to watch the finale fight between Kurt and George get set up, rehearsed, and then watching it being shot. That was nice. Meeting Kurt was also special. He's a great guy. Nice to everyone. From the top to the bottom. The whole shoot was just fun. The Happy Kingdom stuff was all shot on the Universal Studios backlot [Courthouse Square] and for me it's always great to be working on a backlot, particularly Universal's. There are less shows done on backlots these days. Although I had worked three years already as a professional stunt performer, it was under ACTRA [The Alliance of Canadian Cinema, Television and Radio Artists] contracts up in Canada. Working on *Escape From L.A.* allowed me to get my SAG card, so that's a great memory for me as well.

What do you think of the movie personally?

I'm a fan of all John Carpenter's movies and anything with Kurt Russell as Snake Plissken is always going to get a thumbs up by me. For me personally, *Escape From L.A.* wasn't quite as good as the first one, but it's pretty tough for any sequel to top the original. There's plenty of good stuff in this movie for me, so I'll always be a fan of it. And really, you have to love the ending.

What are you currently doing and what do you enjoy doing in your spare time?

I'm still involved in stunt work and try to keep busy with that these days. I've lived down in New Orleans since 2009 and I teach traditional kung-fu and tai chi. It might be a little premature to talk about it, but I can at least say that there are plans in the works for collaborating with Al Leong on a feature film project in the near future. Aside from making movies I love watching them as well. I was a film buff long before I got into the business. I like being outdoors as often as I can, reading and listening to music. I also really enjoy teaching martial arts and I'm currently writing a few books on the subject.

JOHN SENCIO
Extra / MTV Host

How did you end up being a TV host/producer etcetera?

Like most American kids growing up in suburbia I was fascinated with pop culture. Rock and roll, movies, TV, radio, and comic books. As I got older, I realized it was the content that grabbed me. *Mad Max*, Led Zeppelin, *The Twilight Zone*, *Batman*, you name it. I couldn't just "stare at a TV." It had to be compelling. I remember on a road trip from Boston to Florida listening to the radio for hours on end. Shock Jocks to fire and brimstone pastors. Love it or hate it, I couldn't turn it off. In junior high school, my father introduced me to the idea that it was the director and producer [along with the writer and "talent"] who brought the media to life. It wasn't just [Robert] De Niro. It was [Martin] Scorsese. My dad bought me a big VHS camcorder and I started shooting music videos of our band, movies, and wrestling matches. It was absolutely crazy. My brother and I almost destroyed my parent's basement. In high school, I became obsessed with *The David Letterman Show*. It was a bonkers addiction [but safer than others]. I was late virtually every day my senior year because I stayed up so late watching his show. I remember thinking, I can do that.

When it was time for college my parents sat me down and said [I'm paraphrasing], "Trust us. You should not be a scientist. You should go to film school." I chose Emerson College in my hometown of Boston. I studied TV, radio, and film. All aspects of each discipline. It was great. So how did I become a "professional" producer, director, host, and sometime actor? It was the accumulation of all those experiences and luck. I put myself out there and thankfully I got responses. I've been fortunate enough to occasionally make a living doing not only what I actually studied in college [and I use the word "studied" loosely] but also what I'm passionate about.

How did you get cast as an extra in *Escape From L.A.*?

I graduated from college and landed a dream job on MTV. It was an extraordinary twist of fate. I shot a VHS audition tape at my apartment and mailed it to MTV.

L: John Sencio [Extra/MTV Host],
R: John Sencio, Kurt Russell [Snake Plissken/Producer/Co-Writer]
(Photos Courtesy John Sencio)

A few weeks later, I got a call that I was being flown to New York for a screen test, which I thought was a prank. [Seriously, I almost hung up]. Long story short, I got the gig and within a year I was interviewing some of the biggest stars of the 90s. Mel Gibson, Jodie Foster, John Travolta, Halle Berry, the cast of *Friends* and hundreds more. One day, the talent coordinator came in and told me I was going to interview the star of the new movie *Stargate*, Kurt Russell. I freaked out. Snake Plissken! *Escape From New York* rocked. I saw it as a kid and it blew my mind. When Kurt came in for the interview, I was ecstatic, peppering him with detailed questions about every aspect of *Escape From New York*. When you watch that interview, you can see Kurt wasn't sure what to make of me at first. I was this long-haired rocker rattling off *Escape From New York* factoids like an over-caffeinated film freak.

Clearly at some point in the interview, Kurt realized I was the real deal. Kurt actually said on air, "You are a REAL fan." He went on to reveal that he and director John Carpenter were in serious talks about a sequel, *Escape From L.A.* Then, and this was magic for a fan. He said, "If we actually make it, you can be in it." Wow. Then Kurt and his team left the MTV studio. I remember thinking that was an excellent interview, but I had no expectation that if *Escape From L.A.* were made I would actually get a phone call. Almost a year later, my talent coordinator came to my dressing room and said, "Guess what? Paramount Pictures just called. They've invited you to be a part of *Escape From L.A.*" "When?" I asked. Answer, "This week." I was beyond psyched! Obviously, there was a quid pro quo here that I was excited to be a part of. I would help promote the movie. I'd shoot spots on the set, interviewing Kurt and John Carpenter, that would air before the premiere. It was a blast. A little adventure. We had a fantastic time. Those promotional spots look great.

How did you prepare for the role and how was your experience filming?

More often than not, if you do it right, shooting a movie takes a long time. *Escape From L.A.* was no exception. "Hurry Up and Wait" is an axiom during production. We shot extremely late at night. Around 1 AM and we would wrap at sunrise. As for my "role" in the movie. Well, I was really more of an extra with some additional screen time. We did talk about me having some more lines, but all of this was extremely last minute. That said, even the smallest details are taken seriously at that level. That was a big-budget Paramount Pictures production. We went through my little scene over and over with Kurt and John Carpenter. It was crazy having a stare down with Snake Plissken!

How was your experience working with the cast and crew? Is it true that each group that was similarly dressed started to hang out together and really got into their characters?

I love being on movie sets. John Carpenter is the consummate professional and Kurt Russell was absolutely tremendous. Both men are incredibly talented. I'm not just saying that. As anyone who has ever worked in show business will tell you, there can be a lot of egos and drama. There was nothing but creativity and generosity the few days I was there. It was a great memory. At one point at the end of my time there, just before dawn, Kurt looked over at me and said with a dry sense of humor, "Making movies is not all cocaine and sunglasses." I'd never heard that before. I always remembered that line. The cast and crew were also fantastic. Your question "did each group that was similarly dressed start to hang out together" is interesting. I recently watched a behind the scenes documentary on the original *Planet of the Apes*. That exact dynamic occurred on that set. They showed behind the scenes footage from craft services [the actors eating lunch] and at one table you had the chimps, at another the apes, and at another the orangutans. Crazy. I seem to remember some of that dynamic on the *Escape From L.A.* set but I was actually assigned to interview everyone while I was there, so I had to mingle as much as possible.

What's your favorite memory or memories of working on the movie?

My favorite memory of working on that movie? Honestly, it was the overall experience. I was born in Boston then grew up outside the city. The idea of Hollywood was magic, especially to a kid in suburban Massachusetts. As a child, watching a movie like *Escape From New York* was a true "experience." My dad had [and still has] an extensive record collection close to 5,000 vinyl albums. One of them was the soundtrack to *Escape From New York*. After we'd watch the movie, we'd put on that record and reenact scenes straight from the script. As kids, we took our *Escape From New York* seriously. When I graduated from high school, I moved back to Boston. Then after college, I moved to New York for MTV so when I was called for *Escape From L.A.*, it was like a brief *Escape From New York*. Kind of funny in that sense. The overall adventure of my personal *Escape From L.A.* experience [in its entirety] is my favorite memory of the movie. To this day, I still have that excitement when I work on something I'm passionate about.

What do you think of the movie personally?

Like many film fans, my range in movie taste is massive. For me, it starts with the classics. *Citizen Cane, Rebel Without a Cause, The Wizard of Oz, The Godfather, Blade Runner, To Kill a Mocking Bird, Taxi Driver*. It's a long list. I think *Escape From New York* is a dystopian classic. Depending on the reviewer, the film is described as action, sci-fi, fantasy, or post-apocalyptic. The feel of those movies: *Mad Max, Planet of the Apes, The Warriors, Logan's Run* - they all resonate deeply with my psyche and clearly the collective subconscious of millions of movie fans. The arch of those stories strikes a deep universal nerve. When the serious crap hits the fan, how does the hero [or antihero] survive. That is the journey of Snake Plissken.

As a director, John Carpenter has done some amazing work. *Halloween* set the template for an entire genre. *The Thing* is a sci-fi horror masterpiece. The suspense is insane like the Agatha Christie murder mystery *Ten Little Indians*. Then at the other end of the sci-fi spectrum, you have Carpenter's *Starman*. In comparison, it's incredibly understated yet wildly insightful. If you watch *Escape From L.A.* closely, it has some biting satire. It reminds me of one of Carpenter's smart cult classics *They Live*. What many fans don't realize is that John Carpenter composes the soundtrack to many of his movies. That is some serious talent. I actually have the theme of *Escape From New York* on my phone.

I want to make another mention of Kurt Russell. I had the pleasure of interviewing him multiple times. Keep in mind, I have interviewed hundreds of celebrities. You can see a large sample on my website [johnsencio.com]. Not that this makes me special. I don't deserve the Nobel Peace Prize for interviewing famous people. It just gives my opinion on the subject some veracity. Kurt was easily one of the coolest most genuine interviews ever and he just happens to be a movie star. I've read it's Kurt's iconic status from movies like *Escape From New York* and *The Thing* that drew Quentin Tarantino to cast Kurt in *Grindhouse* [*Death Proof*]. When an actor is a "star," their craftsmanship is sometimes overlooked. I suspect Quentin is not arguing these characters are *Hamlet,* but he is recognizing Kurt's obvious talent. In addition to these iconic roles, Kurt has standout performances in understated films like *Silkwood* and *The Mean Season* as well big budget pictures like *Tombstone*. The trailer for Tarantino's *The Hateful Eight* looks very promising.

What are you currently doing and what do you enjoy doing in your spare time?

What do I enjoy? Number one. Far and away my favorite thing in life is my family. My kids, my wife, and my parents. Professionally, I love being creative. Creating and consuming quality media content. Music, books, movies, radio, TV, comics. Obviously I've made most of my living generating TV content either in front of or behind the camera. This past year I've done some rewarding work on talk radio in Los Angeles. As to what I'm doing at this moment, I'm in pre-production on a documentary. What's it about? Not to be a buzzkill, but it's about cancer survival. I know, that's not hilarious especially given much of my work gravitates to comedy.

Follow me here because this topic does have a real *Escape From New York* connection. The first time I was diagnosed was in 1995 during my MTV days. I was treated with chemotherapy and radiation. It was challenging. In fact, months later just as my hair was growing back I did *Escape From L.A.* as a skinhead no less ironic. In fact, some people have seen photos from *Escape From L.A.* and have mistakenly [but understandably] thought those images were from my treatment. Back then, I never publicly mentioned my health. That was then. Seventeen years later in 2012 now with a wife and children I was diagnosed with an entirely different and deadlier form of cancer. This time I thought, I want to do something positive with this experience. Both times I searched for a documentary that followed an actual patient who beat the disease. Seemed natural for a movie fan. Nothing complex. Person gets cancer, person beats cancer, see the gritty journey, gain valuable insight, be inspired. I thought this would be a valuable weapon for survival. I couldn't find what I was looking so I'm making it. A documentary by a patient for patients called *Thryvor*. Long story short. The 2012/2013 battle was hardcore. A far more challenging fight then 1995. The good news is I survived. I'm healthy.

So here's the *Escape From New York* connection! One of the ancillary side effects of treatment is PTSD, Post Traumatic Stress Disorder. One of the techniques we used in dealing with trauma is movie therapy. I would go into a session and recount my reactions to movies I watched during recovery: *V for Vendetta*, *Marathon Man*, *Watchmen*, *The Tree of Life*, *Lone Survivor*, *Into the Wild*. A pattern emerges through this. Recognition of what's lurking below the surface of the psyche then a purging. I came into one session and mentioned that *Escape From New York* popped up in a dream. It only took a few minutes to figure out the connection in my subconscious. In *Escape From New York*, Snake Plissken is hesitant to accept the mission to rescue the President [Donald Pleasence] from the massive prison of New York City. Remember, Snake is an outlaw. However, Snake finally accepts the assignment reluctantly. In preparation for the mission, Snake is injected with what he is told is a vaccine. Well, it turns out the government as an insurance policy has injected an explosive into Snakes neck! It has a 24-hour countdown to ensure that Snake actually rescues the President. Here's the kicker. I had an explosive in my neck. Stage-four cancer. No surprise, *Escape From New York* surfaced from the depths of my psyche. We both had something deadly inside of us. I identified with that survivor archetype. As a kid I remember thinking *Escape From New York* is almost a horror movie. The gang members are like relentless zombies, Snake has this explosive in his neck, the clock is ticking. I kept wondering. How the hell is Snake going to survive but Snake does survive. Awesome. Ideally, the energy of those cool movies I watched growing up where the hero survives comes through in my documentary. The mission of *Thryvor* is to have a positive impact on patients.

JOHNNY TORRES
Extra

How did you get cast as an extra in *Escape From L.A.*?

At the time I was a member of Cenex Casting [now Central Casting] and was contacted by a casting director. I was told that my picture was handpicked by John Carpenter to be a featured extra in the movie as a member of Mescalito gang.

How did you prepare for the role and how was your experience filming?

I worked on the movie for about two months and I was in a few different scenes. The basketball scene, the Happy Kingdom scene, and the Sunset Boulevard scene, just to name a few. In the scene where Cuervo [Jones] [George Corraface] tries to shoot Snake with the sniper rifle after making all of the shots, I was the one that was holding the sniper rifle and handed it to him. I worked two weeks of twelve-hour nights on the basketball scene, which was filmed at the Los Angeles Memorial Coliseum. That basketball scene took so long to shoot because Kurt was determined to make all the shots himself all in the same take. He eventually made all the shots himself.

How was your experience working with the cast and crew? How did Cuervo Jones' [George Corraface] Mescalito gang collaborate and spend time together for instance?

All of the cast and the crew were very friendly and personable. It was pretty much like a family atmosphere. In between scenes, all of the guys in the Mescalito gang would pass the time playing cards.

What's your favorite memory or memories of working on the movie?

I remember on our last night of filming the basketball scene, our dinner consisted of steak and lobster, which we got to eat with Kurt Russell and John Carpenter in the parking lot of the Los Angeles Memorial Coliseum. John Carpenter is an avid fan of the Los Angeles Lakers. I remember one night in particular that he paid a few thousand dollars just to get the big screens turned on so he could watch the

L-R: Johnny Torres [Extra], Steve Buscemi [Map to the Stars Eddie]
(Photo Courtesy Johnny Torres)

Lakers game in between shots. I am one of very few that can say I've watched a Lakers game sitting on the field of the Los Angeles Memorial Coliseum.

What do you think of the movie personally?

I personally love the movie. Not only because I was in it. I think it was ahead of its time in regards to special effects.

What are you currently doing and what do you enjoy doing in your spare time?

I am married and have three kids. I currently work for an automotive tire distributor in the Inland Empire as a warranty manager. Hoping to someday get back into the movie business [hint, hint to any casting directors]. Either in front of the camera or behind the camera. After *Escape From L.A.,* I did extra work on a few other movies and TV shows. In my spare time, I like to travel and spend time with my family. I like go to rock concerts and go to live plays. I also like to play poker with my friends and at various casinos around the SoCal area and Las Vegas.

JOHN CASINO
Stunt Player

How did you end up being a stunt player and Kurt Russell's stunt double?

I started out when I got out of the Army. I wanted to be a sheriff and I applied for the sheriff's department in Orange County, California. I took all my tests and I was on the list. While I was waiting, I was going to college for police science and there's an amusement park in Buena Park, California called Knott's Berry Farm. They have gunfighters out there who do shootouts and little skits out in the streets. I auditioned for that and got hired to do that. Then three years later Universal Studios had a stunt show called *The Western Stunt Show* up there and I applied for that and got hired. I did that for about five years and in between I went down to meet some of the producers on TV shows and got hired on a TV series in 1979 and worked as a stuntman for many years. Then I met Kurt Russell in 1988 on *Tango & Cash*. They were looking for a stunt double for him, so they called me down for an audition and Kurt picked me out and we got along really good and I've been with him ever since 1988.

How did you and Kurt Russell prepare for this project and how did you collaborate?

We both read the script and break it down and figure out what we have to practice up on. The most important thing was that we had to be in great shape. They had a big trailer that they took everywhere on location with a gym in it so we could work out every night. At the studio, we had a gym we could work out in. We also had a person there that put us on a strict diet and gave us vitamins and fed us proper food. We really kept in shape for it, watched what we ate, and rehearsed on a lot of things. We had to do motorcycles or whatever and you'd be surprised. Kurt does a lot of his own stunts. He's a very talented man. We were working six days. You work nights and you work fourteen, fifteen hours. By the time you get home, it's probably six, seven o'clock in the morning. Then you have to be back at work at six o'clock at night, so all you do is go to bed, take a nap, do whatever you can, get up, take care of your bills, do whatever you have to do, and then back to work again. And that was three months of working nights. The

L-R: Robert Carradine [Skinhead], John Casino [Stunt Player]
(Photo Courtesy Robert Carradine)

hours are incredible. I think the shortest day we had was about twelve hours and we go all the way into fourteen hours sometimes, but they have to give us a twelve-hour turnaround. They have to at least give us twelve hours to come back. Yeah, especially when you work night. It's very, very difficult. Especially after working three months of nights and then going back to days again. It's kind of hard to get yourself back on the time schedule.

What kind of challenges did this project provide and which stunts, scenes, or locations were the most challenging, problematic, memorable, and fun to work on?

Most of the stuff we did were fights. There wasn't anything that was major, major difficult. We had to do a lot of running, a lot of jumping, mostly fights. The hang gliding thing we did towards the end with the machine guns, those were all on cables, so we weren't working on hang gliders. We were on cables. That was pretty difficult to shoot because of the timing of coming down on that wire on the hang gliders and shooting the machine guns at the same time. That was a little difficult, but we had a good special effects team.

We did another scene that got cut out where we had to do a mudslide and they dumped 11,000 gallons of water on me and I went flying down a hill with water behind me. That was kind of difficult, but they never showed it in the movie. It was fun to do and then every time they do a master of me doing the big shot, we do close-ups of Kurt and we plug in little shots of him doing the same thing. It was a nice little scene but, unfortunately, it was totally different when they edited it. A lot of things we did with the submarine, that was all green screen. The scene where Kurt is reaching down to grab a hold of the submarine and the earthquake happens, that was all done on stage with green screen and I did most of that myself. We only had one take to do it because if we didn't do it in one take, it was about five or six hours for them to set up to redo it. It was very, very important to do get everything done in one take.

The surfing scene was difficult to shoot. I mean, all of that was done on a green screen with surfboards and a background. When Kurt jumps off the surfboard back of Steve Buscemi's [Map to the Stars Eddie] car, that of course is me and I'm doing that. I'm standing in front of a jeep on the bumper and I was holding on. Then at a certain time when the jeep got up to speed and the car drove by, I jumped off the jeep onto the back of the car and we continued the scene. That's how we did the transition from the surfboard onto the car. It was pretty fun to do. Again, we did that in one take. That thing you were talking about where Kurt got shot in the leg and fell into the water in the sewer? We did that on stage where I got shot in the leg and fell into the water. Everything was made sure. Everything was safe. The water was at the right level and everything was good. The scene where Kurt rides the motorcycle in the back of the truck... I did not do the jump on that one. We had a special guy that only does motorcycles. His name was Jimmy Roberts [Stunt Player] [Uncredited] and he did the jump over the horse and then we did the landing with Kurt. That was all done with special effects on a rig on cables, so that was done really safely too. Yeah, it worked out great.

Were there any accidents during the making of the movie?

Nothing at all. Nothing at all. Jeff Imada was our stunt coordinator, and Jeff is one the best stunt coordinators, second unit directors in the business and he won't allow anybody doing anything if it's dangerous. I mean, we rehearsed and everything turned out great. Nobody got hurt. The only thing that I can say is, it was very cold. Some of the nights we worked in the water. It was very cold, but it was very safe.

How was your experience working with the cast and crew?

I think it was probably my fifth or sixth movie with Kurt. We did a lot of night scenes and everyone worked. John Carpenter always uses the same people. The same cinematographer, the same first assistant, second assistant directors, and so it's almost like a family. The makeup people and everything. We have so much fun when we work. The entire movie was a joyous occasion. At the end of the movie, we all went to John Carpenter's house and had a party and it was a very, very fun situation. Peter Fonda [Pipeline] and everyone showed up and we had a great time. One of the most incredible things that was done on that movie, do you remember the basketball scene? That last time when Kurt threw the ball? That was actually him. He shot across the court and he made it and that was pretty amazing. I've worked with a lot of actors, but Kurt has definitely been my favorite to work with. He's just a very genuine person. He's a nice man and the way you see him on the screen is how he is. He's just a very nice man and it's always a pleasure to work with him.

What's your favorite memory of working on the movie?

Just working with John Carpenter and Kurt.

What do you think of the movie personally?

I liked it. I thought it was great. I enjoyed doing it. There were some things that were a little bit kind of hokey, but all in all it turned out good and, like I said, we had a lot of fun doing it. It's just like the surfing scene.

Do you have any favorite memory or memories of working with Kurt Russell during all the years?

Yeah. I've done seventeen movies with him. We just did *The Hateful Eight,* which is a western that Quentin Tarantino directed, which is coming out in December. Then we did another one called *Deepwater Horizon,* which will come out next year. It's about the BP oil rig that blew up off the gulf coast. I think one of my favorite movies with Kurt was probably *Backdraft. Backdraft* was a really fun movie to do and we had a great time doing it. We were in Chicago for seven months. It was a very tough experience. We worked with genuine fire. Back in those days, there wasn't that much CGI, so we worked with real fire. There were places where we're hanging from the beams and, when it got too hot, we would scream and they would turn on the hoses and cool us down. It's another show that we did a lot of dangerous things on, but Walter Scott was our stunt coordinator and nobody got hurt. We had a great time. I don't think I've ever done a movie with Kurt that I haven't had a good time with. He's always a fun person to be around.

The thing about Kurt is there are a lot of things actors aren't allowed to do as far as stunts go and Kurt is very gung-ho as far as doing things. He always checks with me to find out if it's something that he needs to do and I say, "You know what, this is something we don't need to do because I can do it. When we do a close-up of it, we do it with you, but in the long shots let me take care of it." He always listens to me. He's always been great about that. He just gets along with everyone and the thing is, he's probably the most knowledgeable man I know about the movies. He knows everything about it. He knows about directing, producing, and he's a good family guy. He's just a good friend. He's been very good to me. He's made my career. And the thing about Kurt too. We do movies like *Tango & Cash, Backdraft, Stargate,* and *3000 Miles to Graceland* where he plays kind of a crusty character. When you look at movies like *Captain Ron* and *Overboard* where he just plays this friendly character, he's very verse on different things too. It's just so much fun to work with him. I don't know if you ever saw the movie *Overboard*. That's pretty much how Kurt's character is in real life. He's just a very happy-go-lucky guy. So I have been really fortunate. The movie we just did with Tarantino. That was a blast too. So much fun to do. Doing a western with Tarantino and Kurt Russell is pretty exciting to do.

John Carpenter is another great guy. He's an awesome man. Probably one of the best directors around and just a really nice person too. Probably out of all my forty years of working, my favorite director to work with because he loves stuntmen and he loves to make sure they're taken care of. John and I keep in touch all the time. He calls me to see how I'm doing and I call him to see how he's doing.

What are you currently doing and what do you enjoy doing in your spare time?

I'm sixty years old now, so I've been doing stunts since I was nineteen, so I try not to go on location too often. I like to hang out with my family. My kids are growing up and I like hanging out with my family. I don't do too many recreational things anymore. I used to ride motorcycles and things like that, but I don't really do anything like that anymore because if I get injured, I won't be able to work. I have to kind of keep in shape, eat well and just take care of myself. Go to a good church. I know it sounds kind of boring but that's my life. That's what I like to do. I live in Georgia now. I moved out of Los Angeles years ago and wanted to have a place easier for my kids to grow up.

JAMES LEW
Stunt Player

How did you end up being a stuntman/coordinator and actor?

My very first job was on the original *Kung Fu* series that starred David Carradine. My best friend found out there was a "cattle call" at Warner Brothers looking to cast Chinese talent that are kung fu students. We decided to check it out not knowing anything about the "business". We showed up at Warner Brothers and saw this very long line of people. At first we thought not to wait in this long line and go get a hamburger lunch at Bob's Big Boy nearby but we thought since we were already there to go ahead and wait in line. Luckily, it turned out that we both got cast as kung fu disciples. It was a life changing beginning and I caught the bug to continue in the business. I met my calling and jobs continued to come through.

In the early years, I was the go-to guy that got beat up, shot, falling on the ground. In the stunt business, we call them "ground pounders!" Many shows a stunt coordinator would hire me to be in a fight scene and then frequently ask me to create the fight choreography. This was always an exciting day for me to create a fight scene. It became a regular process, that a stunt coordinator would hire me to be in a fight scene and then have me create the fight choreography. The stunt coordinator would leave for a production meeting. After his meeting with the director/producers, they would come back and have me show them the fight scene. I would hear the stunt coordinator, tell the director/producers that this is the action he put together.

After doing this procedure on many stunt jobs, the light bulb turned on that I should take a step up and pursue work as a stunt coordinator. The opportunity to be in front of camera in a fight/action scene also required many times being asked to say a line. That sparked the passion to expand my skills into the acting world. As in anything I do, my goal is to do my best. I was fortunate to have learned so much from several brilliant acting teachers. I feel the acting classes made me a better action actor, fight/stunt coordinator.

L-R: James Lew [Stunt Player] [Saigon Shadow], Al Leong [Stunt Player] [Saigon Shadow], Stuart Quan [Stunt Player] [Saigon Shadow], Jay Leno [Set Visitor], Jeff Imada [Saigon Shadow/Stunt Coordinator], John Koy [Stunt Player] [Saigon Shadow], Leo Lee [Stunt Player] [Saigon Shadow]
(Photo Courtesy James Lew)

How did you get cast as a stunt player/Saigon Shadow in *Escape From L.A.*?

I have been friends with Jeff Imada [Saigon Shadow/Stunt Coordinator] for many years, starting from the martial arts world and working together many times as stuntmen. Jeff was also one of the stuntmen on *Big Trouble in Little China*, which I was fortunate to be the fight coordinator on.

How did you and uncredited Saigon Shadows' John Koy [Stunt Player], Leo Lee [Stunt Player], Al Leong [Stunt Player], Stuart Quan [Stunt Player] as well as Jeff Imada [Saigon Shadow/Stunt Coordinator] and Pam Grier [Hershe] prepare for these roles and stunts and how did you collaborate? How did you execute the glider scenes for instance and what kind of challenges did this movie provide?

I wasn't involved with the glider scene. It would have been fun. I had a limited schedule because I had another project that I was prepping, so I didn't get to play on some of the scenes. I did have to fall off the helicopter to the ground. No crash mats, just good old dirt. John Carpenter did not give us any specific directions with our characters. We all just stuck with the characters being pure bad ass and in survival mode because of the harsh times of the story.

How was your experience working with the cast and crew?

The entire cast and crew were very talented and professional. It was such a fun and relaxed work environment. I look at a job like this, with so many of my friends working on it, as just a fun get together. It was also such a great reunion to work on a movie with John Carpenter and Kurt Russell. Pam Grier is an icon and she is a bad mofo in person and extremely nice. I admire her commitment to character with her growing her armpit hair!

What's your favorite memory or memories of working on the movie?

Getting to visit and work together with John Carpenter and Kurt Russell was such a pleasure. Both true talented legends in the entertainment business.

What do you think of the movie personally?

It wasn't what I expected and a different vision from the original movie, which I loved. There were some very creative choices and, as just pure entertainment, it was fun.

What are you currently doing and what do you enjoy doing in your spare time?

I recently moved to beautiful Vancouver, Canada from my life long home in Los Angeles, California. I am enjoying life in this peaceful environment. I signed with a top theatrical/commercial agency. I just finished working on a wonderful movie playing a retired general from the Chinese army. Not one bit of stunts involved. My focus between acting and enjoying the beach is to finally finish writing my book. The title is *Fights Camera Action*. It is a "how to book" about cinematic action. It would be a wonderful way for me to give back with my great experiences as a stuntman, actor, Emmy winning stunt/

fight coordinator, DGA second unit director and director. I want to share my knowledge and hard knocks. And all profits go to charity.

DAVID WITZ
Unit Production Manager

How did you end up being a production manager and producer?

I worked for many years for Sandy Howard Productions starting in accounting and worked my way up to producing films for him. When his company stopped making movies, I looked for the best job I could get, which was as a production manager. At that time, there was a lot of non-union work and I was able to do enough shows to qualify for placement on the DGA qualifications list allowing me to work on DGA shows.

How did you get the job of unit production manager on *Escape From L.A.*?

I was hired by Film Finances to oversee a series at Showtime that was having budget problems. This series was being produced by Debra Hill [Producer/Co-Writer]. At first, she was very suspicious of me and the job I was doing, which was basically trying to keep the bond company Film Finances from having to take over the show. Ultimately, it turned out to be a good working relationship with Debra. When she went on to her next project, *Escape From L.A.,* she asked me to come in for a four-week exploratory budgeting and concept period where we tried to figure out how to make the movie for the price the studio wanted. A couple weeks after that, Debra called to say that they had agreed to do the show and that she had to put some of her fee against the budget as a contingency. I don't remember the amount, but at the time Debra told me, "That's as much as a house. Don't lose my house!"

How did you, Alexandra Koch [Production Supervisor] as well as Debra Hill [Producer/Co-Writer] and Kurt Russell prepare for this project and how did you collaborate? Any issues prior to filming and such?

It was an exciting project for me as it was my first big studio project. As I've come to learn over the years, each project is dictated by the way the director approaches their shows and my job is to figure out how to help them make their movie for the budget. John [Carpenter] is a very pragmatic and smart filmmaker. He would not even get out of the scouting van if he thought the location was going to be too hard to shoot logistically.

What kind of challenges did this project provide and which scenes or locations were the most challenging, problematic, memorable, and fun to work on?

Since it was a location heavy show, there were a lot of challenges and problems. The coliseum [Los Angeles Memorial Coliseum] did try and extort us for a completely new field. We had some toxic waste issues at the Carson landfill [Former Cal Compact Landfill] [Sunset Boulevard/Beverly Hills Hotel Exterior/ Santa Monica Freeway]. At the Universal [Studios] backlot [Courthouse Square] [Happy Kingdom by the Sea], we had an issue with gunfire after 10 PM because of the neighbors that border Universal and Universal not wanting to piss them off due to ongoing development they were doing, which later became City Walk.

How did you manage to solve the toxic waste issues at the former Cal Compact Landfill in Carson?

Not very interesting. We just had to avoid the dirt and the construction crew that did work in it had to have disposable suits and all the equipment had to be washed down that had the infected dirt on it.

Was anything discarded due to budget?

I don't recall anything that was planned then scrapped as we had a pretty detailed production schedule and budget before we started.

How was your experience working with the cast and crew?

I have good memories of working on the show as it was a group effort to figure out how to do this huge show for a modest budget with a lot of production challenges. All nights. Lots of extras that needed to have makeup and dressed. Lots of visual/ practical effects. Big stunt sequences etcetera. I enjoyed working with Debra Hill. She was one of the few producers that was involved with every aspect of the movie. Writing the script, casting, marketing, watching dailies every day, cost report meetings. She could do it all. It was a sad day when she passed away.

John Carpenter was a very responsible filmmaker. He never wanted to step foot on a set that he didn't know how the day was going to go and be sure to make his day. I remember one night being woken at 3 AM by a very upset John Carpenter calling to tell me it was raining and he couldn't shoot and asking me what he should do. He was really venting because neither Debra nor I was there most nights as we worked the days and split shifts during most of the filming since he was so dependable and didn't need us looking over his shoulder. I told him to wrap and we'd sort it out. John was upset because he did not want to fall behind schedule, so he made up the time over the next couple of days and got back on schedule. Kurt Russell was great to work with, always up to do anything to help the project. One night he was supposed to ride his motorcycle through a maze of people and stuff. His contacts were irritating his eyes, so he rode the course once with his glasses to see and then did it without them and an eye patch on for the shot. He did not want a double doing it.

Interesting note was that they really wanted to cast Kate Hudson, who was pretty much an unknown at the time [except for being Goldie Hawn's daughter] as the President's [Cliff Robertson] daughter, but at the time she was under eighteen. It would have been almost impossible to schedule the movie around the curfew and hours restrictions for a minor.

What do you think of the movie personally?

I like the movie but have not watched it in a long time.

What are you currently doing and what do you enjoy doing in your spare time?

I am still working as a production manager and line producer. I recently did some additional photography on *Baywatch* and last year I did the project *Dunkirk*. In my spare time, I like to go to the movies and play tennis.

CHRISTIAN P. DELLA PENNA
First Assistant Director

How did you end up being a second/first assistant director?

I was on a show called *Perfect,* which was a John Travolta thing years and years ago in 1983 or 1984, something like that. I wanted to be an actor, but I was a stand-in, so I got to be right there by camera and watch the production assistants and assistant directors working. I helped out the production people checking the background and I kind of got to see what everybody did. After that, I got a job from a guy named Artist Robinson and he brought me on as a production assistant. I worked my way into being an assistant director through the Director's Guild to get my pay days. Artist Robinson hooked into John Carpenter and brought me on as a PA [Production Assistant] on a show called *They Live.* Then I was the second AD [Assistant Director] on *Village of the Damned* and then a 1st AD on *Escape From L.A.* and *Vampires.* I had a chance to do *Ghosts of Mars,* but I just wanted to kind of do something else. At that moment, I was directing television. Larry Franco was John Carpenter's 1st AD and he moved up as I moved up.

How did you get the job of first assistant director on *Escape From L.A.*?

I don't think I was John's first choice. There were some big time assistant directors that applied for the job, but they were saying John couldn't do it in seventy days or something and John didn't like that. I went in there and John liked me as a 2nd AD, but I was kind of quiet around him. He scared me a little bit. He's kind of intimidating. We had a sit down and I just said, "This will be cool. I believe in whatever days you think it's gonna take." So he gave me the opportunity. It was an odd thing. I had some directors to call that I had worked with to talk to him. The studio wasn't really sure. It was my first real go at it, you know. It was a big thing for me. It was a pretty big show at the time, fifty million or so.

How did you, Martin Jedlicka [Second Assistant Director] and Jason Roberts [Second Second Assistant Director] prepare and how did you collaborate?

As a 1st AD, you schedule the motion picture with your production designer

L-R: Shyam V. Yadev [Visual Effects Production Assistant], John Carpenter [Director/Co-Writer/Co-Composer], Benu Bhandari [Script Supervisor], Jeff Imada [Saigon Shadow/Stunt Coordinator], Rochelle Ashana [Stunt Player], Christian P. Della Penna [First Assistant Director]
(Photo Courtesy Shyam "Toast" Yadav)

knowing that certain things have to be built. You have to put those towards the end of your schedule. Certain things are easier to get to, so you want to put those in front and you also have actor restrictions and such. I schedule the movie, break it down into elements, and have meetings with different departments with John. We have a prop meeting, wardrobe meeting, and an effects meeting and a special effects meeting. We chat about the show and get their input. I put that altogether and make a master schedule, my shooting schedule, and such. That was my first real feature. I did a couple of movies before, but I never did anything that big in my life. It was huge for me. The show was so big at the time.

The Sunset Boulevard [Former Cal Compact Landfill] [Sunset Boulevard/Beverly Hills Hotel Exterior/Santa Monica Freeway] set where Snake walks along before he runs into Steve Buscemi [Map to the Stars Eddie], that set was probably a good quarter mile long, the whole thing. I mean, it was crazy huge. They had to make electric cable to accommodate our show. There wasn't enough to rent at the time. For me to talk to everybody and give my safety meetings at the beginning of the day, they gave me a microphone and they had speakers. I could just talk to everybody calmly because we never yell on a John Carpenter set ever. I would talk calmly about the day's events, whatever. I'd prep the show with John and then I'd make sure everything is ready for each scene. That's what I do on set and that's my job. For instance, I start my day with whatever Scene 63 is. It's got Snake Plissken on the bike or whatever. I make sure that all of that is ready and that it's safe. I had my own staff with my second AD and an additional second, so I had a big staff. We had seven, eight, ten guys to help me manage the set every day for John.

What kind of challenges did this project provide and which scenes or locations were the most challenging, problematic, memorable, and fun to work on? Did anything mess up the shooting schedule and such?

The submarine sequence when he lands on shore and Peter Fonda [Pipeline] greets him. Part of that was in Griffith Park [Mulholland Drive/Mountainside] and I think part of that was at Castaic Lake [Cahuenga Pass Shoreline]. John did not like the submarine when we first saw it. He was like, "What the fuck is this?" because Larry [G. Paull], our production designer had it kind of retro. It was cool but John wanted it really bitchin' modern. Somehow John didn't buy into it by the time we got there. He didn't like that, so we didn't shoot much there. That was the only thing that I can say that really messed up one of my nights because we didn't have the submarine. Then we went back and did some stuff on stage with him falling off this little cliff, the submarine falls off, and we had to reshoot that a little bit, so that cost us a little time. Otherwise, we were right on schedule. I mean, we had a lot of days that were shorter than we thought.

Talking about that submarine sequence, we did the interior on stage, I believe. I think it was on stage. I can't remember, but the two guys that are down below there that help him into the sub, that's Mark [Thompson] and Brian [Phelps]. Those are two DJ's and radio hosts from L.A. that are really popular. They were really cool. We treated them really good too, so that was fun. That submarine turned out to be like a bullet, beautiful and sleek. We just did it all CGI from there. That was the only thing that I think really tripped me up like, "Ah fuck. I got to reschedule that."

Another time, we were down in Carson where Snake comes across Sunset Boulevard and there's all the people and stuff there. We got fogged in one night and we just stood there. We had one of those huge lights in the air. You couldn't even see that light, it was so foggy. John was kind of putting pressure on me as a first AD, "What are you gonna do, Chris? Are you gonna pull the plug? Are we gonna go home? Are we gonna wait out the fog? We can't film in this." So we waited for about an hour and half. It was about two or three in the morning and I finally said, "Ok. I'm gonna send you home because we're not being able to get it," and I personally sat there for another two hours just to make sure I made the right decision, but we had to shut down that night. I had like five or six nights for that sequence and we were ahead.

Here's one that was kind of funky and didn't turn out very well. It was the mud sequence [deleted] where Snake slides down the mud. It was a big fricking muddy mess up there. We had these trucks dumping water over this hill. We're trying to make it real. Then you try to do it. It was like 1996 and we had to make a mudslide and it was just a big mess. That was another night that didn't turn out very well for anybody. I just remember me and Jeff Imada, the stunt coordinator, on the hill with shovels trying to dig a path that was safe that wasn't a mess. It was like a nightmare.

When Kurt's standing there and he's got those guys. Bangkok Rules, right? That was my line right there, Bankok Rules, yeah. I love that scene. The wind was blowing so fucking hard on that scene we couldn't keep the flames going. That location was hard for us. It gave me a lot of trouble. I just remember how big some sets were and all the vehicles that were there. This being my first big show, I would get anxiety about how big things were. But I would go to that little set that was lit up at the time. I would just kind of own that moment and not worry about everything else that was happening all around me. There'd be fifty or a hundred background extras getting ready while the sets are being dressed. Then the makeup and all that stuff. Craziness. I had a really good staff that managed that for me. When all those shadowy figures are chasing Snake and he goes into the manhole, two of those guys running after him after my assistant directors. Jason and Martin are both in that scene running. There were a lot of crewmembers in those hoodies making some extra money.

I remember that it was very exciting to get the coliseum [Los Angeles Memorial Coliseum] into your show. The threat of, how do we make all the background? At first we thought we'll fill the coliseum of 90,000 people, but that was impossible. Then we thought, maybe we could do some tie-in, have a bunch of background, keep shooting them in all the positions and then you put all that in. We didn't want to do that either, so John came to conclusion that there's not that many people. I can't remember how many we put up there. Two, three hundred. I don't know how many, just to fill the end there a little bit and I think that kind of worked. It was quite amazing to film in there. We had the basketball court at the bottom and there's never a basketball court at the coliseum. I'd get there early. I'd get there a couple of hours beforehand and just play pick-up games with the production assistants in the coliseum on a basketball court. Who does that? Who gets an opportunity to have that?

John Carpenter is a huge Los Angeles Lakers fan, of course. He's a big basketball fan and very knowledgeable about it. On one of our nights, Magic Johnson was playing his first game back from being HIV positive and so John had it rigged so it was on the coliseum's huge screen for us to watch. When we'd roll camera, we'd turn it off. John pulled that off. Remember in that coliseum scene when Kurt's being taken out and he's got those guys on him and there's guns on him? They're walking him out to those cages to do that whole basketball event. Kurt is like, "These guys are being too easy on me." On one take, he just like totally kicked all their butts real quick. Bam, bam, bam. Took them down. That wasn't in the movie, but it was his point of saying, "You guys better fricking keep on me because I'm Snake Plissken!" After that, those guys were scared shitless. Kurt would do that every now and then. The coliseum was a tough one for sure, but it was cool filming there.

We didn't like the treadmill moment because Kurt could, at anytime, just stop walking on the treadmill. He would just do it. He's like, "I don't want to keep walking on this thing. I can just step up to the side," and just like put up his feet up to the sides a bit. He's like, "This is bullshit." He didn't like that. That was dumb. That got cut way down, that treadmill. That wasn't the smartest idea really in that respect. I know that.

When we got to the square [Courthouse Square] at Universal [Studios Lot] [Happy Kingdom by the Sea], we took the tree out and stuff. I mean, *Back to the Future* was known for that square and we went in there, lined up all our Latina cars with all those wonderful paint jobs and all those guys. I must have had more than fifty or so people with M16 rifles. To reload everyone's weapon would take us forty-five minutes, almost an hour, just to get another take. Back then, you really used weapons. You used blanks and stuff. Rick Dees was a big DJ in L.A. at the time and he lived close to Universal. He would try to shut us down after ten o'clock. He was all mad about us because we'd fire fifty or sixty M16's at once. John would have seven, eight cameras on that and I had two big walkie-talkies. I was talking to everybody on the ground and to the helicopter in the air, which was being shot at the same time. It was very coordinated for us to manage all that. I have to say we did all that very well my team and I. We managed the whole sequence really, really well. That was really cool for me to do. At the time, it was such a big thing. I mean, *Seinfeld*, all those actors would come up to meet John and watch the set. It was a big event at Universal. It was the set to go and see at the moment.

Then there was the night that we were out at that horse ranch [Ventura Farms] doing the ending where the helicopter crashes and he walks away from it. What Kurt did was cool. He got it from some other movie. I can't remember the name of the movie, but he goes, "Pour me down with a bunch of water!" and we got his jacket all wet. Then he got by that fire and it started smoking and he walked away. That was Kurt that did that. He was like a kid in a candy shop when he got that jacket smoking. "Check it out now! It's like I walked out of this thing!" He was really excited about that. He's fun to film with that stuff. He's funny.

Now that we're talking about it, there was a lot of shit that night that happened to be bad. When we got there, [the set] was like a cutout kind of bullshit thing. We wanted real helicopter parts there and it wasn't really that, so they scrambled to put something else together. I know that John was upset about that, once again with Larry the production designer. It wasn't a big enough hull. They should've done it more like a real helicopter. I don't remember how we fixed it that night. They brought out a bunch more shit or something. We were doing some other stuff and we blew it up at the last moment. They had to keep working on making the crash sequence a little more real looking. We couldn't afford to put in a bunch of CGI helicopter stuff in there. I remember it was a big thing. The helicopter itself was funny because the guy who was renting it to us was really particular about it. It was this high-tech helicopter we were using. Kurt is like, "What do you mean I can't touch this shit?" and he started touching all sorts of shit. He's like, "Fuck that, man. Keep that guy away from me." "Yes, sir." We didn't damage anything, but Kurt was like, "What do you mean we can't touch anything? Dammit. This is bullshit. I'm driving this thing."

Once we got on stage, the green screen got us fricking sick. It was one of the biggest they had ever put together. We had to put these yellow glasses on because we were all getting nauseous because the screen was so much green. Once we put the glasses on, we weren't sick. That doesn't happen anymore, but it was a really big fricking green screen and we were still having two or three o'clock afternoon calls. John just didn't want to turn around. He's purely a vampire, man. He eats breakfast for dinner and dinner for breakfast. He's a vampire. We could've all gone back to 7 AM calls in the morning, but he's like, "No way, we're staying on nights." For another twenty days or whatever on stage, we stayed on afternoon call, which is so rare. You would never do that, but of course, we did it for John.

We spent a long time sitting there by that green screen. We spent days on that. You learned a lot. It was still the breaking age of it all back then. They'd done a little bit of it, but we were trying to figure out what we could afford and do, especially with stuff like the surfboard sequence. When we put water on the surfboards, they would disappear because of all the green. So we did it again dry and put all the water in later, which we weren't expecting to do.

How was your experience working with the cast and crew?

With *Escape,* it was all nights. We lost a good twenty-five, thirty percent of our crew the first two weeks of work because they couldn't handle all the nights we had. They had children at home that wouldn't let them sleep or they had construction by their house or something. Once we settled into that, we went seventy days or something. We went a long time. It was an odd thing. I couldn't call my friends. You shop in the middle of the night at grocery stores. It was like the earth was a lot less crowded for all of us. We all kind of got used to it, actually, I have to say.

John and Kurt and Peter. Those guys were cool. Peter was really great. I worked with Peter before, so it was nice to see him again. He's awesome. He likes the set real quiet. When you work with Peter, it's real quiet, man. John's sets are always quiet. John's real quiet anyways on the set. There's never any yelling or any kind of talking loud on the set with John ever. He's really great. I kind of like that too. Kurt is just one special person. At least for us, he was. I've never heard a bad story about him. Since he's been a kid he's been acting and he was really great.

The relationship that Kurt and John have is special, so to be around that was really a neat moment for us. I don't know if you've heard this story before but we're in a production meeting. It's me and John and Gary Kibbe the DP [Director of Photography], Larry the production designer, and some of their assistants taking notes. We're just kind of going through the script. John had a very specific way how Kurt travels to Los Angeles in that moment, so we're kind of tracking that at the time. Kurt busts in and he's wearing Snake Plissken's original stuff from *Escape From New York* and he's like, "Look at this! It fits me still!" We were laughing because it still fit him. He was so proud. He was really special.

I saw him later, years later, at Warner Brothers when he was doing *Poseidon* and he remembered me and we had a big chat. He's really a cool guy. I remember one time, it was late and we were down in that street in Carson. He had to do that sequence where he jumps on all those cars and gets on the motorcycle and he takes off and does this wheeling. It was probably four in the morning and he had kind of gone back to sleep a little bit. He was always out. Kurt is ready and comes out and hangs on the set all the time. He's out there the whole time hanging out just like an old-time actor. He had gone back to sleep and we're all set up. "Let's get this shot." I got it all set up and we had all those people on the background, so I said, "I'll go get him," so I got in a golf cart and cruised down. I knocked on his trailer and I had to go in and wake him up and stuff. He's like, "What's up?" "I really need you for this thing. For this shot. I'm sorry it's so late and had to wake you up." He puts his fricking arm around me and goes, "Chris, I'm making so much money and I love you buddy and I'll do anything you want. Let's go down and get this shot." That was a special moment for me. He loved filmmaking. He loves being an actor and it didn't matter. Some actors are like, "What the fuck, man! Why are you waking me up?" He was like, "Let's go do it." I said, "Kurt. You're awesome, dude."

I didn't have any trouble with any of the actors. I had worked with A.J. Langer [Utopia] years before. I did a show called *In the Heat of the Night* and she would play this girl that was distraught. She was really, really good and so when John was thinking of her I said, "I don't know if this is the right look, but she sure can act." And I thought she did really good. He worked with her a little bit, but he'll like get all the actors to come to his house and hang out with Sandy [King] and have a big meal and they'll have a one-on-one with the actor talking about the script. Then they'll have them all back together and they'll have a big meal altogether and they all talk about it, so when you get out there on the day there's no conversation why we're doing this like this. None of that happens. It's already done. He's already worked that out. That's old school directing and that's the best way to do it. The cast is great. No complains there, man.

John shoots very efficiently and works with many cameras at once. He doesn't really make it complicated at all. I mean, if there's a complicated sequence, we talk about it way in advance. John is very organized and it's really special working with him like that. For an AD to director relationship, it was awesome. He works with his AD and lines it up and every morning you go in there and you just kind of talk about the day with him as he's looking through his work. You tell him what you got for him and then he just works through it. He's all prepared.

I knew Gary Kibbe as a DP. I worked with him before. It was hard for him. It was one of the biggest things he's ever tried to accomplish for sure. He got mad at me one night. That was pretty tough. He wasn't very happy with me. I was maybe goofing around or something like that. We had to have a meeting between all the three of us and John's like, "He's my guy. He's not going anywhere." It was an odd thing. I kind of got on Kibbe's nerves and it was because he and the production designer had different opinions about lighting and looks and things and so. That was getting on to his nerves and I think that I maybe fueled that. I'm not sure, but Gary is a wonderful guy. I did *Vampires* with him after that. We had a good ol' time. He's old school, man. He's cool.

Do you know if John Carpenter got his first choices regarding actors and crew members on the movie?

I don't know if he got his first choice with her [A.J. Langer] particular. I know that the Cuervo [Jones] character, that guy [George Corraface]. They wanted him and they fought for him a little bit. I think the studio wasn't really into him, but John was but the girl was a bit of an issue. I think Kurt had something to do with that too because Kurt produced it too. Kurt and Debra [Hill] [Producer/Co-Writer] and John were all in cahoots together. I don't really remember too much of that. He wanted Gary Kibbe and he got his wardrobe people that he always use. They work together all the time. We all did four or five movies together so he got all the people that he wanted.

What's your favorite memory or memories of working on the movie?

I had a lot of good times on that show. There's one moment of Kurt walking away that I wish I could freeze frame. It was a green screen shot and he's walking into L.A. and he said, "Chris, when I do this, I'm just gonna be laughing and calling out your name so when you see it on the show, you'll know that I'll be thinking of you." And he did that. I said, "That is super cool, buddy." That's my little secret moment with Kurt that he did for me.

Just being around Kurt and Peter were my favorite moments. Hanging out with Kurt, Peter, and John when they were doing lighting and just the stories those guys told and the personal stories that Peter Fonda would talk about, his father and stuff. You really don't get that anywhere else but on a set when you're all hanging out like that. Kurt talking about his younger years at Disney. Those are some special moments that you don't get anywhere else but right there when you're standing right with them. I haven't worked with John or spoken to him in years. We're not mad at each other or anything like that. Out of set, Johnny kind of gets quiet, so I never bothered him or tried to get in touch with him. If I wanted to get in touch with him, he'd probably talk to me. I did truly love working with him and that was a really great moment in my life to be a part of that kind of groundbreaking thing and be part of his thing with Kurt Russell.

What do you think of the movie personally?

I thought it was a fun movie. It was a little before its time. I wished we could do it now and really fricking light it up with the CGI effects like surfing, you know what I mean. Taking that wave and stuff. I wished we could have done a few things. We just didn't have the money that we needed to do it and we were big dreamers. At that time, Buena Vista [Visual Effects] was going out of business and we got the best out of them, but it really wasn't that great. I'm not disappointed. I think it's a really fun show. Everything John does is a western. He loves westerns. That was a true western, man.

What are you currently doing and what do you enjoy doing in your spare time?

Well, I'm still firsting quite a bit. I'm doing this pilot right now called *Mission Control* for CBS. It's kind of like that movie *Gravity* but in a TV show. Mission control on the space station and stuff. I'm kind of groundbreaking it right there and stuff. That's kind of fun. I still enjoy doing what I do and that's first assisting directing, but I plan on retiring in a few years. I'm a triathlete. Swim, bike, and run. Meditate, yoga. Try to just survive. Most assistant directors, because of the stress, we die at fifty-five to sixty years old. I'm fifty-six. I'm trying to last it out, man. I really just stay outside. I've got a few more years, but that's about it. I mostly just do television now. I don't do features anymore. I'm always filming for eight days at a time and I prep for eight days when I'm filming and stuff like that.

MARTIN JEDLICKA
Second Assistant Director

How did you end up being a second/first assistant director?

I started in locations as a location assistant. My first job was on *Viva Shaf Vegas* with Paul Shaffer from *The David Letterman Show*. I drove a fake New York City taxicab to Las Vegas and scouted places like trailer parks and cafes. I found out about the Directors Guild [of America] Training Program and decided that the ADs [Assistant Directors] worked better hours than the location managers. I got in the program in 1988 where my first assignment was *Star Trek: The Next Generation*. Two years later, I was an AD working as a 2nd 2nd on [Francis Ford] Coppola's *Dracula*.

How did you get the job of second assistant director on *Escape From L.A.*?

Chris Della Penna [First Assistant Director] and Jason Roberts [Second Second Assistant Director] both called me. Chris wanted as his 2nd Jason Roberts but the studio and UPM [Unit Production Manager] felt that *Escape* was a complex show with many locations and required a veteran. Jason knew me socially, so when Paramount suggested me based on my experience doing *Fire in the Sky* for them and also *True Lies* for [20th Century] Fox, he reached out to me at my home in Utah. David Witz, the UPM was the husband of Patty Witcher who was the UPM on *True Lies,* so he was a supporter of mine. Jason became the 2nd 2nd and we put together a production team that included guys like Mauritz [Pavoni] [Production Assistant] who worked with me in Miami and Jey Wada, an AD that I had done extras coordinating with as well as guys that Chris and Jason had worked with on their earlier collaborations.

How did you, Christian P. Della Penna [First Assistant Director] and Jason Roberts [Second Assistant Director] prepare for this project and how did you collaborate?

The 2nd AD does a lot of the organizing of what the crew is going to shoot as opposed to the 1st AD, who focuses on what is being shot. I ran the call sheet, which is the logistical menu for the cast and crew that shows where and when

L-R: Martin Jedlicka [Second Assistant Director], Jason Roberts [Second
Second Assistant Director]
(Photo Courtesy Jason Roberts)

and what we're going to do the next day. I also organized and set the background
extras with Jason. I'm very particular about background action and *Escape* was
the chance to do some really fun and interesting work.

**What kind of challenges did this project provide and which scenes or locations
were the most challenging, problematic, memorable, and fun to work on?**

We shot a scene on the Universal [Studios] backlot [Courtyard Square] where we
had all these low-riders [tricked out and lowered Chevy Impalas] and a couple
hundred gang members firing guns for some rally of Cuervo's [Jones] [George
Corraface]. Props handed out over fifty AK-47s, which were all full auto. Another
forty handguns as well. We broke some record that day for blank ammunition used
by a non-war movie. Hot brass was flying everywhere. It was crazy. An ejecting shell
broke an extra's tooth, but that guy was like, "It's just a tooth. Gimme more ammo."
It was a real party and those guys didn't have to do a lot of acting. I'm probably a
little deaf from that night. You can't monitor a walkie-talkie with earplugs.

The location in Carson [Former Cal Compact Landfill] [Sunset Boulevard/ Beverly Hills Hotel Exterior/Santa Monica Freeway] turned out to be a former Monsanto plant and had been condemned by the EPA. We would wrap before sunrise and these guys in hazmat suits would spray down our shoes and car wheels so we wouldn't track the contaminated dirt out of the site. My wife was pregnant at the time and she was pretty upset I was working there, but it was a spectacular location. You can't shoot in places like that nowadays. The Queen Mary hull is now off limits to shooting due to asbestos, so it was a rare opportunity to have filmed in there.

How was your experience working with the cast and crew?

John [Carpenter] is a great old school director. He knows exactly what he wants and shoots just that. There's no dithering or musing with him. Just, these are the shots. He shoots fast so you have to be up on your game in terms of having the actors and sets for the next scene ready. Sometimes actors sit around in trailers for hours waiting for all the coverage to be completed for the prior scene. With John, the coverage was minimal, so the scenes would shoot quickly and I was always speeding people through makeup/hair/wardrobe. I wasn't used to that fast pace then but that's pretty much how we shoot TV shows now. John's a huge basketball fan and I'll never forget how the whole crew and 400 extras all watched the Lakers game on the Coliseum jumbotron while shooting the shot-clock scene.

Kurt was very friendly. Another job of mine is cueing actors and background extras so that we can replicate action across takes. I wore a headset that received the recorded audio so I could hear the dialogue. There's a scene where Snake enters in the hull of the Queen Mary, a decommissioned ocean liner in Long Beach. I talked to Kurt about giving him a hand cue behind some set dressing when he told me couldn't see me without his glasses. So I got into costume as a Saigon Shadow and stood on a ship's ladder where I could wave my AK-47 to cue him. Except now I'm blind also since I wear glasses and forgot my contacts that day. We had a laugh about that, both being barely able to see each other but the timing worked out every take.

What's your favorite memory or memories of working on the movie?

I remember shooting in downtown L.A. at an old movie theater [Los Angeles Theatre]. We filmed in an alley behind the theater where there were all these extras playing prostitutes and drug dealers and customers. After setting the background all night, at dawn I was wrapping the extras. I collected all the fake money and piles of fake drugs. The prop guys had gone home, so I took all this stuff home and just dumped it on my desk. The next morning was Saturday and I flew home to Utah. When I came back to L.A. on Sunday my house was broken into. All that was missing was the fake cash and drugs. Someone had spotted it through the window. The cops were fascinated. They told me they'd know who stole it when that guy would turn up dead from trying to sell it.

Under a modern high-rise in L.A., we shot in an abandoned red car station from L.A.'s old subway system [Subway Terminal Building]. Gary Kibbe, the DP [Director of Photography] was born and raised in L.A. and we were looking at this rail station half buried in dirt and he told me about how he would, as a kid, board a train right here and ride all the way to Santa Monica to go swimming. I certainly knew that L.A. had public transit in the 40s and 50s, but that made history come alive. It was something to think about in traffic on the way home.

Shooting nights turns you into a bit of a vampire. My neighbors got used to seeing me on my porch at nine in the morning drinking beer. I didn't sleep a whole lot on that show since people are always calling and I was dealing a lot with the production office, which had daytime hours. Driving home in heavy morning traffic after working sixteen hours was tough. A camera operator told me this trick of using one hand to reach over to hold your other shoulder blade while driving. If you fall asleep the hand falls and you'll wake up in time to grab the wheel. It works!

What do you think of the movie personally?

It's very entertaining, but it's not exactly my taste. I'm more of an *English Patient* or *A Very Long Engagement* kind of viewer. It had decent performances, but not great ones. It is a fantastic tribute to L.A. Every landmark is in there and, considering that I was moving to Utah while we filmed, it I certainly related to the title.

What are you currently doing and what do you enjoy doing in your spare time?

I currently am the 1st AD on ABC's comedy series *Speechless*. We shoot on the Fox Lot in Century City. I play rhythm guitar for a couple industry-related bands on the weekends. I'm a skier and snowboarder. I used to mountain bike, but have no collarbones left to break.

JEFFREY BERK
Production Coordinator

How did you end up being a production coordinator/supervisor/manager and producer?

I went to school in New York and I graduated and I was gonna be working at CNN. Well, I did some work at CNN, so I got the bug. I got the excitement of production and then I came out to Los Angeles. I thought I would have a job in production with CNN, but the company downsized when I got out here, so I panicked a little bit and decided maybe I should do film production. I picked up a book called the *Hollywood Creative Directory,* which is a book of all the production companies and I started calling them. By the time I got to B, I got ahold of a company called Keith Barish Productions. Keith Barish produced a number of films. He hired me to come in and help him out with a restaurant called Planet Hollywood. I worked on Planet Hollywood for a little while and then I was looking for a job again.

I spoke to somebody named David Witz, who was the [unit] production manager on *Escape From L.A.* I've done ten or eleven projects with David. He's always hired me to work with him. The first movie I did with him was called *Critters 3.* It was a low budget horror movie that starred Leonardo DiCaprio. He doesn't promote or talk about that movie, but it was the first movie he did, which is an interesting story. I've run into him a few times and he remembers me, which is nice. Then I did *Critters 4,* which starred a woman called Angela Bassett and the time that I spent there learning production was, I guess, early 1990s. When I was doing these jobs, I was the assistant coordinator, making little money and just struggling and dealing with production. Then David did a movie called *Buffy the Vampire Slayer,* which was a bigger movie and then he did a movie called *CB4.* Then he did a movie called *Bad Girls* and he started doing more and more movies. The more movies he did, the larger the movies became. The budgets, the actors, and the production.

I first production coordinated and then started production supervising. I just worked my way up the ladder. I started production managing and then I myself did low budget pictures. In order to make the jump to line producer, I needed to do lower budget pictures and I started to do reality television. I made the switch to television because I got married and had children and it was much less of a challenge to do television. The hours weren't as long. The conditions weren't as difficult. The projects weren't as complicated, so I started doing reality.

How did you get the job of production coordinator on *Escape From L.A.*?

Maybe my eighth or ninth movie I did with David was *Escape From L.A.* It was my first job making the jump from assistant coordinator to production coordinator. They needed a production coordinator to work at night. They also had a production coordinator working during the day. That was Diane Ward [Assistant Production Coordinator], so she was the day coordinator and I was the night coordinator.

How did you, David Witz [Unit Production Manager], Alexandra Koch [Production Supervisor], Diane Ward [Assistant Production Coordinator] as well as Debra Hill [Producer/Co-Writer] and Kurt Russell prepare for this project and how did you collaborate? Any issues prior to filming and such?

A production coordinator handles all physical aspects of a production. My job involved a lot of boring stuff like paperwork, dealing with SAG and DGA, actor movement and logistics, equipment ordering, assisting the director and producers, etcetera. Essentially, I ran the production office. The production office was in a bungalow at Paramount. I think it was Bungalow 11. I could be wrong about that. It wasn't a proper building. It was kind of a semi-temporary structure.

I think it was like a fifty-million-dollar budget. I had never worked on something that big before. I had to struggle to get the title production coordinator because I had only had assistant coordinator to my name, so this was a big deal. The company didn't want to pay me production coordinator salary. They only wanted to pay me assistant coordinator salary, so I made a deal with Debra Hill, who I thank and who was fantastic to me. She said, "If you work at a lower assistant production coordinator rate, then I'll give you a production coordinator title when the movie comes out," so she got a good deal for me. I was able to get a big jump to production coordinator and then, once I'd done production coordinating on a fifty million dollar movie, it was easy to start coordinating on other movies. Diane, I think, was working on a picture called *Kiss the Girls*. I think that was the name of it and she was working in the bungalow next door to my bungalow for *Escape From L.A.* I remember going next door to the *Kiss the Girls* bungalow and asking the production coordinator if she knew any good assistant production coordinators and she said, "I have a woman here named Diane Ward and she's fantastic." I met with Diane and hired her right away and she became the assistant coordinator during the day. That was like my big start. My first production coordinating job. I remember how nervous I was and how excited I was. I got to work with John Carpenter. I was a big fan of John Carpenter. Big fan. I saw all of his movies. Rewatched his movies when I got the job. I was really excited about the visual effects. It was one of the first films that I had worked on, one of the first projects that had such big effects. 1996. That was still pretty early for visual effects and they turned out great for the show.

What kind of challenges did this project provide and which scenes or locations were the most challenging, problematic, memorable, and fun to work on?

It was a very smooth production because David and Alex both were professional and very fantastic at what they did. Shooting went smoothly because the actors were so awesome, because they were so down to earth. They had no egos. I mean, that was one of the things. The whole film was shot at night and there were never any complaints or any problems or difficulty with the hours that we were shooting. The hours would be from like five or six o'clock until like three, four in the morning, sometimes later. Sometimes, they would shoot until the sun came up and nobody really complained. The actors were all cool.

It was challenging to do the locations because we were shooting at night and, with safety, that became an issue. People get sleepy and they fall asleep driving home after working ten or twelve hour days. I remember that was a challenge. I talk about how smooth it was shooting at night, but it really does a toll. It was a grueling shoot. Grueling meaning that they were working really hard at night for long hours. Safety was paramount. I don't think anyone got injured. I dealt with that too. That was one of my job responsibilities. Dealing with medical issues related to people getting injured, but I don't really believe that there were that many injuries or insurance claims. We shot *Buffy the Vampire Slayer* at night. That was a lot of nights as well, but I've never known any movie that just shot all at night. That was the biggest challenge on *Escape*.

I remember we shot at Universal Studios [Lot, Courthouse Square] [Happy Kingdom by the Sea], the big scene at the end with the big battle and that went smoothly too. I think the hang glider was a big challenge. Getting that to work was a challenge, but the visual effects were great for the show. The mechanical effects were fantastic. It was a top notch very sharp production crew. All professionals.

Did anything went over budget?

We stayed on budget.

Did you have to negotiate with any of the actors?

We didn't have to worry about any strange requests for food or any strange requests for their living arrangements that some actors have or their drivers for the hours that they work.

How was your experience working with the cast and crew?

Kurt Russell was a really cool guy. I liked him a lot. He was very friendly to everybody on the production. He would always come in. No ego. He and John worked together really well, just because neither of them had an ego. Both of them are kind of like cowboys in a sort of way. They get their hands dirty. They do what it takes to get the job done. Work long hours, work really hard. Just very supportive of the crew. Everybody was nice on that show. It was such a positive experience. Peter Fonda [Pipeline] was fantastic to work with. He would tell me stories on the phone. He would just have these long, wonderful stories that he told. Same thing with Pam Grier [Hershe]. She was fantastic, a very sweet lady. She lived in Colorado at the time. One of my jobs was to make airplane arrangements for the talent. For the cast. We would have long conversations that just would go absolutely all over the place. She is very down to earth and humble and just fantastic. Same thing with Steve Buscemi [Map to the Stars Eddie]. Down to earth and friendly, a very nice guy to deal with. I remember the girl who played the President's [Cliff Robertson] daughter [A.J. Langer] [Utopia]. She was great because she was kind of a newly discovered person. She was fantastic as well.

Alex was the production supervisor. We got along really well and she ended up doing some of the production coordinating work, but she basically worked with David. He and her were a team. Alex worked hard. She was supportive of me and the team. David is very good at what he does. Having worked with him on ten feature films, I'm very lucky. Diane was amazing. I am in awe of Diane. She's a little crackerjack and we worked together really well. I haven't talked to Diane in many years. We were good friends. I did a movie with her afterward called *My Giant* with Billy Crystal. I think she had the harder job during the day because she had to try and accomplish things when everybody was at sleep and, for me, it was easy. I would just drive to the set if I needed information or needed to have a meeting. Chris [P. Della Penna] [First Assistant Director] did a great job. He was good, a really cool guy.

Debra Hill was amazing. She was one of the biggest workaholics I've ever seen. She was a very tireless worker. Very, very focused, very high-energy. ALWAYS running around. Very spirited, I guess, is a good word for her. It was very much different than the energy that John had. John was much more chilled and relaxed and kind of easy going. He related to everyone. You wouldn't recognize him that he was a movie director walking down the street or talking to him for a little bit. He just had no presumptions. He had no conceits of being in the entertainment business. Very down to earth is a good way to describe him. He was just a good guy. He would come into the office and just greet everybody and ask how they were doing. He was a great leader. I got some stories about him. John is a big liberal and very much against the conservatism of government. He smoked non-stop cigarettes. I don't think I ever saw him without a cigarette in his hand. He loved eating junk food. Almost every meal he had was a hamburger. He just loved meat. He loved meat so much and he loved smoking so much that it entered into the picture because he thought that, in the future, the government would not allow smoking or eating meat anymore. He turned that into the movie a little bit about how strict and how right-wing the government had become.

It was probably the only film I've ever done where I absolutely enjoyed working with everyone. It was just such a pleasure to go to work in the morning and look forward to the day. It contrasted very sharply with other productions that I've done. The last production that I did in feature film was working on a movie called *A Man Apart* with Vin Diesel and it was a very bad experience. I saw all the worst of Hollywood in that movie. Egos, eccentricities, demands, things that were bawled, budgets that were blown away, so I quit that job to go work in television. I was done working in films with the egos and all the bullshit that went along with working in these movies. What's really nice is, again, I can look back on *Escape From L.A.* as being one of the most pleasant experiences I've had working, if not the most pleasant experience I've ever had on any movie. I just remember having a lot of fun too.

What's your favorite memory or memories of working on the movie?

I remember that we would go out and have the most amazing meals at dinner time because the studios pays for your meals. They pay for the catering for everybody on the set, but what David and Alex had told me was that we could spend the same amount of money on the meals in the office as they spent for catering. We would order from all over around the city and have a big party with the food at night, you know, with our feet up on the table. It was a good life. It was really fun. Ordering from the best restaurants in L.A. Not the best restaurants, but just places that we really enjoyed going to and eating at. It was a lot of fun.

What do you think of the movie personally?

It's a total fun movie. I remember the first time I saw the movie and I saw the shark. Universal Studios had Bruce, the shark from *Jaws*. I think Kurt was underwater with the vehicle and he was riding the vehicle and the shark snapped at him. The shark was like electrically still working and I remember thinking to myself for the first time, "This movie is kind of like a cartoon. It's not real life. It's a silly sort of a fantasy movie like a Disney movie with you know, animated characters." I remember thinking to myself, "That's really cool that John made that scene in the movie." I thought that was really, really nice. The studio loved the picture. Everybody loved the picture, but I think the picture turned out not to be a big success. Everybody thought it was gonna be a hundred million dollar picture, but I don't think it made very much money. I think it was a picture that they were very unhappy with.

There were challenges with the way the movie was marketed and I don't know if the John Carpenter fans really came out to the movie. It wasn't like raw. *Escape From L.A.* was a fifty million dollar slick. That's a word that I would use for that movie. A slick production with high production values and highly-paid people on the show that were working on it, but John is kind of low budget. *They Live* which is a great movie he did was kind of shot low budget. *Assault on Precinct 13* was a low budget picture and *Halloween* obviously. He did all these really raw, very sort of gritty pictures. I remember working on *Escape From L.A.* and being so impressed because I loved the movie *Assault on Precinct 13*. I was so impressed that he had done that movie and *Halloween,* obviously, that it was a pleasure just to have him call my name. I remember him saying, "Jeff, Jeff," if he needed something and I would say, "Hey, that's pretty cool. John Carpenter is calling out for Jeff."

I'm very proud of the way the movie turned out. I'm proud to be associated with it. I just wish that more people saw it. John was ahead of his time with it. One thing that's interesting is that he had a scene in the movie where the police are escorting Kurt. They've just gotten Kurt and the police were walking him out. Every single police officer had an accompanying person with a video camera following them and following Kurt. Everybody was filming everything and I thought to myself, "That's so strange. Why are there so many camera people filming?"

Now I understand it. Everybody is filming these days. Everybody is filming to make sure that they're protected. In the [United] States, we have George Floyd going on. George Floyd is just the most recent incident where somebody with a camera was filming the police and filmed the police officer kneeling down on the neck of George Floyd and killing him, essentially. Now I understand that. When these things happen and people are filming everything to make sure that things are protected and saved and backed up by video, I just always remember John having done that in the movie. It left a big memory with me about how prescient, how ahead of its time he was.

What are you currently doing and what do you enjoy doing in your spare time?

I've been working in reality. I worked with a company called Original Productions doing projects like *Deadliest Catch, Ice Road Truckers*. I did all of these manly man shows. I got out of films because films just became too stressful and too bullshit for me with the egos and the personalities, so I started doing reality television right around the time reality television was getting hot. I think it was around the year 2000 and I was burnt up by films and I got an invitation to work on a reality show called *Dinner & a Movie* and I started doing reality shows. I started doing documentaries. The last documentary I did we shot for Vice, a company in Panama. I've done a lot of traveling around the world doing production, which has been exciting but very stressful. It's a very, very stressful job being a production coordinator because you're dealing with everything related to the movie. Insurance and production reports and budget and talent and travel and everything that happens behind the scenes the production coordinator has their finger in. In my opinion, other than maybe the director, it's the hardest job. It's a really challenging job. I think I just got stressed out with production and now I've left production and I'm a teacher for kindergartners. I'm taking a little sabbatical.

LEO NAPOLITANO
Camera Operator

How did you end up being a camera operator?

Actually, I kind of stumbled into it. I was a machinist in the Navy after high school. I didn't go to college. I took a class in school for the United States Navy and, after I graduated, I was taking coach courses. As I said, I was a machinist mate for the Navy, so I happened to hear about a job at Technicolor, which was a company that processed all the color films for Disney, Warner, all the biggest studios. Everything was colored by Technicolor in those days. I had an opportunity to meet the hiring manager, and I told him one of my jobs was in the Navy and he hired me because they built process machines. Those are the machines that do the developing and processing on the film and they use a lot of machinists, so I started working there and, at night, I took film classes because everyone was telling me to take three classes. To make a long story not too long, eventually I got a job at Universal Studios in the camera repair shop. I would build parts for different cameras and stuff like that and learned all about the cameras inside and out. I became a technician for Universal Studios, but I realized what I really wanted to do was to become a cameraman.

After I became well-known in the studio business, I put it out there to people that, if there ever was an opportunity, I would like do it and I would be willing to start all over and work my way up. In a short time, I was offered jobs and got into the camera local. That was a very big deal in those days. There weren't that many studios. It was a closed operation, but because I knew how to fix the camera and work the camera and test the camera, I became first choice for the people that were renting new equipment. At that time, a lot of new cameras were coming out. Arriflex was getting big in the business. They had the BL's [Blimped] and Mitchell's and Panavision had the Panaflex, Panagold and stuff like that. I knew these cameras inside and out so camera crews would hire me so that I could be with them in case they got troubles with the cameras and eventually I worked my way up to camera assistant. I only did one movie as a second assistant then I moved to first assistant. Then after about five years, I was offered a job as a camera operator with Paul Lohman, who was a notable camera man at the time. It was for a big project in Israel called *Masada*. Thirteen hours of television all shot in the desert and stuff like that. Anyway, so I went to Israel with him and eventually became his camera operator and people get familiar with you, good work and stuff like that, so I worked for the next twenty years. I've done over eighty movies and I've probably done about a thousand commercials. I've done various photography because of my technical skills.

How did you get the job of camera operator on *Escape From L.A.*?

Any large-scale picture like this one had troubles. They had to work in the rain, the wind, the dirt, and stuff. Somehow, I got the reputation for doing rough projects that were difficult for the cameras because I knew them really well. I knew the camera, knew when to fix it or not to fix it and this and that. Gary Kibbe, who I knew from Universal Studios, was the DP [Director of Photography] for John Carpenter at the time and he had somebody. Actually, I must confess I did not start the picture. Somebody else started it and, being honest, I don't know what happened to them but after a few weeks on the production they called me up and said, "We need you, Leo. Are you available?" And I was finishing up another project and it worked out. So I went over to Gary and did the picture with John Carpenter. The rest is history.

How did you, Jud Kehl [Camera Operator], Chris Squires [Camera Operator] as well as John Carpenter and Gary B. Kibbe [Director of Photography] prepare for this project and how did you collaborate?

I've since worked with John Carpenter on other pictures. He's pretty much a laid-back guy. He knows exactly what he wants, which is the best thing for a camera crew. Some directors are more difficult to understand and get what they're trying to achieve, but John is pretty specific and so is Gary, who is my immediate boss. John works very... how do you say it? He doesn't work by status or things like that. He'll go talk to everybody and makes himself known. Camera, actors, stunt men, anything. He's a man of few words, but you understand those few words because he's got a vision in his head. He's a reserved person. He's not a loud leader type. He's very knowledgeable. He's very easy to work with and so is Gary Kibbe. So we all worked together. We all knew each other. Jud Kehl I knew the least. Chris Squires had worked for me as an assistant and I'd hired him on many pictures before. Of course, I told you I knew Gary Kibbe from Universal Studios. We just became a team right away. We become like a football team, if you can imagine.

We didn't have any preparatory because, like I said, I was replacing someone, although when they hire you the first thing they do is to send you a script. In those days, you had to drop by the office to pick up the script and then you have a meeting with the production manager and, of course, with Gary Kibbe, the director of photography. He would explain what we're doing, how we're doing it, how it's going, what to expect, what to look out for, and what to prepare for.

Is it true that it was a tough project for Gary B. Kibbe?

It was for cameramen, especially in those days. Nowadays, it's at least fifty percent easier to do anything because the electronic cameras are so much more forgiving. Ours required much more light. Everything had to be lit. Luckily, Gary had an old school background. He started out as a very young man and he knew about the big lights and lighting. When you light for that scope, it takes dozens of men and dozens of huge lights that we set and you can't move them around. You have to make a decision and stick with it. And you'll be making decisions during broad daylight. You're standing there, it's nine in the morning, broad daylight, and you're trying to figure out what it's going to look like in the dark. It all has to be visualized. It was difficult for any cameraman to do that project. It took a lot of preparation. Huge electrical department, maybe a hundred men.

What kind of challenges did this project provide and which scenes, sequences, and locations were the most challenging, problematic, memorable, and fun to work on? Any technical issues and such? The Sunset Boulevard, Beverly Hills Hotel Sewer, and Los Angeles Memorial Coliseum scenes come to mind.

Out of the ordinary, you mean? Well, during the rain sequence and hang gliding sequence, which was very difficult, I became much more important because of the technical aspects. Protecting the cameras and stuff like that. I would operate in some difficult circumstances. I actually flew. John came to me first and asked me if I was afraid of heights and flying and I said, "No. What do you mean?" He says, "We want to put you in one of those hang gliders." By the way, I was also the smallest person of the camera operators. Anytime you're dealing with flying, weight is a factor, so if you're going to carry a camera, you want to pick somebody that knows what he's doing but you pick somebody that's not too large because of the weight of it. So John asked me if I would do a favor and get in there and fly one of these things carrying a camera and looking down at the ground and stuff like that. Do what they call POV, the point of view of the actor. That was something that was unique to myself. It was very adventuresome.

I like the adventure of these things. The best analogy would be a sport during the exciting part when the clock is running out and everyone gets their adrenaline going and, after a while, you like that part of it. It becomes the part you look forward to, when things are exciting. I've never flown in a hang glider. I didn't know how to operate it or anything and, of course, it was all done with wires and stuff like that. I wasn't completely set free, although it seems to be when you watch the movie. They were all controlled very much by the technicians and stuff like that. I enjoy this stuff.

The hang gliding sequence was one of the most difficult. We did it at Universal Studios on the backlot [Courthouse Square]. We would come in six in the evening and go home six in the morning when the sun was coming up. That was pretty fatiguing day after day. It was a big sequence and had a lot of technology involved for those times. That was one of those things that took extra effort, plus everybody is tired. Nights are the most difficult because you have to work from sunset to sunup. It's harder to adjust at first, especially with water and rain, lightning, explosions, and fires, so that was the tough part of it. If you remember the picture, except for the straight up dialogue, it's a lot of action. Going from places to other places, running through hallways and corridors and junkyards. There were a number of technical issues, but they were all minor and they didn't have any big consequence in the movie. We had cameras that got wet and dirty. Things like that. We had cameras that water got into the batteries and stuff, but we're prepared for that. They had duplicate equipment.

Sunset Boulevard: That was also a very big deal with coordinating all those cars at night. You also have stunt crews and a stunt coordinator and all that. Just imagine all the building that went into creating those images. It was much more difficult in those days. You actually had to do it. Nowadays with electronics, they can make it look like Paris if they want to.

Beverly Hills Hotel Sewer: Well, that was very interesting. It was something we've never been around before, but I can't think of anything unusual. There were no accidents or anything unpredictable. It was all handled by top people in the industry. They knew what they were doing and were prepared way in advance.

Los Angeles Memorial Coliseum: It was planned out. It wasn't complicated at all. It seems so but it was all set up and had been rehearsed by Kurt before they even started production.

How was your experience working with the cast and crew?

It was a very good crew. A lot of us knew each other. In fact, my son was on it. He was a camera assistant. We had a long history and it was a joy to get together and do it because it was such a great project. I have good memories on it. I've worked with John Carpenter since. I did *Vampires* some years later, so I already had a working relationship with him and I enjoyed that. He called me to do another picture with him. I've never worked with Peter Fonda [Pipeline]. I'd worked with Kurt Russell years earlier [*Captain Ron*], but we never knew each other as friends. We did recognize each other and said hello. I don't think I was a camera operator then. I was an assistant. He's a great guy to work with too. Easy going guy. He's as good as you can imagine and also funny. If something goes wrong, he makes a joke out of it and keeps the crew in a good mind set. There wasn't a tough person in the project. Everyone was very professional. They knew what they were doing.

What did you film additionally for the movie?

There weren't any retakes really. There were pick-up shots where the editor and director decided we needed some more cuts of like the car sequences. I think we also did some more explosions and additional shots for the hang glider sequence. We also did some establishing shots at the end, a picture of a city or something like that. We do shots like that later because we want to stay with the action and do the most difficult shots first. So we did some afterwards. I can't remember anything significant. It was kind of routine stuff at the time.

What's your favorite memory or memories of working on the movie?

Working with Kurt Russell because he was such a joy. He made it easy for us. He knew where the camera was at all times and we didn't have to do shots that were awkward. You know, retakes and stuff like that. He just had a sense about my job as I did with his job, so he became very easy to work with under those difficult circumstances. Like I said, night, rain, wind, fire, and explosions. Some of that stuff is pretty dangerous. It was a lot of stress, but Kurt Russell made it a pleasure and so did John, but John is a more quiet man.

What do you think of the movie personally?

I like it. It's fun. I mean, you gotta like the movie. It's a great action movie and it's got humor. It's got drama. It's got twists and turns like a murder mystery and stuff to think about too. We had a virus. We had an atomic weapon. We had an earthquake. It's all in this movie, which makes it very timely.

What are you currently doing and what do you enjoy doing in your spare time?

I'm pretty much retired. I worked much longer than most people do in the industry. I worked into my seventies as a camera guy. I became an action kind of guy because I enjoyed that and I don't have to work as much. They pay me a little more to do it. My last picture was done in China. It was a picture for the Chinese called *Streets of Fury* and I pretty much retired after that. It was time to finish then. That was difficult enough. I've worked on, like I said, eighty movies. I've worked on three of four Clint Eastwood movies. I know Clint very well and his family and those guys over at Warner Brothers. I did *Star Wars* too. *Return of the Jedi*. *Fast & Furious*. I worked on three or four of those. I do aerial photography with helicopters. Now they use drones. I've done a lot of that remote stuff with the high-tech cameras.

I'm living in San Diego now with my wife. My son is still a camera guy in Hollywood. My daughter-in-law is a makeup person. She was a makeup person for this new movie called *Tenet*. It's a big picture that's about to come out in a month or so. I'm still attached to the business because of that. I have a lot of people and friends that contact me but I moved away from Hollywood to just give myself a break somehow so not every conversation was about movies I've done and stuff like that. Although now I've learned to embrace it. It's a pleasure to share. I'm currently doing a thing called *Arlington Cemetery*. It's a big cemetery in Washington, DC with all the heroes and soldiers and it's got an old history that goes back to the civil war. I'm doing a documentary using this one person as a guide that takes you through what happened there and more of this man Bob Hammerquist who died recently. He was buried at Arlington which is a big honor. He had five purple hearts. He had fought in the second world war, Korean war and the Vietnam war. He's been wounded five times. He was an army coronal. His life was so historical. It's amazing and nobody ever heard from him. He's like an unsung hero. Nobody knows who Bob Hammerquist is. I've been in the Vietnam a little bit before while I was in the Navy and the destroyers. I'm doing his life and how it ends in Arlington Cemetery. It's different than fantasy because we're dealing with a real story with real people. A friend of mine who is an editor and I just shot the whole funeral and now we're in post-production. Kind of a work of love rather than money. I mean, it's possible it might be on television and stuff like that.

JEROME FAUCI
Camera Operator [Uncredited]

How did you end up being a Steadicam/camera operator?

I went to film school in San Francisco in the early 90s. Francis Ford Coppola's brother August was the dean of the creative arts department and promised us that this film school would be different and wouldn't be so commercially geared to the industry like the other SoCal schools. He was right. It took me a much longer time to get a job!

I started as a writer. I was a two-time quarterfinalist selection from the Academy of Motion Picture Arts and Sciences awards program, a Walt Disney writing semifinalist selection, and a MTV/Latino Film Festival screenwriting semifinalist selection for a really popular feature that took place in Belize. It was a simple little "Faux-Foreign Film" like *Il Postino*, *Cinema Paradiso,* and *Slumdog Millionaire*. It was called "Faux-Foreign Films" because they had the charm, subtitles, and lush locations but were directed by English speaking directors who saw how these films charmed the smarter demographic of movie-goers. There was only one problem. While I was in development of my film called *Boy*, a feature-length drama that follows a poor, orphaned sweetbread delivery boy as he explores his Latin family's dark past to prove that he is heir to his beautiful tropical island to stop the bulldozers of an American resort developer. One of the producers nonchalantly mentioned that, after I sold this script, it'll be probably the last time I ever saw it or was even allowed to do anything involving the project. In fact, he said I probably wouldn't even be invited to watch the actual filming. Hmmm. I decided that would suck and started training on cameras.

In the 90s, the only real way into the camera departments at most studios, which were ruled by politics and nepotism, was to buy and learn how to use the Steadicam. It was the latest and greatest camera system every director wanted to use on their films. So I bought one, practiced on my dog and girlfriend and got good on it. Besides that, I got lucky on my God-given name. You see, during the early to mid-90s, diversity was the name of the game for Hollywood and many hiring companies that wanted to *Do The Right Thing*. Although I was a short white guy, my name was Jerome. I started getting hired on every feature that had black producers, black stars, and anyone that wanted to "level the playing fields." As my resume started having names like Denzel Washington, the Wayans Brothers, Samuel L. Jackson, Tyler Perry, people just thought I was black. They only seemed a little surprised when they saw me on set, but of course they didn't really want an embarrassing situation or a lawsuit, I guess. I actually got a gig the day after the L.A. riots for a very anti-white music video by Tone Loc in the smoldering wreckage of what was a federal store on La Brea. The mood was pretty tense all over the city that day and the only other white guy in a ten-mile radius was a motorcycle cop who screamed at me like I was mad. When I arrived at the location and someone demanded to know who I was, I simply said, "Hi. I am Jerome, the Steadicam operator." It took a while for the entire black crew to adjust, but I can tell you that Tone Loc had very powerful motivation that day as he fired off anti-white rap at the short white dude with the camera in for of him.

How did you get the job of camera operator on *Escape From L.A.*?

Chris Squires was the B-Op/Steadicam operator who had been working on nights for a few months. Chris was big time. *Forrest Gump, The Usual Suspects,* etcetera. I don't think his leaving was because of a bad experience. It was probably a scheduling problem. I think the Carpenter film went way over in shooting days and Chris is really sought after and had to leave. It happens all the time, especially when you're forced to work nights for three months. He knew I was good and he let me have the existing few weeks that were the interior studio scenes and reshoots.

What kind of challenges did this project provide and which scenes, sequences or locations were the most challenging, problematic, memorable, and fun to work on? Any technical issues and such?

I remember shooting a scene where the Steadicam slowly tracks behind the President, Cliff Robertson, as he turns slowly and faces my camera. Carpenter was drawing from his 110s and yelling out, "Everyone knows what they doing? Right! Alright, last looks!" I stood there and shut my mouth and prayed that the hair and wardrobe people would see that the camera was very close to Cliff's back of his head where the seventy-plus actor, God bless him, was terrifically thinning. It was obvious that someone in hair decided to spray black paint on his sparse scalp. Well, all of that was fine, but I remembered very well that during the last rehearsal that his beads of sweat were making the back of his head look like one of those bad 1950 movie transformations of the werewolf. I stood there and tried to politely tell my concerns to hair and makeup without pissing anyone off, but what I got was, "It's fine. It won't read on film."

The stage's buzzer goes off and red lights beacon all across the giant stage. Sound calls, "Speed!" and my 2nd AC [Assistant Camera] claps the sticks, "Steadicam only!" Carpenter draws about two inches from his glowing embers and says quietly, "Action." My Steadicam smoothly comes behind Cliff with the perfect speed and just about when he is about to turn, I see the back of his head that clearly shows brittle wirily thinning hair matted down with black spray paint. I remember that this movie is in anamorphic, so what I am watching on my Steadicam monitor will be about forty-five feet wide by twenty-eight feet tall. The man in front of me looked like a scrotum in a pin stripe suit. I decided I couldn't do it to my Cliff or his heirs who would have to stomach this scene for hundreds of years, so I let go of the camera and the Steadicam dipped towards the floor thus ruining the shot. "CUT!" It was Carpenter and he was pissed. He came running to me and demanded why I dare ruin one of his shots. Cliff was there too and I wanted to tell Carpenter without embarrassing Cliff, whose work I respected for so many years, but Carpenter was not helping. "His what is showing!? Scrotum!?" After a minute and with the help of the AD [Assistant Director] who helped translate, Carpenter walked away understanding. Presumably to find another cigarette, but as he walked into the darkness of the set he turned and announced to the hair and wardrobe department, "Next time the kid tells you about a problem, listen to him for Chrissakes!"

How was your experience working with the cast and crew?

The stage was near some funky casino off the I-5. Most of the crew were still on nights and were walking like zombies. I was pretty rested. Mostly these final weeks of shooting are to fix and reshoot some scenes that some didn't like the performances or the photography. The first thing I noticed was that, on a John Carpenter set, you were not only allowed to smoke cigarettes indoors on stage, but it was encouraged. Every time Mr. Carpenter stuck one of his 110 Marlboros in his face, he looked around and watched as the DP [Director of Photography], the first AD, and even the operator lit up. I wasn't really a smoker, so since Carpenter was right there, I bummed one from him, but as I looked around the room, I remember I saw the horrified looks of the first AD. I figured it probably wasn't a good idea, but John flipped me his pack and asked in his crusty deep tone, "Need a light too I suppose?" Three lighters came from three different directions with a chorus of, "No, he's good, John."

You see, I think Mr. Carpenter was kind of tithed that I replaced his first operator. Especially someone he didn't know and someone who didn't look like an old Hollywood veteran. He was probably even expecting that I was black. He never learned my name. He called me "kid" or "the kid" or "that kid." He really liked my Steadicam, but he hated my conventional camera operating on the dolly and tracks. I don't think it was the quality of the framing. It was that I didn't look or sound like a camera operator from the studio periods of the 60s and 70s. Guys whose only job was to execute the director's and the directors of photography's visions. I was used to being a Steadicam operator where the DP or the director allowed the Steadicam operator to "design his own shot" since they had no idea how to direct a camera that'd no boundaries. I quickly learned that, when I was seating on back on his dolly in conventional camera mode, I was to zip it and listen to exactly what my Carpenter wanted. The DP Gary Kibbe sometimes jumped on the dolly when he thought John was in a bad mood trying to save me from getting yelled at.

What's your favorite memory or memories of working on the movie?

The time we were doing a big tracking shot with Kurt Russell and I had a chance to chat with him. I was a little uptight since I would be making or breaking this important shot when Snake gets the poison that spins the movie's plot into action. There were a lot of opinions on how the shot should be blocked. I was told how Mr. Carpenter wanted the shot and, to make it believable, I had to place the camera in the exact spot at the exact time when a female character runs her tiny finger nail across Snake's hand. We're talking about a spot as small as a postcard, but the shot starts showing the entire room with panning from the guards and prisoner background artists. This was going to be the hardest shot I tried in the movie and, after Carpenter left, I was more than half nervous. I bummed a cigarette from someone and saw Kurt Russell. Man, the dude was icon but here he was chilling just before a pretty important shot with his lifetime partner Goldie Hawn and their young son. They reminded me how California was when I just got there as a child. People had mid-western manners and were on laid-back beach time. They never changed. Maybe that's why so many fans still love them. Anyway, we spoke for a few minutes and the cute little family left me totally relaxed. Kurt said, "Put me anywhere you want to make your shot." I nailed that damn shot in two takes.

I immediately fell in love with Michelle Forbes [Brazen] in her femme fatale bob. She was the reason I actually continued to going to work since all that yelling and cigarette smoke was getting to me. Forbes was not only a knock-out, but she was an absolute pro. Helpful, really helpful and one of the most down to earth actresses I've ever worked with.

What do you think of the movie personally?

It's a comic book movie, so the characters could play a little. Carpenter must have an interesting persona to be attracted to this tough guy, tongue-in-cheek, anti-social genre. I was always impressed that he did most of his own musical scores. My favorite film of John's was *Starman,* which really showed his talent with character development and human emotions without the special effects. Maybe he was really just a softy behind that gristle.

What are you currently doing and what do you enjoy doing in your spare time?

Still doing features and TV. Not a kid anymore. Guess I am a "vet." Still get black movies, but I think the word is getting out. To this day, I remember the old camera operator replies that Gary and John taught. Example: If you get busted by the director about totally screwing up a blocked scene, you're supposed to reply proud, "I'm still working it out, sir." Or if you really screw up framing, at the video village the proper veteran operator says to the director, "Sorry, sir. I can do better." Works like a charm. In any case, doing more writing these days while picking out features and TV I think I'll have fun on.

MARK J. COYNE
Second Assistant Photographer

How did you end up being a second assistant cameraman and Steadicam operator?

I grew up loving movies, especially sci-fi, and after completing an Associate of Arts degree at the local college, I headed off to Columbia College in Hollywood to study cinematography. I thought the best way to learn movie making was in school. I was mostly incorrect, however. Real moviemaking is learned on the set, not in the classroom. Sometime around 1987, while I was still in college, I attended a big cinema expo. I don't remember the name of the expo, but at the time it was a yearly event that took place in Los Angeles. At any rate, while strolling around the expo I came across a young Guy Bee who was showing off his Steadicam rig. I was very impressed by him and his expertise with the relatively new tool of the industry. I actually played with the idea of dropping out of college, buying my own sled, and jumping into the business.

In the end, I decided to finish up my college education. I took a right at the fork in the road which, many years later, merged back to the same road. To sum it all up quickly, after college I decided to get a job at Panavision. It was there that I learned a great deal about the premiere cameras, lenses, and support equipment used in the camera departments for the biggest Hollywood pictures. At that time, Panavision had been dominating the Hollywood industry for many decades and I wanted to know their equipment inside and out. I wanted to meet the people behind Panavision and I wanted to know the artists, craftsman, and technicians who chose to use it. This turned out to be a good strategy.

Shortly after leaving Panavision, I was offered a job to work on a big-budget movie as a camera technician. Although it was a big-budget movie, it was a non-union movie, an oddity in California. That being said, it was a prime target for the unions to flip. So here are the moving parts. One, I wanted to work on the big Hollywood films, but I was not in the union. Two, IATSI [International Alliance of Theatrical Stage Employees], Local 659 was a difficult union to get into. Three, one back door entry to 659 was to be on a non-union film that flipped to a union film during production. Four, not many camera assistants knew how to service the equipment as well as I did. Five, production did not want to pay for a camera technician. Six, production knew they needed a camera technician. Seven, being a non-union film, production did not have to hire an expensive camera technician, but they could hire me cheaply as a camera loader and then give me the work duties of a camera technician. When the parts all came together, *Stargate* got their camera technician and I got into the cinematographer's guild [IATSE 659]. Flash forward a decade or so and I'm bored with being a 2nd AC [Assistant Camera] and I have the cash to buy a Steadicam.

How did you get the job of second assistant camera on *Escape From L.A.*?

I believe Strad [John Stradling] [2nd AC], a buddy and fellow 2nd AC recommended me to Dominic [Napolitano] [1st AC] who was looking for a 2nd AC.

How come Leo Napolitano [Camera Operator] replaced another camera operator after a few weeks and can you remember who it was he replaced?

Nothing comes to mind. It is not uncommon for crew members to leave shows early. It doesn't mean that there was some sort of problem. At that time, Hollywood was very busy and the name of the game was to keep working. With so many shows going on at the same time, you sometimes had to leave one show to secure a longer gig on another.

How did you prepare for this project and how did you, Jud Kehl [Camera Operator], Leo Napolitano [Camera Operator], Chris Squires [Camera Operator], Dominic Napolitano [First Assistant Photographer], W. Steve Peterson [First Assistant Photographer], Steve Ullman [First Assistant Photographer], Brian Kibbe [Second Assistant Photographer], Ron Peterson [Second Assistant Photographer] and John Stradling [Second Assistant Photographer] collaborate?

I feel pretty confident of the following. A camera: Jud Kehl [Camera Operator], Steve Peterson [1st AC], Brian Kibbe [2nd AC]. B camera: Chris Squires [Camera Operator], Steve Ullman [1st AC], John Stradling [2nd AC]. C camera: Leo Napolitano [Camera Operator], Dominic Napolitano [1st AC], Mark Coyne [2nd AC]. All crews and shows have their own parameters and dichotomies. Above-the-line decisions are not always made by the same person from show to show. For example, usually the camera positions are decided by the cinematographer and or camera operators. With John Carpenter films, that responsibility was largely undertaken by John. Even for C camera, John would walk us over to an exact position, tell us what to mount the camera on [hi-hat, baby sticks, dolly and track etcetera], what lens to put up, and even the camera speed. Normally the A and B crews will stay on but C and up the alphabet not so much. As camera assistants we prep the equipment at Panavision and ready it and the camera truck for shooting.

What kind of challenges did this project provide and which scenes, sequences or locations were the most challenging, problematic, memorable, and fun to work on? Any technical issues and such?

Working as a 2nd AC on a show, my primary responsibility is to get whatever the 1st AC needs to get the shot in focus. There are many other things a 2nd AC does, but if the 2nd AC can't help the 1st AC in this capacity, then he will find himself on the chopping block and for good reason. All that said, when you are working on the C camera crew, you are usually given long-lens shots. As you know, the longer the lens, the shorter the depth of field, hence the more difficult it is for the focus puller [1st AC] to keep the subject in focus. To help Dominic out, I would often place distance markers on the ground for references. A and B cameras usually had the wide-shots and they would see the ground. The markers needed to be things that would not stand out to them. Items that would fit into the scene. Things like [on that show] a tin can, a shotgun shell casing, a rock. All of which would need to be visible to Dominic and firmly held in place. Sometimes I would stand ninety degrees off-axis to subject [or camera] movement and call off distances on the walkie-talkie to Dominic.

How was your experience working with the cast and crew?

It was a challenging and fun show to work on.

How did John Carpenter and Kurt Russell collaborate and were there ever any disagreements between them?

They seemed to get along very well. I did not see any incident that was particularly out of the ordinary, interesting, or funny.

What's your favorite memory or memories of working on the movie?

Favorite memories for me are usually ones that were no fun when they are being made. They seem to be the more lasting. Here are a few. On the first night of shooting Cuervo's [Jones] [George Corraface] arrival into Disneyland [Happy Kingdom by the Sea] or whatever they called it in the movie, there were so many guns being fired on set that several hours into the shoot someone way up the food chain at Universal ordered that our production be banned from any further gunfire on the backlot [Courthouse Square]. So, some of the gun flashes you see in the final film were put in during post-production.

On the night we shot the hang gliding landing scene I was called out and received some ire by John Carpenter. As I mentioned earlier, I would often place markers out for Dominic's focus pulls. Well, it just so happened that John was kicking around and came upon one of my carefully placed markers. A shotgun casing spiked to the ground. He was very angry because he saw it as a hazard, the spike part. He was genuinely perplexed as to what it was and why it was there. After I explained how and why, he calmed down a bit but ended the conversation with a stern, "No more spikes."

It was a wicked cold night when we shot the helicopter crash scene. For it, the effects crew ran some underground pipes to an old wreck of a chopper and then they would pump in propane, and I think it was liquid not gas, and light it up. The fire was spectacular and when the director called "Cut!" they would halt the propane and the fire would go out pretty quickly. After a long take, just shutting off the propane flow failed to halt the fire and hence they had to move in and extinguish the fire with CO_2. The explanation given was that the fire got so hot that the magnesium parts in the chopper began to burn.

What do you think of the movie personally?

I like it because it is fun and campy. If taken seriously, the magic vanishes. If I want a serious Carpenter film, I'm watching *The Thing*.

What are you currently doing and what do you enjoy doing in your spare time?

I currently make my living investing in real estate, something I've always done. I'm an outdoors kind of person, but I like to return home to my creature comforts after a good hike or kayak ride.

ROBERT ZUCKERMAN
Still Photographer

How did you end up being a still photographer?

Well, that's an interesting story. I had always loved photography as a hobby and, in the late 1980s, I was a partner in a small production company in Los Angeles. I was the sales person. There was a director, producer, and myself and I was the one responsible for bringing business in. After about a year in business, my two partners decided they didn't want me in the company anymore. It was very distressing at that time, so I went through a lot of stuff and I just decided, "What am I gonna do now where I don't need any partners?" Like I said, I had been doing photography as a passion and a hobby for probably about sixteen years at that point. I said, "I'm gonna be a photographer now," so I just got some business cards printed out and put together a portfolio.

I got one job right away. I was shooting a jewelry advertisement for a jewelry store in Beverly Hills. Shortly after that, I got a call from a woman that I knew who was a secretary to a television producer. She called me and said, "Do you wanna try doing some stills on a set?" I said, "Yeah, I'll do that," and I ran out and got myself the equipment that I needed. I borrowed some stuff. It was a television show that was being produced by ABC television that never made it to the air. They pre-ordered about three or four episodes then they cancelled it. It got me my beginning. One of the actors in that show was a guy with long hair, at the time down to his shoulders, George Clooney. That was my first job.

My second job was a very big job, actually. On a lot of movie sets, they'll have a set photographer that's part of the crew and is there every day. They also have someone who comes in and does the big poster shoot that's a very high paid, high-end photographer like Annie Leibovitz or some big famous person. I happen to be friends with the assistant to Oliver Stone and he was filming the movie *The Doors* at the time. The assistant got me a meeting with Oliver Stone and I had no celebrities in my portfolio, just a lot of my black and white portraits that I did on my own. Oliver Stone really liked that, so he hired me to be that big portrait photographer on the movie *The Doors*. So basically, a nobody got the biggest job at the time in Hollywood. For the next couple of years, I did small independent films.

In 1991, I had gone to a book signing. There's a pretty famous bookstore in Hollywood called Book Soup. They had a book signing with David Mamet, who's a director and writer and I stayed afterwards. We somehow struck up a friendship and we're hanging out and I photographed his wife and did headshots. Then about the fall of 1992, I get a call from a producer, Edward Pressman, his office. They're getting ready to do a film called *The Crow* with Brandon Lee and they say, "David Mamet recommended you to be the still photographer." At the time the film was being done by Paramount Pictures. They were the original distributor and I had done one film for them earlier that spring, but they didn't feel that I had the experience. This is gonna be a dark action film with very rugged conditions and they wanted someone with more experience, but the producers stood behind me. They went back and forward and back and forward and suddenly I made a deal with Paramount. I said, "Look, just give me a three-week trial period and if you don't like the results of what I'm doing then I'll step down."

So I just got there in North Carolina and it was very cold and rainy. The conditions were very tough, but I had really practiced a lot. I was very determined to do a good job and Brandon Lee really liked what I was doing. I was showing him some of the results. The three-week trial period passed and Paramount was liking what I was doing. Are you familiar with the tragedy that happened on that film? They disbanded after Brandon Lee was shot. They were gonna figure out how they're gonna end the film and so they gave it like a six-week hiatus and I went back to Los Angeles. The same guy at Paramount who was resisting me being hired said, "You know, we have photographers we worked with for 20, 25 years that we wouldn't have hired on this job. You did an amazing job and we're very proud of you." It got me into doing. I was the guy that could do dark action films so from there I did like a *Hellraiser* and some other stuff. Anyway, I'm talking my head off. The moral of the story is that, even though I was doing other things, and I had a very negative experience with those earlier business partners, I actually look back twenty-six years later and I thank them. It pushed me into something that's been a really amazing career for me.

How did you get the job of still photographer on *Escape From L.A.*?

I can't quite remember the chronology. In 94 or 95, they did the sequel to *The Crow* and I worked on that and then did another couple of other films. Then Paramount was getting ready to do *Escape From L.A.* and so they called me to do that movie. It all came out of the experience on *The Crow*.

How do you work with people to get the photos you want?

Well, you just have to be present and be there and treat it very professionally. I feel if you give respect to people then they give it back to you. Being on a movie set is always a dynamic. Some actors are very comfortable with a still camera around. Other actors get distracted by it, so you have to try and be aware of that and respect that. I've learned through experience and through making mistakes. I also try to think about the end result. In other words, a certain part early on you're very eager. You want to get every photograph, but you kind of learn what becomes used and what doesn't become used. The main usage for the imagery that we shoot is for advertising, for poster or for publicity in a publication or online or the other thing they use it for, merchandise, so I just try to think about that. If I feel there's something of a really durable photograph of an actor that maybe is hard to get when we're actually filming, I'll ask the first assistant director who's running the set if he wants to hold the lights for me in the end so I can grab some stills that way.

Another thing I've done is what they call in the business, the pull away shot. If I see a cool piece of a wall or texture or lighting or something that will be great for a portrait, I'll ask the actor or the actor's representative if they can just step aside for a minute so I can get a really nice portrait. That can be useful down the road as well. When I was working on the movie *Any Given Sunday* in Miami which is very rugged with an amazing cast of people I made it a point to go before they were filming. They do what they call lighting and makeup test. They have the actors in full makeup and the camera and director of photography have them in nice lights where they don't have to worry about saying their lines and remembering dialogue. They're just there for the look. That's also an opportunity very early on in filming or before filming to get some really cool portraits so I do that as well. Just working hard and be respectful and I also try to treat the actors not as models when I photograph them.

I was on one film in 1992, my first film for Paramount before *The Crow*, called *The Temp* and they had a very big name photographer come on and do some special portraits and one point one of the actors. I was kind of observing from the side and saw the main actor Timothy Hutton get really pissed off and walk away and he was saying, "I'm an actor. Not a model." That gave me an insight very early on to treat it like an acting job and not a modeling job and I think you know the actors appreciates that when you do that.

What kind of challenges did this project provide and which scenes or locations were the most challenging, problematic, memorable and fun to work on?

They were all challenging in a way. It was a pretty rugged film. That mudslide that you spoke about. That was, like I said, the first night. That was kind of like getting, they say, "Throw the baby in the pool until it learns how to swim." That was one of those things we knew was gonna set the tone for the whole film. Just dark, night, cold, and rugged conditions. The other one is the outdoor action scene shot in a landfill in south L.A. [Former Cal Compact Landfill] [Sunset Boulevard/Beverly Hills Hotel Exterior/Santa Monica Freeway]. Of course, we're hearing all this talk about the landfill being toxic and we had to have the environmental protection agency come out to test the land before we went in there. Welcome to Hollywood! That was a pretty challenging scene, but enjoyable. Peter Fonda [Pipeline], you know. The one scene where he's like surfing on a tsunami, that was kind of fun as well. That was a good one also. Inside the control room was pretty cool and when Kurt Russell and Valeria Golino [Taslima] were like tied up, that's an interesting one.

For me, it was just fun because I had been a fan when *Escape From New York* came out. I thought it was a cool film and it was really cool to work on the sequel to that. It was also kind of cool on the set when Kurt Russell was there and Goldie Hawn and the kids would come and visit. I got to see a very young Kate Hudson at the time, so that was kind of cool as well. I did some stuff outdoors like in a football stadium [Los Angeles Memorial Coliseum] and they came. The big landfill was probably the most challenging, but also very visually compelling and just a lot of stuff there to photograph. It was very dark, so I was also trying to figure out the best film stock to use in those dark conditions in the days before digital cameras. I think the landfill was probably the one we spent the most time at.

What's your favorite photo or photos and how many photos did you take?

I can't remember. I mean, back in those days when we were shooting film, I was shooting 35mm film. The way I worked then, I had these pouches on my belt. One side was unexposed film and, when I expose it, I put it in the other pouch. I would estimate that I probably took about 30,000 frames of film throughout the production. I liked the photo I did with Kurt on the motorcycle that became a poster. I also did some cool stunt photos of the motorcycle in mid-air. Some of the long shots of being on that outdoor toxic waste dump, because you just kind of put everything on a telephoto lens and it compresses everything, so you get to see some of the scenery best. That is kind of a cool effect. Some of the things inside with Kurt Russell when they're in that control room and Kurt Russell and Valeria Golino being tied up. Those were pretty cool. We did some big opening crowd scenes in the Universal [Studios] backlot [Courthouse Square] [Happy Kingdom by the Sea] and I felt those were kind of fun as well. There's some cool photos of Cuervo Jones [George Corraface] on a truck with a lot of people around him. I kind of enjoyed those photos.

How was your experience working with the cast and crew? Which people did you enjoy the most working with for instance?

That was a long time ago. I can't believe it. It's about twenty years. I really enjoyed them all. Kurt Russell was very cool and a very hard-working guy and really open. Like I said, in your previous question, if I saw something really cool, a cool photo or whatever, he'd be very compliant of that. There's one shot that actually went on one of the posters for the movie where he's kind of sitting on a motorcycle with a bunch of flames behind him. I thought that was a cool shot and it was just something on the set at night with him sitting on the motorcycle and they put the flames in later in the post-production, so Kurt Russell was great. Another actor in there was Cliff Robertson [President]. He was a really, really nice guy to me. He came from like my parents' generation, so that was really an honor to meet him. He wrote me a nice letter afterwards. They were all pretty good. Pam Grier [Hershe] was really nice. Steve Buscemi [Map to the Stars Eddie], obviously he's gone on to great notoriety. He was very cool. They were all very cool.

John Carpenter, the director, was a very kick back guy and obviously a veteran to film sets, so it was very easy to be around him. He let me do my work. Kurt Russell's stunt double is a really cool guy. The sound mixer, his name was Thomas Causey. Actually, the film was shot, I think with like seventy-three all-nighters pretty much in the winter time, so the nights were longer. We go in like four or five in the afternoon and leave like six or seven in the morning and drive home in rush hour traffic being tired. Pretty grueling experience. Tommy Causey was a sound mixer and we'd sit around like three o'clock in the morning telling each other stories and just bullshitting with each other. Just telling good stories of our lives and stuff. That was interesting.

The stand-in for Kurt Russell was a guy named Travis Burrell. We became really friendly. Again, we were there in the middle of the night just trying to stay awake. We always found ourselves doing exercises like push-ups or dips. Things like that and out of that experience we actually created a portable exercise machine that has been patented and sold. That was out of that experience being on *Escape From L.A.* We've been friends ever since that time as well. I haven't really seen some of the other people. Valeria Golino was great, but I haven't seen her since then. It was cool to work with her. Like I said, Pam Grier was great and all the cast members were really kick back. There wasn't anyone who was anti-photography. Everyone was really cool.

What's your favorite memory or memories of working on the movie?

Like I said, that setup shot I did of Kurt Russell. They had another guy, Greg Gorman, come in and do a big photo shoot. I'm a little disappointed because I did that cool shot of Kurt Russell sitting on the motorcycle with the flames behind him and what not. I showed them a print and someone goes, "Man, this is really cool. We're gonna have Greg Gorman do this in the studio." Of course, Greg Gorman made more than I made in seventy-three nights of filming, so I was a little ticked off by that. They made two posters, one from Greg Gorman's photo and one from my photo. So, I have a little vindication there.

I enjoyed watching Kurt Russell and Goldie Hawn in their relationship together. I worked on one film with Kurt Russell subsequently back in, I think, 2002. It was a movie that ended up being called *Dark Blue,* a cop movie. When Goldie Hawn would come to the set, I really enjoyed watching them and I learned from them too. A lot of times when people who are together for many years, they kind of just go on autopilot. They don't really talk and, when she was talking, Kurt Russell would just really sit back and pay attention to her and really listen to what she was saying like another person. It's not about the film so much, but it was a good lesson in life to watch that. I'm fascinated with a lot of the stuff that goes on behind the scenes in making the films.

The key grip, Norman Glasser, was a really good guy. We used to tell jokes to each other, another thing you just do on a movie set when you're waiting in between setups or whatever. There's a lot of idle time on film sets. It takes like months to put something together that's only gonna be like an hour and a half or two hours on the screen. Norman was a great guy. He's now the rep for the grips union.

What do you think of the movie personally?

I really enjoyed the movie. It created a whole other world. It's just interesting because 2013 has come and passed and it's interesting to live through that. When you spend like seventy-three intense nights on a set with people working, it becomes like your family. I really enjoyed that. I did like the film. I was a little skeptical at first. I didn't know how they were gonna pull it off, but I think they did a good job with it.

What are you currently doing and what do you enjoy doing in your spare time?

I live in Miami, Florida now. I used to commute back and forward because I had two disabled sisters and my mom there to support for a long time. I continued working since *Escape From L.A.* on movies up till about three years ago. In the early 2000s, I began having issues with my mobility. I would fall and lose my balance and so forth. I went about eight years, almost eight years of testing, until I was finally diagnosed in late 2010 with a very rare genetic disease that has put me in a wheelchair and rendered me paraplegic. So once I got in a wheelchair, it seemed like Hollywood stopped calling me, so I decided to come over to Miami full time. Now I'm really pursuing what I love doing, which is teaching. I have a position with FIU, which is Florida International University. I just try to do what I say, teaching and world betterment. Making them do things that are gonna help the world get a little better.

One of the things I have started back in 2002 is a body of work called *Kindsight*. *Kindsight* is kind of like the original. I don't know if you've ever heard of the photo series *Humans of New York,* which also is a photo and story book about random encounters. I started *Kindsight* about ten years before that. That's been something that has been ongoing for me. I got books. I exhibit the work in hospitals. I also try teaching and empowering young people right now. You know, showing my experience in photography. That's kind of what I'm doing now. In 2005 I started exhibiting and I probably had about maybe in the last ten years about thirty or more exhibits between New York and Los Angeles and elsewhere.

Even if I'm on a wheelchair now, I keep the camera with me at all times, and so if I see something that inspires me I'll make a photo of it or just always be ready for stuff. I really enjoyed the film business. I have like almost a twenty-five year career. I think the thing I enjoy the most part is like the comradery and the connection of the people you spend all that time with. Trying to be a good person. Try to take care of my family. Teach others. I've also taken on an apprentice, a seven-year old boy who has leukemia and going through some very hard times. I did a workshop with him and I made him to my apprentice and associate and now he comes along on jobs with me.

JASON ROBERTS
Second Second Assistant Director

How did you end up being a second second/first assistant director?

I started my production career early while I was still in high school. I worked for several years as an intern and then production assistant before being accepted into the DGA Training Program where they trained me to be a DGA 2nd AD [Assistant Director]. After graduating from the program in the early 90s, I worked as an assistant director on a variety of shows. You can find my credits on IMDb.

How did you get the job of second assistant director on *Escape From L.A.*?

I had worked with Chris Della Penna [First Assistant Director] as his 2nd 2nd AD when he was a key 2nd on *Black Sheep*, which was a Chris Farley and David Spade comedy for Paramount. Artist Robinson was the first AD on that film. Chris asked me to be his key 2nd, but Paramount didn't think I had enough experience at that point in my career to handle what was then a bigger budget feature. So I told Chris that I knew a really top notch key 2nd AD, Marty Jedlicka, and thought he would be a good fit with Chris. He was just coming off of *True Lies,* which was a much bigger budgeted picture than *Escape From L.A.,* so I knew the studio wouldn't have any issues with him. The only condition of bringing Marty into the mix was that I would be kept on the film as the 2nd 2nd AD. I wasn't disappointed at all. I wanted to do the movie and I found a way to bring a friend aboard and help put a really solid team together. Making movies is such a collaborative effort that being a part of the production team was enough for me. Both Chris and Marty are terrific ADs and really good-hearted guys!

How did you, Christian P. Della Penna [First Assistant Director] and Martin Jedlicka [Second Assistant Director] prepare for this project and how did you collaborate?

I was in charge of setting the background artists [extras] and helped run the production team on set. I also did the production reports and sometimes assisted with the call sheets.

Jason Roberts [Second Second Assistant Director]
(Photo Courtesy Jason Roberts)

What kind of challenges did this project provide and which scenes or locations were the most challenging, problematic, memorable, and fun to work on?

Overall, working seventy plus nights in a row was a challenge for everyone. I craved sunlight and had a lot of trouble getting any for five months! A lot of people started getting an orange hue to them, probably due to lack of sunlight and vitamin D!

Many of the locations were difficult due to unforeseen variables. For example, the part where Snake meets up with Pipeline [Peter Fonda] before they get on the surfboards was one of our first days of shooting. It had been raining the previous few days before we started. When we arrived, all of our production trucks got stuck in the mud and it took the transportation department a long time to dig them out. It also made it difficult to get access to the shooting areas with all the equipment. The actual surfing part of those scenes were shot on a green screen. At some point, we sent some surfing doubles to Texas to a newly designed wave riding park [Schlitterbahn Waterpark & Resort] to grab footage of them surfing on controlled waves [FlowRider]. The main company wasn't there, but I think that was what was cut into the footage of the actual water and feet on the boards.

I loved shooting the Surgeon General of Beverly Hills [Bruce Campbell] scene. We shot that at the P&E Lofts [Pacific Electric Building] on 610 Main Street in downtown L.A. It's been used on tons of movies. I've shot there on three separate movies, myself. The cool part of that was all of the prosthetic effects we had done to the actors and background artists. It was amazing work by Rick Baker [Special Makeup Effects] and his crew. Really cool stuff. Bruce Campbell didn't even look like himself. So great. And Valeria Golino [Taslima] was super nice too.

Working on locations that were outside of L.A. proper presented traffic issues for the crew. We would go to work in rush hour traffic and drive home as the sun was coming up in the morning rush hour traffic too. That was pretty miserable, morale-wise. It was also hard to stay awake while driving, which now taken as a much more serious safety issue these days. I do recall that I had the studio put up the PAs [Production Assistants] and myself at a hotel in Carson where we shot the motorcycle sequence and the Map to the Stars Eddie [Steve Buscemi] meeting amongst other things since we were shooting there multiple days in a row. We were working too many hours to drive back and forth to our homes. So we were able to get some sleep and then, as a team, we would meet for lunch before heading off to set.

There was one moment during the motorcycle sequence that stands out for me. We were doing a half-mile insert car shot. We had about 300 background artists to set from one end to the other. I remember John [Carpenter] said he would be back in forty-five minutes once everything was ready to go, so Marty and I each took half the background. He took the front half or first 1/4 mile of the run and I took the back 1/4 mile run to the end. I set up really anarchic background action. I am talking about waaaaay left field kind of stuff. Fights, rapes, bondage scenes. General anarchy reigns type thought. Once I had set everyone and had set the action to happen as the insert car was driving by, I told Marty that I had to head to base to work on the call sheet or some paperwork stuff. He said, "Okay." Chris wanted to do some test runs and check everything out before John came back to set to make sure everything worked camera and motorcycle-wise with all the elements working including the background action. Marty told me he would run it with Chris and make any changes before John came back, so I headed to base.

About ten minutes later, I get a call from Marty on my radio freaking out. I rush back to set and he proceeds to tell me that my action is out of line. He said I can't set such violent background and that I had to change it. Just as he's telling me this, we get word that John is coming to set and we're going to shoot. Marty looks at me and says that he's going to make sure that John knows it was me and that he'll figure out a way to state this background action was not set by him. I tell him it'll be okay. Anyway, I head back to the start of the run and John jumps up on the insert car with Chris and they do a run where John sees the action. I'm at the start with Marty and when they get to the end of the run, I hear Chris call me on the radio. He tells me to rush over that John wants to talk to me about the background. I thought, "Oh no. Marty was right and I'm screwed. I am in for a beating." So we bolt over to the end in a golf cart, I get out and John is standing on the insert car looking like [George S.] Patton. Chris is right next to him. He looks down on me and says, "Did you set this background action?" I told him, "Yes, sir," thinking he's going to yell at me for messing it up so bad. Instead, he says that he loved it and to amp it up more and, in fact, try to get more of that on the first part of the run too! I couldn't believe it. I don't know if my look to Marty was as much as his look to me was at the same time, but we all had a laugh about it afterwards!

The end sequence where everyone gathered at "Happy Kingdom by the Sea" was fun to shoot. We did that at Universal Studios on their backlot in the *Back to the Future* square [Courthouse Square]. I remember working with Central Casting on getting the look right for that. Jennifer Bender was our background casting director [She now is the head of Central Casting and runs the entire operation]. I told her I wanted every kind of person that never gets cast for any other shows, the ones that no one wanted. We conceptually asked for a scruffy/homeless/any kind of gang related tough look. We booked 300-500 people for a week with the exception of the model type girls. We didn't want any pretty people or faces on this show.

On the first day, as we were getting everyone ready for the scene [this entails moving each background actor through hair, makeup, wardrobe, props and finally into a big circus type tent for a meal before heading to set], I found the two biggest, most intimidating background guys I could find. These guys were built like linebackers for the Oakland Raiders football team, really tough, hard looking guys. So, while everyone is busy getting everyone ready, I pull these guys aside and tell them that I am going to give them a pay voucher for the day but not have them work. I asked them to act up in front of everyone during the get ready process where I explain to everyone what we would be doing that evening. I told them to talk back to me and that I was going to fire them in front of the whole group of 500 people. They would then leave when I threatened them with security. They agreed to help me out with this little plan and, in turn, I also promised them I would give them other work days on the movie.

When it came time during my speech to all the background artists, these guys were causing trouble and talking loudly and not paying attention, doing exactly what I had asked them to do. I stop my speech and told them come up to where I am standing in front of everyone. They were towering over me. I asked for their pay vouchers. They handed them over to me and I ripped them to shreds and threw them on the ground. I told them to get off the lot, that they were fired. They protested just that little bit and I threatened to call security. Then they left with their heads slung low. Every single other background actor was staring at me with their mouths open. They couldn't believe that this shorter AD stood up to and handled the two biggest guys in the tent. I turned to everyone else once they had left and told them that I don't want to have any problems with anyone or they will end up with the same thing. Fired with no pay! I said they better pay attention and keep their heads up since a lot of action was going to be going on. I'll never forget that moment since about ninety-nine percent of them stayed in line that whole week. You have to remember, these people weren't cast very often and I had to think outside the box to keep them in line. It was easier, at that point, to keep them interested through each night too. Sometimes you have to think outside the box.

I remember a couple of other moments that stand out. One day I was the photo and hand double for Steve Buscemi. I was his hand in the movie that put the red nail polish dot on the disc. I also doubled him in the car on a wide driving shot. What can I say, we were pretty much the same size and the clothes fit me! Marty and I were also two of the robed guys chasing Snake and Taslima from the Beverly Hills Hotel. I also put my dad in the movie. He's in the opening sequence when the earthquake strikes L.A. He's the guy running at union station with the briefcase just before it blows up. I also put my stepbrother in the movie too at the end sequence. He's one of the two guards with the black masks that drag A.J. Langer [Utopia] into the scene. It was funny because it was so cold out at Ventura Farms that all the masks fogged up. It was already hard to see since they were tinted and we were shooting at night. Combine that with very uneven ground and small trenches, my stepbrother and the other guy tripped bringing her in a couple of times.

Top and Bottom: The Donald C. Tillman Water Reclamation Plant
[Firebase 7 Exterior/Access Tunnel]
(Photos Courtesy Jason Roberts)

How was your experience working with the cast and crew?

Getting a chance to continue my working relationship with Chris Della Penna was something I wanted to do. As an AD, finding a production team you can be a part of is one of the best feelings in the world. I think most ADs seek that. There is a comfort level of knowing your team has your back and vice versa. Since this was Chris' big break moving up to 1st AD, I wanted to be on that rollercoaster with him. Working with John Carpenter was a treat. I loved *Starman, The Thing, Big Trouble in Little China, They Live,* and of course *Escape From New York.* Having the opportunity to work alongside him and Kurt Russell, who was and is just plain cool, was a big part of my desire to do the movie in the first place. Kurt didn't have an entourage and was very accessible to the crew. He's a what you see is what you get type of guy. He was always kind and sincere. John had his moments, but overall was a director with a vision for the movie. It was his baby through and through. The crew bonded and worked strong together to get through the tough schedule. Everyone was at the top of their game, so it was hard since you had to keep up with them but also inspiring as a learning experience too.

How did you collaborate with the extras and how were they chosen for the different scenes?

On *Escape From L.A.,* I remember picking the different gang types. There was one guy in particular. William Peña [Jacket Mescalito]. He actually got a line in the movie and a few small moments. He was the guy who picked up Snake's jacket at the end of the motorcycle sequence and later Snake retrieves it back from his dead body before getting on the chopper. He had a great look and a great attitude. I made him and one other guy the leaders of the Mescalitos. That's what we called them. Robin [Michel] Bush [Costume Designer] did a great job of designing this semi-retro zoot suit look mixed with a *Mad Max*/World War II type vibe. Those guys lived their characters and really brought a lot to each of the scenes. They were great on camera. I loved working with everyone of them.

Other than finding a few of the background artists asleep around the sets in the abandoned cars, I didn't really have any issues on the movie. Everyone was excited to be working and John and Chris created a very well-run set. Everyone had a job to do and knew where to be. I work well with background artists. Setting background action is one of the most creative jobs for an assistant director. When done well, it enhances every single scene. Imagine any movie without the background and just the actors. Those scenes will lose the believable atmosphere and they won't have the same feeling. The ADs work is tangible and it's right there up on the screen, so there is a ton of creative satisfaction to that work. I treat everyone with respect. I don't yell and scream or push and shove. I try to uplift people to give the best performance they can for any scene. It's in the best interest of the movie to make sure that a background actor knows how they fit into a scene and how they can subtly enhance it. Remember, being part of the AD department is managing the crew. We are the only department that has to get people who sometimes have never been on a set before perform perfectly on camera from the get go. That can take a lot of skill and sometimes requires a little magic and tricks up your sleeve to make it happen.

What's your favorite memory or memories of working on the movie?

Well, I have a pretty crazy story that I don't think I ever told anyone except for A.J. Langer. I might as well tell it now. Originally, John had cast Kate Hudson as Utopia or at least was planning to. I think Kurt was in line with that too. This was during prep, but Goldie Hawn, her mom said, "No way." She was staying in school and not going to be a full-time actress yet. I guess Kurt and John agreed with her. The only problem was that we were starting production and didn't have a Utopia cast yet. Since that character wasn't scheduled to work right away, John and Debra Hill, the producer had time to cast the right actress.

While we were shooting in downtown L.A. for a two-day period, they had the studio bring in about twenty actresses. The ones that weren't in L.A. were flown in from New York and London. They held auditions for them in a trailer in basecamp. They needed them videoed so, for whatever reason, I drew the short straw and videotaped all of the auditions for them, which means I was in the trailer with John, Debra, and each actress as they came in to audition. Once each audition was over and the actress left, I would sit quietly while John and Debra discussed them. I remember one of the actresses was Bridgett Wilson, who is married to Pete Sampras, the tennis player. Anyway, during these discussions Debra and John would complain that none of the actresses were hitting the right moments in one of the three scenes that they were auditioning with. I took a mental note of that to see if any of them did that. There was a break when John and Debra were called to set, so I stepped outside to get some fresh air and tell the next actress that they would be back shortly. I got to talking with her and she seemed super cool. As we were waiting for John and Debra to get back, I asked this actress if she would like some unsolicited advice. She said, "Sure," so for whatever reason, I told her what John and Debra had been looking for in the three scenes and not getting thus far. Simply stuff I overheard them talk about in the trailer. To this day I don't know why I did that. It was very out of character for me.

Anyway, John and Debra come back and we go into the trailer and this actress auditions for it. She leaves and John and Debra are excited that this girl hit the right notes and gave a good audition. They pretty much decided on the spot, but went through a few more auditions to solidify it. That actress was A.J. Langer, who got the part. I want to clarify that I didn't get her the part at all. She did all the work and gave the best audition, but I thought it was pretty neat that my advice might have helped just a little bit. A.J. was very cool with me on the movie and we became friends and here is the crazy side note to this already surreal story. A.J.'s best friend was this girl named Susie and Susie was A.J.'s de facto friend/assistant to help her on the movie. Since we were shooting nights, I hired cast PA drivers to get the actors to and from set on the long hours. One of my buddies was A.J.'s driver/cast PA. His name is Kevin. Well, Kevin and Susie fell in love and, in the intervening twenty plus years, are married with two lovely children, so I would also like to think that my actions caused the stars to align for them too!

What do you think of the movie personally?

I think it's good campy fun. Not as good as *Escape From New York* as it had some underdog feeling that made you root for him the whole way through. Maybe because that was new then. I always have high hopes for the projects I work on. You have to believe in them when you are in the midst of it working so many hours and giving so much of your time day in and day out. You always give it your best effort and sometimes it works out and sometimes it doesn't. I think the majority of the shows I worked on in the 90s don't hold up anymore. The advancement in CGI and other film technology has opened up the possibilities of so many different realities that wasn't possible back then. A lot of the VFX shots from *Escape From L.A.* look a little cheesy and retro. It wasn't even groundbreaking back then so all in all it was a little bit disappointing.

What are you currently doing and what do you enjoy doing in your spare time?

At the moment I am the first AD on a series for Fox called *Orville*. It is created, produced, written by, and stars Seth MacFarlane. I still bounce around from movie to movie as an AD. Strangely due to reshoots, VFX post-production schedules and the ever shuffling of releases, I have six projects coming out this year. Just recently the Scarlett Johansson movie *Ghost in the Shell* was released. I did the U.S. portion on that one. Next I have Michael Bay's *Transformers: The Last Knight opening* in June. Then sometime in September I have a Doug Liman and Tom Cruise movie coming out called *American Made*. Although I think the title may change for that one. Then I did Angelina Jolie's latest directorial effort which is called *First They Killed My Father*. We shot that in Cambodia and I think it's a really special project about the Khmer Rouge's takeover of the country and the subsequent genocide of their people. It's told through the eyes of a nine-year-old girl. That should also be out in the fall.

Finally I did an Alexander Payne movie with Matt Damon called *Downsizing*. I think that is going to be released in December. *Orville* by the way will be out in the fall on TV. I enjoy hiking with my wife and reading and photography as a hobby. We have been traveling a lot lately too. I have also been giving back by teaching at schools and doing online seminars about the mechanics and art of being an assistant director. If anyone is interested they can check out my webinars at Stage32.com in their education section.

PATRICK M. SULLIVAN JR.
Set Designer

How did you end up being a set designer, art director, and production designer?

I studied architecture but always loved movies. When I learned I could be creative, design, and build cool architecture for film, that's what I pursued.

How did you get the job of set designer on *Escape From L.A.*?

It was my second union film. I had no support network yet. No one to call to get my next job. I had just completed *Twister* and was in the union office finally getting sworn in. A production underway at Paramount had called the union office looking for an availability list to get crew. I got my name in there to meet with Larry Paull [Production Designer]. We got on well. He saw that I had managed to be successful on *Twister* with a demanding designer, had some good drawings to show, so he figured I could handle working for him.

How did you and set designers Nathan Crowley, Richard Mays, Christopher S. Nushawg and Darrell L. Wight as well as Lawrence G. Paull [Production Designer] and Bruce Crone [Art Director] prepare for this project and how did you collaborate?

Larry Paull oversees and conceptualizes and we all help him flesh out his ideas. Props, ships, vehicles, and weapons are generally in the realm of the illustrator. Tim Lawrence [Illustrator] handled a majority of that. Joe Musso [Illustrator] was great at creating the overall wide establishing shots and setting the mood and scale of the film. Richard Mays was brought on to specifically handle the construction drawings to build the helicopter set piece. Chris, Darrell, Nathan, and I handled the set design drawings. They were doled out mostly based upon schedule and size of build, whomever finished their previous set as the next one needed to get drawn. The drawings were done entirely by hand. Construction documents, illustrations, and concept art. The key here is that these were all pre-digital realm. Markers, inks, lead, paper, vellum, glue. In

L-R/BG: William Hiney [Assistant Art Director], Carol Kiefer [Art Department Coordinator], Lawrence G. Paull [Production Designer], Patrick M. Sullivan Jr. [Set Designer], Nathan Crowley [Set Designer], Darrell L. Wight [Set Designer]/FG: Bruce Crone [Art Director]
(Photo Courtesy Carol Kiefer)

short, messy. Pre-production, the design and planning phase of the film, may have been as much as twelve weeks before filming began.

Did you have any reference material?

Research was entirely collaborative. We knew what we were going for and the texture and tone that it required. A few reference books, namely *City of Darkness* and *Unterwelten,* factored heavily in the development of our ideas. Some sets were full builds on a sound stage such as the interior Sewer [Beverly Hills Hotel] and interior Detention Center [Firebase 7]. Others were partial builds of various sizes to augment locations chosen by Larry and John Carpenter such as various locations in downtown Los Angeles as well as the backlot at Universal Studios [Courthouse Square] [Happy Kingdom by the Sea]. The exterior Detention Center with the entry, the perimeter walls and guard towers were built at the [Donald C.] Tillman Water Reclamation Plant.

Were any ideas discarded?

Certainly a lot of material gets discarded in the process. That being said, a lot also get saved and archived by the studio. Constructions drawings and illustrations take days to weeks to complete. It varies based upon complexity, medium and its place in the process. Some ideas get worked out THROUGH these drawings. Others are just output to present for approval.

What's your favorite memory or memories of working on the movie?

My favorite memory has to be seeing Kurt Russell in full Snake Plissken costume, eye patch and all. I was a big fan of the original so I felt fortunate and grateful to be a part of the lore and the legend.

What do you think of the movie personally?

It's great fun. It had the perfect tone and quality that it needed to have to sustain and continue the cult status of the saga. I've always felt that the story almost beat for beat is like a retelling of the original. Characters, their meaning, purpose, and importance align across both films.

What are you currently doing and what do you enjoy doing in your spare time?

I'm still staying busy in the industry always trying to find new creative challenges. I enjoy spending time with my family in my spare time.

CAROL KIEFER
Art Department Coordinator

How did you end up being an art department coordinator?

I became an art department coordinator by accident. I had been a university instructor of corporate finance and moved to L.A. after a personal crisis. After working unsuccessfully in a consulting firm I decided to take my life in a different direction and took some classes at UCLA film school as the film industry seemed to be the biggest employer in L.A. I had a degree in English with an art minor and I had an MBA [Master of Business Administration] in finance and a good sense of story and budgets. I was introduced to someone who needed a hair model for her union test and I needed a job. We became good friends and in time she introduced me to J. Michael Riva, a production designer. He was looking for a coordinator for a Rob Reiner film called *North* and he gave me a chance because my non-film background was interesting to him.

How did you get the job of art department coordinator on *Escape From L.A.*?

After *North* I worked with Michael on *Congo* and then was hired by Lawrence Paull [Production Designer] to do *Sgt. Bilko*. He and I got along well and he asked me to work on *Escape From L.A.* Bruce Crone was the art director on both projects with Larry.

How did you, Lawrence G. Paull [Production Designer] and Bruce Crone [Art Director] prepare for this project and how did you collaborate?

To prep for this we studied *Escape From New York* because the character of Snake Plissken was going to be revived and screened other John Carpenter films to get a feel for John's style. We studied graphics from the original movie through screen grabs. The internet was barely a tool at that time. We were just entering the digital age. We still used pagers. Few people had cell phones. Based on the script Larry hired a few artists to illustrate key frames in the movie. These illustrations helped him develop the look of the film. Although we were based

L-R/BG: William Hiney [Assistant Art Director], Carol Kiefer [Art Department Coordinator], Lawrence G. Paull [Production Designer], Patrick M. Sullivan Jr. [Set Designer], Nathan Crowley [Set Designer], Darrell L. Wight [Set Designer]/FG: Bruce Crone [Art Director]
(Photo Courtesy Carol Kiefer)

on the Paramount lot the film was shot on local locations. I don't remember if we built sets. If we did they were small.

What kind of challenges did this project provide and which scenes or locations were the most challenging, problematic, memorable, and fun to work on?

There were challenges. Budget was always an issue. I don't remember what the number was, but I know it was a struggle to stay within the numbers.

Was anything discarded due to budget?

I don't remember if there were props that didn't get made or if scenes were cut. I'm sure there were last minute requests. That happens on all films, so it isn't something that made an impact. I do know there was a lot of tension about the budget.

How was your experience working with the cast and crew?

Kurt Russell was very hands on with respect to the prep of the film. He wore the same costume from *Escape From New York*. It still fit. He and John seemed to have a good relationship and were together a great deal of the prep, going over scenes, planning the action. I had good working relationships with the crew. I'm still in touch with several people. Both Larry Paull and Bruce Crone have retired. Bruce moved to Santa Fe and Larry retired right after *Escape From L.A.* and moved to La Jolla. I think he teaches at San Diego State University [Chapman University]. I like Bruce and Larry. They worked together a lot and had a good relationship. Bruce was an excellent art director and was someone Larry could depend on and trust to have his back. Larry has a colorful Hollywood history and told me great stories about experiences on his former films. My favorite was hearing about *Blade Runner*. At one point, he had a *Blade Runner* art department reunion of sorts at his house and he invited me to join them. It was a thrill for me.

What's your favorite memory or memories of working on the movie?

One of my favorite memories was going to the main locations and watch everything come to life as they filmed. We filmed the low riders on the Universal backlot [Courthouse Square] where the *Back to the Future* clocktower scene was filmed. The more industrial prison scenes were filmed in a water power plant [Donald C. Tillman Water Reclamation Plant] [Firebase 7 Exterior/Access Tunnel] near the Sepulveda Basin.

What do you think of the movie personally?

When we started the project, I know we were all excited to make a sequel to a cult movie. Personally, I think the movie was *Escape From New York* light. They were too similar. I haven't seen it in over twenty years. I should look at it again. Technology has changed so much over the decades since this was made. What we thought was cutting edge VFX is crude by today's standards.

What are you currently doing and what do you enjoy doing in your spare time?

I'm currently finishing *Black Panther* in Atlanta. I've had some wonderful experiences working in the industry. Two films actually allowed me to work overseas and that was life changing. *Rendition* [Morocco] and *X-Men Origins: Wolverine* [Sydney].

FIREBALL TIM
Illustrator

How did you end up being a production illustrator and storyboard artist?

I went to school as a transportation designer at Art Center [College of Design] but ended up at Disney's Imagineering. While there for three years I did concept art for five different parks and built a pretty good repertoire. By the time I went into film [1991], I could pretty much work in any genre. Disney was a great place to bounce daily from sci-fi to western to fantasy and adventure. In an average week, I'd do cars for Autopia, Indiana Jones paintings, Toontown props, and *Beauty & The Beast* architecture. It was awesome. For storyboards, I just wanted to learn to direct. The best way to do that was to board and make as many mistakes as possible, some very painful. I've boarded with David Twohy in his house, Guillermo Del Toro in an editing bay, and even created fight scenes on a lawn at Universal Studios. I have a background in martial arts which helped me get hired doing those. Nothing like beating the crap out of the director! But all in all, I'm had wonderful teachers and great experiences.

How did you get the job of illustrator on *Escape From L.A.*?

I don't remember how it actually happened, but once John [Carpenter] found out that I was the son of Anthony Lawrence, who wrote/produced *Elvis,* which he directed, we hit it off. But the production designer Larry Paull got me the interview. We had worked together before, but John wanted someone who could board and do concept also. Our personalities fit and we both liked twinkies.

How did you, Joseph Musso [Illustrator] as well as Lawrence G. Paull [Production Designer], Bruce Crone [Art Director] and John Carpenter prepare for this project and how did you collaborate?

Concept and boarding are very different animals. Concept artists rarely work with the directors, but work consistently with productions designers and art directors. I'll read the script and the PD [Production Designer] will dole out key

L-R: Sean Clark [Set Visitor], Tim Lawrence [Illustrator]
(Photo Courtesy Fireball Tim)

frames he wants me to concentrate on for money shots or I'll be assigned props and just go to town on them without direction. Just come up with cool shit. Guns, costumes, props, vehicles. Boarding is done directly with the director and I don't ever see the PD. Honestly, Larry didn't give too much creative direction nor did JC [John Carpenter]. I just pumped it out like there was no tomorrow for nine months.

By the time I got together with John Carpenter, he was directly shooting my boards shot for shot. I was really creating the shots as per his request, but the angles, lens and actions dynamics were mine. That experience led me into directing commercials. I appreciate that from him. Collaboration with Larry and Bruce was great. Bruce was always cracking jokes but was very good at what he did. Options weren't explored too much as time didn't allow it, but we were all on the same page. They just built what I did and even Larry gave it the thumbs up. Pretty much everything I designed was built and Larry's only input other

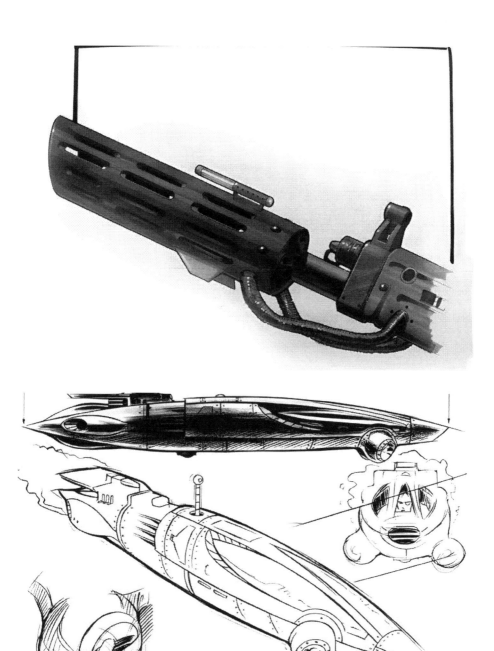

Top: Concept Art [Coreburner]
Bottom: Concept Art [Submarine]
(Art Courtesy Fireball Tim / *FireballTim.com*)

Top: Concept Art [Denizen]
Bottom: Concept Art [Denizen]
(Art Courtesy Fireball Tim / *FireballTim.com*)

Top and Bottom: Concept Art [Cadillac]
(Art Courtesy Fireball Tim / *FireballTim.com*)

Top: Concept Art [Cadillac]
Bottom: Concept Art [Helicopter]
(Art Courtesy Fireball Tim / *FireballTim.com*)

than saying, "Do this page." was "Nice job." I went on to *Plasticman* with Larry at Warner Brothers after that, so we did several projects together until he retired. Joe and I worked well together. We would sometimes work on a similar piece from a different angle or John wanted two interpretations of the same thing. Joe and I would crack each other up all day. He was [and is] a funny guy. Pretty sure he just did concept as I did both concept and boards. A great working relationship as he was the head of the union and also worked on one of my dad's TV shows *Jean LaFitte: Part 1-2* [*Swiss Family Robinson*] in the 70s. He's an old-timer!

Did you have any reference material when you drew the Los Angeles landmarks for instance and did John Carpenter, Lawrence G. Paull, and Bruce Crone have any favorite of your drawings?

We always had a lot of reference in designing landmarks, so we knew what we could destroy and what should stay. Larry's favorite piece was the one that was finished. Relief was in his eyes more than anything and we were all very proud when we saw it get shot.

What's your favorite illustration or illustrations for the movie and which were the most challenging and fun to work on?

I'm always most proud of the cars. I love vehicle design, although weapons and wild props are fun too. I did a bunch for *Mouse Hunt* as well. Larry Paull let me run with the cars and oversee the builds. Once I did that, I really didn't want to do much else and got known for that. I'm not a builder like my famous buddy George Barris, but I am the guy who sends him the sketches. I've done cars for about 400 films now and it never gets old plus I get to share them in books.

How come some of the designs were never used in the movie like Cuervo Jones' [George Corraface] monster truck Cadillac for instance? Was there something you were disappointed to see go?

Always, but movies come down to budget. We create at one hundred percent, but fifty percent gets used. Many times I've had designs turned down only to re-introduce them into another film.

What's your favorite memory or memories of working on the movie?

I worked at Paramount Studios and it's a really cool lot. They were shooting *Star Trek* there and I'd always see funky characters walking around. Along with Paramount being next to a really awesome pasta place, I think working with John and Kurt was the best thing. Kurt was very humble and easy to be around. On set at Universal Studios [Lot, Courthouse Square] [Happy Kingdom by the Sea], he suggested that one of the hotel facades be called the St. Lawrence because he appreciated the weapons I created for him and there were going to be a lot of holes rocketing through the hotel. Everyone on the shoot was kind and easy to work with. We had a great time and I was given a long leash to play. I am very grateful for the experience.

What do you think of the movie personally?

The movie is more of a comedic version of *Escape From New York*. Everyone knew that. John just really wanted to have fun with it and make it a bit of a mock to the first one. He knew it would not surpass it as *Escape From New York* was very strong. He wanted *Escape From L.A.* to be hip, fun, relaxed in tenor, and visually cool. I think he achieved that and Kurt had a good time too.

What are you currently doing and what do you enjoy doing in your spare time?

I really enjoy doing my talk show *5Minute Drive* and traveling for automotive events. I host the only Automotive Film Festival in Monterey for Pebble Beach and travel across the world to other car shows. When I'm home, I surf, do my books, and play with my pups and family. It's chill.

JOSEPH MUSSO
Illustrator

How did you end up being a production illustrator and storyboard artist?

When I was five years old in Vineland, NJ, I wanted to be a cartoonist for Walt Disney. After I saw *King Kong* when I was ten, I decided that someone had to design and lay out the compositions for its scenes, so I decided that I wanted to work on live-action films instead of cartoons. I then focused my life to that goal. I went to the Philadelphia Museum College of Art [now the Philadelphia College of Arts] and received a BA [Bachelor of Arts] in illustration. After finishing my military service, I eventually moved to Hollywood, CA and started phoning the heads of the art departments in the various studios. I finally got an interview with Lynn Sparhawk at 20th Century Fox, who was impressed with my portfolio to recommend me to the illustrators union IATSE [International Alliance of Theatrical Stage Employees], Local 790. They in turn sent me to work for Frank Sinatra's company, Artanis Prods. [Sinatra spelled backwards] with art director Leroy Deane at Warner Bros. While at Warner's, I then worked on *Brainstorm*, *A Big Hand for the Little Lady*, and *Who's Afraid of Virginia Woolf?* before going to Fox for *The Blue Max*. Eight months of working with Alfred Hitchcock at Universal was next on *Torn Curtain* and then came *Caprice*, *In the Heat of the Night*, *Uptight*, and *Tora! Tora! Tora!* before working on the effects sequences and matte paintings for *Flesh Gordon*. I then went to work for Irwin Allen in 1973 on *The Towering Inferno* and continued working with Irwin off and on for the next eighteen years until his death of a heart attack in 1990.

How did you get the job of illustrator on *Escape From L.A.*?

Larry Paull [Production Designer] contacted me to work on *Escape From L.A.* I'd worked for Larry in the past on *Naked Gun 33 1/3: The Final Insult* and he was well aware of my precise storyboards and concept illustrations that I did for Hitchcock, Irwin Allen, and others. When director John Carpenter said he wanted precise concepts for the various sequences, scenes, and matte paintings Larry said that the job was mine if I wanted it. I agreed and started immediately.

How did you, Tim Lawrence [Illustrator] as well as Lawrence G. Paull [Production Designer], Bruce Crone [Art Director], and John Carpenter prepare for this project and how did you collaborate?

Larry would usually let me know what John Carpenter was looking for. Although in some cases, John would let me know directly. Besides doing the detailed concept illustrations, Bruce Crone, on behalf of Larry and John, would occasionally have me back project some other concepts, photo montages, etcetera to give John the positions as to where to place the camera. Once John approved of my pencil concepts, it would take anywhere from a few hours to a day [or two days depending on the detail] to finish my color illustrations using felt tip pens and some acrylic paint. Fireball Tim had his own assignments separate from mine.

Did you have any reference material when you drew the Los Angeles landmarks and did John Carpenter, Lawrence G. Paull and Bruce Crone have any favorite of your drawings?

Larry told me on more than one occasion that his favorite was my illustration of "the car pile-up on the 405 Freeway [Santa Monica Freeway]." I don't remember John or Bruce ever singling out one in specific other than they really liked everything I did. However, in the beginning John was really concerned about getting the view down Hollywood Blvd. right as well as my concept of the Queen Mary Downtown.

What's your favorite illustration and which were the most challenging/fun to work on?

The scene where the Queen Mary is depicted amongst the ruins of downtown Los Angeles, the scene looking down Hollywood Blvd. in ruins, and the pile up on the 405 Freeway are my favorite illustrations because of their visual sense and the challenge it gave to do something visual and creative but at the same time very realistic. I enjoyed doing the woman on the girder. I think the "Queen Mary Downtown" and "Snake being escorted through the L.A. coliseum" took the longest as far as I can remember to execute.

What's your favorite memory or memories of working on the movie?

How nice everyone was on the film crew. Not only with Larry, Bruce, and Fireball Tim, but also with John, Kurt Russell and Cliff Robertson [President]. I was told that John personally asked for me when he was prepping for *Ghosts of Mars*.

What do you think of the movie personally?

Well, it is kind of bizarre and it's most enjoyable on that level. Of course, I'm proud of the fact that the visual conceptual scenes contribute to the fantasy drama elements for the basis that makes the film's plot work so well.

What are you currently doing and what do you enjoy doing in your spare time?

Researching history and collecting historic artifacts as well as painting detailed historic scenes from all periods. I'm especially interested in researching the historic James Bowie and the Texas Revolution.

This Page: Concept Art [Queen Mary]
Opposite Page: Concept Art [Hollywood Boulevard, Santa Monica Freeway,
Los Angeles Memorial Coliseum, Tops of Skyscrapers]
(Art Courtesy Joseph Musso)

GINA DEDOMENICO
Illustrator [Uncredited]

How did you end up being a costume illustrator?

When I graduated from Parsons, New York, I worked as an assistant designer for a sportswear company in downtown L.A. I realized quickly that I did not like the fashion industry, so I decided to break into designing for movies. I learned quickly that, to work on feature films, you must belong to one of the unions [there are many different ones depending on what you want to do], so I joined the CDG, the Costume Designer's Guild. The CDG consists of costume designers, design assistants, and costume concept artists. It's a bit tricky to get in and I realized that I was able to get in quickly as a concept artist. Once in and working, I was so happy as an illustrator that I never even considered another classification.

How did you get the job of illustrator on *Escape From L.A.*?

Once in the CDG, you become part of a network and we all hire from within. I met Robin [Michel Bush] [Costume Designer] and Bob Bush [Costume Supervisor] early in my career and we hit it off. She and her husband Bob were so fun and lovely to work with. Such good people! We worked on John Carpenter's *Vampires* and *Escape From L.A.*

How did you and Robin Michel Bush [Costume Designer] prepare for this project and how did you collaborate?

I start by reading the script and really getting a feeling for the characters. Robin provided me with all her ideas, her quick sketches, tear sheets, and head shots of the actors. She then went character by character and we discussed her vision for each. Probably took two days per sketch. It is my job to bring her vision to life on the page and to make it look so cool that the producer and director love it so that it can be cleared and go straight to the workroom to be made. If that happens, I have done my job.

Concept Art [Snake Plissken]
(Art Courtesy Gina DeDomenico)

What's your favorite illustration or illustrations for the movie and which were the most challenging and fun to work on?

The most challenging costumes to illustrate are the simple ones. The more complex, the more interesting the silhouette, the easier it is to create a striking illustration. I am proud of all the ones I sent you, but my favorite is Snake!

Were any ideas discarded?

All of Robin's ideas were used if I remember correctly. She's a brilliant designer!

What's your favorite memory or memories of working on the movie?

Laughing with Robin and pining for Kurt as I was illustrating him. I've been in love with him since seeing *The Computer Who Wore Tennis Shoes* when I was a little kid!!!

What do you think of the movie personally?

I liked the movie a lot. I love sci-fi movies. I was a HUGE comic book collector when I was younger. You know, I LOVED *Escape From New York*.

What costumes have you enjoyed the most illustrating in your career so far?

I think my favorite character that I got to illustrate [other than Snake] was Sarris from *Galaxy Quest*. The original illustration was very detailed and a blast to do and working with Albert Wolsky a dream.

What are you currently doing and what do you enjoy doing in your spare time?

I was trained at Parsons, New York to illustrate with gouache. I spent most of my career making designers very happy with the pencil and paint, but as of three years ago, the entire industry went digital. Paint is now a thing of the past. I had to go back to school. I spent an entire year crying. I was so frustrated and desperately fought the switch over, but now I am a digital illustrator and the thought of paint a distant memory! I am currently working on a film called *The Solutrean* designed by Sharen Davis. Albert Hughes will direct the survival tale set 20,000 years ago in the Ice Age. Such a blast to illustrate ice age costumes!

Last year I finished *The Magnificent Seven, Pitch Perfect 2, The Hateful Eight, The 5th Wave,* and *The Ridiculous 6.* All movies with numbers!

ROBERT ZULLO
Second Company Rigging Grip

How did you end up being a movie grip?

Well, basically, right place at the right time. You don't get in if you don't know somebody already there and then you don't keep your job if you don't work hard and learn fast.

How did you get the job of second company rigging grip on *Escape From L.A.*?

The key grip l worked with worked with Charles Saldana [Key Grip] for years and I was kind of his protégé, so he took me with him to do *Escape From L.A.* as his best boy, which is basically like the foreman or 2nd co. [company] rigging grip.

How did you, Bud Heller [First Company Rigging Grip] and Charles Saldana [Key Grip] prepare for this project and how did you collaborate?

Whenever we do a movie, we prep trucks, we read the script, go over a shot list, attend a couple pre-production meetings, plan out anything special, then we load our truck and get started rigging. Collaborations between director and key grip are usually done in a production meeting on the tailgate. But usually Charlie would communicate to Bud who would pass it on to me and l would run the crew.

What kind of challenges did this project provide and which scenes or locations were the most challenging, problematic, memorable, and fun to work on?

For the most part, this movie didn't have much complicated rigging. One thing we had to do was build a wall of black to block out the Don Kott Ford sign next to the 405 freeway as they kept it lit all night a 1/4 mile behind our exterior set. This wall was 40" high and 120" long constructed out of 24" box truss 21" lengths of 2" pipe seven camera towers [which is just scaffolding that stacks along with tons of concrete on the bases to anchor them down] along with three or four 40" shipping containers [to cable off too]. When all was said and done it was a pretty impressive rig. And as we came to work four days later at 5 AM in the dark l saw it. The Don Kott Ford sign!!! Bright as can be. Apparently, the wind came up early and blew my rig over backwards. Damaged every single piece in the rig. But, of course, the show went on.

How was your experience working with the cast and crew?

Cast and crew were fine as we usually end up being a small family by the time we wrap. We had done a lot of big shows by that time. *Hook, Death Becomes Her, Batman Forever, Titanic, Sphere, The Perfect Storm, Deep Blue Sea* to name a few, so each one has its own highlights.

What's your favorite memory or memories of working on the movie?

One of my favorite memories, however, is one morning l showed up early to the coliseum [Los Angeles Memorial Coliseum] and was alone. I was able to ride my bicycle from just under the iconic L.A. coliseum clock all the way down to the playing field by basically hopping my bicycle row after row after row till I hit grass. Then rode my bike all the way across the same field I used to watch the Los Angeles Rams play on when l was a kid going to games with my pop. It was quite surreal.

What do you think of the movie personally?

Personally, l enjoyed the movie. Thought it was pretty well done. Well, except for the surfing scene. I grew up on Venice Beach surfing and that just looked so fake to me. But, all in all, entertaining.

What are you currently doing and what do you enjoy doing in your spare time?

Today I'm retired but wish l was still working. I went on to key five features myself and after thirty years called it a wrap.

DONALD FLICK
Sound Effects Editor

How did you end up being a sound/effects editor?

I ended up being a sound editor because of family. My father was a teacher of radio and television and head of the department at San Jose State University, California. He created the radio station KSJS in 1963 and it is still on the air. My older brother Stephen was a sound editor out of USC film school and had started a business with two friends of his, Richard Anderson and Mark Mangini [Dialogue Editor: *Escape From New York*] with their assistant editor John Dunn [Supervising Sound Editor] just out of Paramount Studios editorial. It was called Thundertracks. They had met while working on *Star Trek: The Motion Picture*. I learned the basics of our business by working for lots of people doing different parts. I worked as a picture assistant learning to sync dailies and how to set up code books and how to set up the 35mm reprints for editorial use. I learned how to build units which are rolls of 35mm film used in mixing with sound effects or dialogue with fill leader in between recorded takes to maintain sync. I pounded the pavement telling bosses I'd work for them if they taught me something. One of those people was David Yewdall [Sound Editor: *Escape From New York*].

How did you get the job of sound effects editor on *Escape From L.A.*?

By the time *Escape From L.A.* had been made, I was working at Weddington Productions, which was Thundertracks under a new name and many years down the road. John Dunn had been supervising many projects for them and had gotten *Escape* with the help of the bosses. He had supervised *In the Mouth of Madness* and *Village of the Damned* for Carpenter earlier, which I had cut with him and Carpenter liked us. We also did *Vampires* and *Ghosts of Mars,* so being one of his team, that's how I got to work on *Escape*. I think I've worked on at least eight Carpenter shows. I was not a sound editor on *Escape From New York,* but an apprentice/assistant who built the units and carted them to a dub stage and rewrote cue sheets in legible script so the mixers could read what was going on. Though it's not on my resume, I started as an apprentice on *Raiders of the Lost*

Ark. Remember that credits were eighteen cents a foot on scroll, so not everyone who worked on shows got a credit. Only crew who worked from beginning to end received credit. Not like today where most credits can be adjusted quickly through computer upgrades. On *Escape From New York,* David's place was a large one room editing area with a back room for a transfer room where sound was moved from one format to another. Usually 1/4" tape or cassette to 35mm film for editing. As FX were transferred, I would "break down" the 1000' to smaller usable rolls and give them to the editors. While I was doing this task, David was also teaching me to become an effects editor on smaller projects he had running at the same time at his shop.

How did you, John Hulsman [Sound Effects Editor], David Whitaker [Sound Effects Editor] as well as John Dunn [Supervising Sound Editor] and John Pospisil [Sound Designer] prepare for this project and how did you collaborate? Any disagreements and such and did John Carpenter have any specific input? Here were some of the sounds assembled for the movie for instance?

John [Dunn] had meetings every week to discuss what he and Carpenter had talked about in his room. John Pospisil was also in the spotting and from his wondrous mind came all the effects on that show. He created the sub, the tracker, and the hang gliders by recording large blocks of cloth and canvas being shaken and the sub by using equipment hums. The earthquake material was all low-end generated with rocky avalanche material. We would drop boulders, record the impacts, slow them down and beef them up. Snake's gun was a combination of science fiction weapons and real handguns. It was said that John Pospisil had a magic toaster and everything just popped out of it ready to be used.

I was not privy to how things were done on *Escape From New York,* but I can say this. Every single effect that went into that movie WAS David Yewdall. David also cut *The Thing* for Carpenter. He was a master of sound. Not only what you hear but what you FEEL too. His use of low-end rumbles and airs created a feel for every movie he made. The alarms were his recordings. He would find devices that made odd noises. In the early days of sound, there were no libraries that could be used, so they went out and recorded everything everywhere. I myself had a Sony TC-D5 cassette recorder which ran at crystal sync and Sony microphones. We'd go out in the daytime and after midnight when things calmed down in the city. David liked rough sound and it gave his soundtracks a quality that even today is wondered at. And yes, John Carpenter came by to listen to stuff and he and David and Warren Hamilton [Sound Editor: *Escape From New York*] would discuss things. Almost every single director has spotting sessions [as they are called] with the sound crews. Warren Hamilton cut the bridge scene [69th Street Bridge]. Remember, we were on mag film, so it took nearly three times as long as it does today with computer. Each effect was cut individually. About a week or more to cut that sequence.

What kind of challenges did this project provide and which scenes or sequences were the most challenging, problematic, memorable, and fun to work on? Any technical issues and such?

Most of the problems in TV and features are results of opticals and visual effects being rearranged or even updated as the editing and mix continue. On *Escape From L.A.,* the visuals kept being updated with the effects in the wrong place. Along the waterway, the window kept exploding in different places than the day before. The sub had been done early, but now it scraped along the bottom and so a new effect had to be added. Many little things were showing up at the last minute out of previous sync because the optical house was folding. John Carpenter was not happy with these circumstances and sat in his chair on stage rather than walk around the dub stage when he was not nervous. We mixed over the July 4th holiday that year at Universal while, outside the stage, *Jurassic Park* was blaring the music for a ride that had not opened yet. I was there along with John Dunn and Mike Chock, a dialogue editor on the show [uncredited]. The mixers did their best asking for "sweeteners," a term meaning added sound to help the soundtrack.

What's your favorite memory or memories of working on the movie?

My favorite memories of both shows are working with the people. I loved working with these guys. They were the cream of the crop. They were my friends and family. The crew's worked days on end through the weekends and nights. David had a mattress under his editing bench and I would find him there many times when I would show up for work in the morning. He had been cutting all night. I worked for him for years. He was a great man with a big heart and a wonderful creative mind. Warren Hamilton was a mentor and a dear friend and I miss him terribly. John Dunn I've known for forty-three years and still keep in touch with him. We were like gypsies going from show to show and sometimes our paths would cross many times and sometimes few. I have lost contact with John Hulsman.

What do you think of the movie personally?

I love both movies and am proud to have worked on them. Kurt Russell IS SNAKE PLISSKEN!!! I love John Carpenter films. He has a vision that no one else has. His shows require a sound that is unique to each movie.

What are you currently doing and what do you enjoy doing in your spare time?

I have just finished *Extraction 2, Citadel, A Friend of the Family, Super Giant Robot Brothers* [animated series with Kaiju monsters], *The Gray Man* and a variety of commercials for car companies, all done at IMN Creative in Glendale, California run by Mark Binder. An old friend also. It's a small business, but they do Atmos films and other things. All fun and games and several projects for the Holocaust Museum L.A.'s virtual shows. When I'm not working, I sleep or go to Grateful Dead shows. Since the WGA and SAG/AFTRA strike is ongoing now in its third month, I am not working. Collateral damage. Nothing to work on means no income.

RON BARTLETT
Re-Recording Mixer

How did you end up being a sound/foley editor and re-recording mixer?

I moved to L.A. in 1983 to be a rock drummer. As I was playing gigs all over town, my brother mentioned I could cut sound effects as a day job and keep playing drums the whole time. I started cutting sound at Canon Films and then got into the union. Weddington was my next stop as a sound editor and it was there that I started mixing. It was the next step for me creatively. I really loved putting together a track. I was able to use my music background as well. During this time, I mixed a small independent film called *Reservoir Dogs* for Quentin Tarantino. That put me on the map. I moved to Todd-AO and continued my career as a re-recording mixer.

How did you get the job of re-recording mixer on *Escape From L.A.*?

I was working at Weddington cutting and mixing sound and *Escape From L.A.* was one of the films they were working on at the time. One of the mixers was going on vacation, so I filled in for him and mixed the sound effects over at Universal.

How did you, Michael C. Casper [Re-Recording Mixer] and Steve Maslow [Re-Recording Mixer] prepare for this project and how did you collaborate with the music department? Any disagreements and such and did John Dunn [Supervising Sound Editor] and John Carpenter have any specific input?

I had only worked with Mike and Steve as an editor, so this was the first time I got to mix with them. I did most of the premixing at Weddington and then went to Universal for the final mix. John Dunn and I had worked on many projects together and had a great rapport. Of course, John Carpenter, the director had a lot of input and was the composer as well! He was a very nice man and we had a lot of fun mixing. It's always tough with sound effects and music because they need to give and take depending on the scene. Mike and I worked hard to get a good balance. Steve was very fun to work with and always making me laugh.

What kind of challenges did this project provide and which scenes or sequences were the most challenging, problematic, memorable, and fun to work on? Any technical issues and such and how long did it take to mix the final soundtrack for the movie?

The big action scenes were always tough trying to balance a dense track of big sound effects with the score, especially when the director is the composer! I remember trying to fit his big Harley motorcycle sound with the score was very difficult at times. Surfing the L.A. river [Wilshire Canyon] was a unique one too. Not every day you get to try that one. Water and surf is a very "white noise" type of sound that eats up everything. It's a challenge to get the movement of the water and dynamics in the scene without covering up all the other departments.

What's your favorite memory or memories of working on the movie?

Laughing with Steve and getting to work with an iconic director. I loved *Escape From New York*! Mixing with John Dunn was always a lot of fun and very creative.

What do you think of the movie personally?

It's a lot of fun and a bit silly of course. The character of Snake Plissken is so good. Kurt Russell is bigger than life. Just gotta go with it and have fun.

What are you currently doing and what do you enjoy doing in your spare time?

I just finished *Transformers Rise of the Beasts* and I will start *Dune: Part 2* in about a month. After that is a really nice biopic of Bob Marley called *Bob Marley: One Love*.

KARIN COSTA
Assistant to Director

How did you end up being assistant to John Carpenter?

His wife was my best friend growing up, so I got the job from Sandy [King]. I worked for John from 1987-2000.

How did you and John Carpenter prepare/collaborate for this project?

I can't say I prepared too much other than production meetings. I did all the expected duties, kept his calendar, accompanied him on all appointments, etcetera. John is a phenomenal person, so he was great to work for.

What kind of challenges did this project provide and which scenes or locations were the most challenging, problematic, memorable, and fun to work on?

The biggest challenge was working seventy days of all night shooting. Going to work when people were coming home and trying to get home before the sun was fully up. John never has problems on his sets. As they say, it goes from the top down and every single person respected John and his talent for directing.

How was your experience working with the cast and crew?

I spent time with everyone on the set. It was my goal to know every single crewmember's name by the end of shooting and I did. I do not now, however.

Did John Carpenter have any specific requirements?

Coffee. Lots of coffee and breakfast for whatever time the meal was.

What's your favorite memory or memories of working on the movie?

The people. It was a great crew and cast. There is something very bonding while working nights. It's hard.

L-R/FG: Kurt Russell [Snake Plissken/Producer/Co-Writer],
Karin Costa [Assistant to Director]
(Photo Courtesy Karin Costa)

What do you think of the movie personally?

I think you are always proud of something you worked on.

What's your favorite memory or memories of working with John Carpenter?

I cannot pick one out. As I mentioned, John is a great guy and has an amazing sense of humor. I adore him.

What are you currently doing and what do you enjoy doing in your spare time?

I work for Marta F. Kauffman [Marta co-created *Friends*] as her personal assistant and we are currently just back in the writer's room for season 4 of *Grace and Frankie* for Netflix. In my spare time, I have Darrell Pritchett, my boyfriend who is a special effects coordinator on *The Walking Dead* and my German shepherd dog, Gian Carlo. I play tennis and I have ridden horses all my life.

MAURITZ PAVONI
Production Assistant

How did you end up being a production assistant?

My father married a Swedish-American woman, so he and my brother moved there. Then I got a green card because I was under eighteen. Then I met a girl who had lived in Miami, so we moved to Miami together. Her friends there worked in the film industry, so I started giving out sodas. You know, craft service. Then it was production assistant and then I worked on props. I also worked on lighting and most stuff behind the camera for commercials, music videos, and movies. I moved to Miami in '92 and started almost immediately and got some work. I got work on a movie and one thing led to another. I became a production assistant for a good while. It was a good job. Well, it was funny having been a painter in Gothenburg [Sweden] you know. All of a sudden, I got to work with girls and celebrities. You worked all the time, but it was ok. The first movie was *La Florida*, a French-Canadian film. Then I worked on *Wrestling Ernest Hemingway*. Then I worked on, Oh my God, I can't remember all the movies. It's around a dozen movies. Then came Marty [Jedlicka] [Second Assistant Director] with *True Lies*, the Florida part.

How did you get the job of production assistant on *Escape From L.A.*?

I came in good contact with Marty and another guy in L.A., so I moved there. Then Marty fixed a job for me on *Escape From L.A.* I came to L.A. on Friday and we partied on the weekend and on Monday I stepped into Paramount Pictures and said, "I'm like gonna see Martin." Then I sat and talked to him and got the script and call sheets and stuff like that. It was pretty cool actually. Marty treated us with wine from [Francis Ford] Coppola's courtyard. He had worked on *Dracula*. It was an experience.

How did you and production assistants Danny R. Carter, Christian Clarke, Cecily Gambrell, Paul Hackner, Jeffrey M. Howard, Erica Pearce, Angelica Sini, Marcus Taplin and Benjamin Zura prepare for this project and how did you collaborate?

L-R: Mauritz Pavoni [Production Assistant], Andreas Johansson [Me]
(Photo Courtesy Daniel Johansson)
(Author's Note: Believe it or not, Mauritz is a customer in my workplace in Sweden! What are the odds? Small world, huh? He has lived an interesting life, indeed!)

Before filming starts, every extra is going through hair and makeup, you know. Our task is to get them where they are supposed to be, the set. It's a lot of people wrangling and blocking during filming, so people can't get in. The call sheet should be done every day. You're a delivery boy, more or less, so to speak. We split up the duties. I was responsible for the walkie-talkies and extras. Some took care of Kurt Russell and the main actors. It's the assistant director's job and their assistants are we.

All the production assistants were very ambitious. They had done this in many movies, so I had to step back and do these other jobs that no other wanted to do. We and the assistant directors worked longer hours than everybody. It was sixteen to eighteen hours every day. The location managers worked longer, but they aren't on set as much.

What kind of challenges did this project provide and which scenes or locations were the most challenging, problematic, memorable, and fun to work on?

When we worked on the day with the motorcycle skidding in front of the hotel there [The Westin Bonaventure Hotel & Suites]. That was an incredible experience, having worked so many nights. One scene was funny: There was one guy who was gonna be shot and fly backwards [Robert Carradine] [Skinhead]. There was a lot of talk about it before, but they couldn't figure it out. The machine didn't work properly. That wasn't in. They couldn't do it. Driving to Carson City [Former Cal Compact Landfill] [Sunset Boulevard/Beverly Hills Hotel Exterior/ Santa Monica Freeway] was just bothersome. The [Universal Studios] backlot [Courthouse Square] with the helicopter was easier to work at.

[Note: While watching the movie with Mauritz the following information was also revealed: He met and dated a Swedish girl who was an extra at the Donald C. Tillman's Reclamation Plant [Firebase 7 Exterior/Access Tunnel] set, Kurt Russell's assault rifle [Coreburner] kept malfunctioning in the reclamation plant while filming the scene with Plissken firing blanks at Malloy [Stacy Keach] and Brazen [Michelle Forbes], the doll heads on Cuervo Jones' [George Corraface] Cadillac were John Carpenter's idea, Kurt Russell made the full-court basketball shot earlier than expected, which surprised the crew, real shootings delayed the filming in Long Beach [Street Under Santa Monica Freeway Overpass/Santa Monica Freeway Parallel Street/Queen Mary Exterior] and police cars showed up, and Pam Grier's [Hershe] dress was bothersome.]

Was there any drama or tension on the set?

Not particular. Not in that way. It was night work and everyone was just concentrating on their jobs.

How was your experience working with the cast and crew?

We worked nights. I think we worked four hours total in daytime. It wasn't that nice, actually. Everyone was mostly cranky. You didn't get to see the best side of anyone. It wore everyone out. I didn't manage to sleep properly during the days in Los Angeles. It was helicopters, police cars. You drove home every morning in shining daylight to get to bed so that you had strength to work in the afternoon and drive through rush hour traffic when everyone was on their way home stressed. You stand in traffic jams all day in L.A. Everybody just did their job. It was one of the absolute most boring movies I've worked on in that way. Having worked in Florida, it became more of a fabric. It was simply turn up for the job in time and deliver. A couple of the Mescalitos breathed while playing dead under the helicopter, you know, and got scolded. It was Marty who had to do it. They weren't happy about it. There's high demands, but they get well paid in Hollywood.

There was always things to do. The boring thing, when you had set up for filming the production assistant's job was to stand away and keep people silent and from not walking into the set. Sometimes you could stand far away and it's not that much you can do. We had no cell phones back then. We had beepers and walkie-talkies. They were nice to us production assistants in that regard that one time we got to sit with John Carpenter and watch the dailies. They were good in that way. They wanted to develop people. They took care of us production assistants. It's a shit job, you know. I didn't get particularly close with anyone. It was just a lot of hard work. I didn't work on the whole movie. Marty's other assistant was on a movie in Chicago. We were in downtown somewhere and that was my last day. The next day, I flew to Chicago and started working on *Chain Reaction* with Keanu Reeves, then we continued with *Speed 2: Cruise Control* after that.

Valeria Golino [Taslima] was nice to work with and professional. Steve Buscemi [Map to the Stars Eddie] was fantastic. He nailed his lines in the first repetition. He wasn't really famous then, but it was no surprise. He's a really good actor.

What's your favorite memory or memories of working on the movie?

One positive thing was the Mescalitos. They were real gang members that we had for extras. We became pretty close. I got to take care of them and they were pretty funny. I had some fun with them. They were nice guys. They were just ordinary people you know. I thought it was cool of Kurt Russell in the opening scenes where he comes with that jacket, the original jacket from *Escape From New York*. It was funny when one of the production assistants was told that it wasn't ok just to say Snake when he walked in and that it should be the whole name. She said she was sorry for that. That's a situation I remember.

I was there [Hollywood] almost six, seven years and it feels like one year. I can't remember all the movies. They blend together. I remember some from *Escape From L.A.* because it was the first movie I worked on after my move from Florida. It was a boring job, actually, to shoot movies. There was so much wait. Sometimes it was exciting with explosions, but that got pretty regular. I didn't know many of the actors I worked with. I had no knowledge of movies that way. Of course, I've seen movies but I'm not one of those guys that memorizes lines or names and such. I'm not a film fanatic. It was just a lot of work and you were only as good as your previous job. I had no life. I went home to sleep and then drove to work again. Sometimes we went down on the weekends. Back then, I was young. Then all of a sudden you were out of a job, so you had to look for jobs. There was very little time to enjoy my stay there. Even during the nicer jobs in the Bahamas and around Caribbean. Not much time to enjoy yourself.

I actually had a breakdown and got bipolar disorder. I've had it since 1999. That killed my career. I just couldn't do it anymore. I worked too much. That's why a lot of the things I've told you aren't that positive. My life has been awesome, regardless. It was exactly what I wanted. I went for a career and just kept going. I've been asked about these jobs during the years and people have always thought that it was a very glamorous job. It's not. Not even the actors have it that glamorous. Everyone just works hard. Sure, some diva behaviors were there but that wasn't the main thing. I never liked Los Angeles. I moved there because of my career. Then I met a couple of Swedes in Los Angeles and decided to move to Stockholm. My escape to L.A. made me come closer to Sweden, simply put. There I started working for advertising agencies.

What do you think of the movie personally?

I think it's boring. I think most movies are boring. Everything is fake. It's nothing against that movie. *Escape From L.A.* isn't a bad movie, but it isn't an Oscar winner. I just think it's boring to watch movies and TV. I watch sports during EM [Europamästerskapet i fotboll] [UEFA European Football Championship] and OS [Olympiska spelen] [Olympic Games].

What are you currently doing and what do you enjoy doing in your spare time?

I'm a painter. I fish. I pick mushrooms. I enjoy being outdoors. Those are my interests.

What went through your head when I found out that you were a production assistant on *Escape From L.A.* in the store where I work where we have met many, many times before?

If I could write down the things that's going on in my head, I wouldn't have to work as a painter.

KEN LAVET
Location Manager

How did you end up being a location manager?

I was recommended by a producer friend and started on *Hill Street Blues* in 1983.

How did you get the job of location manager on *Escape From L.A.*?

I knew the producers and they brought me on.

How did you and location managers Gregory Alpert, Don Garrison, James McCabe and David Thornsberry prepare for this project and how did you collaborate? How extensive was the location scout and how were the locations chosen?

As I remember, I was the location manager and the other people listed above were assistant location managers. It's not really a big deal, but I believe that was the accurate lineup. I did most of the scouting and had those guys prep it, which included reaching out to property owners, municipalities, street works, talking to affected property and business owners, etcetera. Los Angeles offers the most diverse and varied locations of any city I've ever worked in, so finding locations that would match the requirements of the script was fairly easy. John [Carpenter] chose all of the locations after looking at two or three choices for each. He was a confident and decisive director, so there wasn't a lot of time wasted with drama.

What kind of challenges did this project provide and which locations and tasks were the most challenging, problematic, memorable, and fun to work on? Which locations were the hardest to get permission to film at and were there any places you wanted to film but weren't allowed to? You originally planned to film at El Camino College instead of Los Angeles Memorial Coliseum for instance.

It's been a long time and I don't remember any major issues. Back then, the process was simpler with less legal issues, environmental requirements, mean personalities, etcetera.

How was your experience working with the cast and crew?

It was a great experience working with everyone on the show. John Carpenter is a gentleman. Debra Hill [Producer/Co-Writer] was a smart experienced producer who knew how to make a movie.

What's your favorite memory or memories of working on the movie?

My favorite memory was when I was driving away from a street location we were using. I looked across the street and saw John setting up a shot. He looked up and our eyes locked and I gave him the finger. He cracked up laughing. That's his sense of humor.

What do you think of the movie personally?

It was a good innovative film shot before anyone had access to visual effects.

What are you currently doing and what do you enjoy doing in your spare time?

I'm trying to retire. In my spare time, I work on my art.

DAVID THORNSBERRY
Location Manager

How did you end up being a location manager?

My father and grandfather were both in the entertainment industry as big-time transportation coordinators. They had some of the first honeywagons in the business. I went to college and received a degree in economics, but would work as a driver for my father during summer and winter breaks to make money for college. When I graduated, I floated around and wanted to get into the business. My father helped me get on *Indecent Proposal* as an assistant location manager because he thought being in locations would drive me crazy and wanted me to get a "real job." To his dismay, I took to it like a fish to water and worked nonstop.

How did you get the job of location manager on *Escape From L.A.*?

I had been an assistant for about two and a half years and a colleague and friend of mine that I worked as an assistant for, Murray Miller, was the original location manager on the film. He called me up and said it was time for me to move up and co-manage with him on the movie. I readily accepted and, to my shock and horror, he was let go two weeks later. They brought in Ken Lavet who, at the time, I did not know. I met with him and he wanted to bring in his own team. When you move from assistant to location manager in the Los Angeles teamster union, you cannot move back down for one year. I was stuck as a new manager without any managing experience, so I felt if I lost this opportunity, I would be unemployed for a while. I knew that the whole movie was going to be shot at night and there were going to be about seventy-five of those. I met with Ken and the first thing out of my mouth was, "I will work the night shift but please keep me here." It worked and I worked every night on that show.

How did you and location managers Gregory Alpert, Don Garrison, Kenneth D. Lavet and James McCabe prepare for this project and how did you collaborate? How extensive was the location scout and how were the locations chosen?

Murray, Jim, and I did most of the early scouting and had most of the locations chosen prior to Ken and Greg joining the show. John Carpenter had everything visualized in his mind and we tried to turn his vision into a reality as much as possible. He was a mad genius and very difficult at times, but it was the process back then. We had to bring locations that could fit into a "wasteland" vision and, fortunately, there were some iconic places that fit that bill. The old Subway Terminal Building [Beverly Hills Hotel Sewer] was one of our best ones. Then there was the water treatment plant [Donald C. Tillman Water Reclamation Plant] [Firebase 7 Exterior/Access Tunnel], which is ultramodern and worked well for the futuristic police state vision. We spent tons of money to control the L.A. [Memorial] Coliseum and literally trash it for the "games" sequences. There was this old waste area in the south bay that had a road running through it but was otherwise desolate, which created the perfect scenario for the freeway [Former Cal Compact Landfill] [Sunset Boulevard/Beverly Hills Hotel Exterior/Santa Monica Freeway]. Visual effects and the brilliant Lawrence Paull [Production Designer] really helped craft everything together.

What kind of challenges did this project provide and which locations were the most challenging, problematic, memorable, and fun to work on? Which locations were the hardest to get permission to film at and were there any places you wanted to film but weren't allowed to? You originally planned to film at El Camino College instead of Los Angeles Memorial Coliseum for instance.

When we filmed at the coliseum, I showed up one night and it happened to have rained really hard during the day. The entire field of the coliseum, where our set was, was underwater and so much so that you could have jet skied on it. The assistant directors were freaking out on me to "fix the situation." My first response when I arrived was to not laugh out loud. I had to work with special effects and some of my crew to clear the drains from our set decorating trash that had clogged them up. Special effects provided pumps to pump out the water. It was a process, but we were able to rectify the situation and still film that evening. I don't remember what happened with El Camino. It was probably about scheduling. That is usually the issue if it wasn't money. It could have been both! I would say that, working all night long for seventy-five nights, not one location was "fun" for me. I can say that there were certain crew members using certain substances and certain attractive extras getting some extra attention on the show. The gossip is what kept me entertained.

How was your experience working with the cast and crew?

Kurt has always been great to work with. My father sort of had a relationship with him from prior projects and we all knew Goldie [Hawn] as well. John and Debra [Hill] [Producer/Co-Writer] were difficult and not too approachable unless there was a problem. You wanted to stay on their good sides. Overall, I just did my job and kept everything moving as smooth as I could so that they wouldn't know there was ever an issue. It was my first go as a manager so I didn't know how to do everything, but I faked the rest and it worked out okay.

What's your favorite memory or memories of working on the movie?

I would say the coliseum flood was my favorite.

What do you think of the movie personally?

I don't like it as much as *Escape From New York*. I love most things Carpenter did, but I felt this came out very short of what he usually produces. Not one of my favorites.

What are you currently doing and what do you enjoy doing in your spare time?

I was working on a new TV show for Peacock entitled *Hysteria* in Atlanta when we shut down for the strike. I am currently doing whatever I can to survive after over three months out of work due to the strike and hoping it ends soon. Once it does end, I will return to Atlanta to finish the series. I enjoy golfing, spending time with my wife, three daughters and two dogs. I also love to travel and drink really good wine. I am also a huge foodie and the go-to guy for restaurant recommendations. I have also started a TikTok offering advice to those who want to pursue location management.

GREGORY H. ALPERT
Location Manager

How did you end up being a location manager?

That's a good question. I only know one person who actively sought out to be a location manager. I "fell into it" like most location managers. Producers, directors, writers, actors, camera department, casting, special effects, etcetera. These are all well-known roles in the industry. Location management is not something known by many. Once you work on your first film or TV show, you get to see first-hand all the different positions there are in filmmaking that are not known by those outside the industry. How I wound up being an LM [Location Manager]? I was finishing up work on my first show in L.A. as a production assistant. Entitled *Never Forget,* it starred Leonard Nimoy and released on TNT in 1991.

The UPM [Unit Production Manager] on the show, Valley Via Reseigne, was about to start working on her next show and asked me if I wanted to join her. Of course, I did! She told me that I was too valuable to her to simply work again as a PA [Production Assistant], so she asked me what I wanted to do. I did not know what I wanted to do, but I knew that I wanted to stay with her and work on her next show. She thought about it for a moment and then stated that the position of assistant location manager was available and asked if I wanted to do that. I responded by saying "Sure," but I didn't know how to do that job. She said that I was smart and that I would figure it out along the way and that the location manager Ken Lavet [Location Manager] was a very strong location manager and I would learn from him. I did just that. I learned a tremendous amount about the job on this show and from one of the top LM's out there. I stayed with Ken for the next six years as his assistant. That was thirty-four years ago. I will always be in debt to both Valley and Ken for literally changing my life.

How did you get the job of location manager on *Escape From L.A.*?

Long story short, early in prep, Jim McCabe was the principal LM. He was a big-time LM back then, having just done *Speed*. Don [Garrison] [Location Manager] worked with him and there were a TON of assistants on. Producer Debra Hill wanted to streamline the location department, so she called Ken Lavet to come in and take over. I'm sure there is more to this story, but I don't know beyond that. Ken had a previous working relationship with Debra and John. Ken came in and then brought me on as the #2 location manager. This was my first gig as a full-fledged location manager. Crazy right? I worked my ass off. Ken and I made a great team!

How did you and location managers Don Garrison, Kenneth D. Lavet, James McCabe and David Thornsberry prepare for this project and how did you collaborate? How extensive was the location scout and how were the locations chosen?

When Ken and I came on, Jim and Don decided to leave the show. Ken and I spent a few days surveying the state the show was in. We let go all of the assistants and brought in one assistant [Valerie Jo Burnley] [Assistant Location Manager] to work in the office. Ken and I finished scouting and prepped the show. When we got closer to shooting, another LM [David] was lined up to come on the show. He would be the on-set guy since we shot for sixty-nine nights and one day. Crazy to think that two of us ran the show. One ran the set and one handled the office. Ken and I would meet for breakfast on set with David [approximately 6 PM] and hand over all our notes, keys to properties, and the like, and talk through the night's work. Then David would be the LM for the night. As we got deeper into the shoot, I would split my days between day and night set work. At the end, I worked the nights as well and Ken stayed on days.

The producers wanted to give screen credit to Jim and Don as they found a number of the big hero locations for the show and rightly so. They should be credited for their work, even though they were not there for the shoot. Jim had also taken numerous meetings with various city agencies and paved the way for getting permissions for some of the big set locations where we did huge builds and big stunts.

Is it true that it was hard to find filming locations that suited the movie's post-earthquake environment due to L.A. being too beautiful?

Actually, NO. It was just the opposite. We were able to incorporate some of the [Northridge] earthquake damage into the film. In many ways, we were able to take a devastating situation and turn it into a positive. I know it sounds odd to say, but we got very lucky because of the earthquake. We shot in Northridge, California. The big quake in L.A. on January 17, 1994 was centered in Northridge. We found a long block of houses in Reseda that had their backsides completely sliced away. It took a lot of convincing for the company, studio, and insurance company to sign off before we shot there because we placed people inside of the unstable houses for picture. If I remember correctly, they needed to be stuntmen and stuntwomen for safety reasons. We shot in both directions so that when we looked towards Snake Plissken from the drivers side or at Map to the Stars Eddie [Steve Buscemi] from the passenger side it would look like there were dilapidated buildings on both sides. It looked really good! The shot where they are standing on the deck of the ship [Queen Mary] before they fly off. This was a huge set piece set in a parking lot in downtown L.A. in front of an old government building [The Hall of Justice]. The building was red tagged because of the earthquake.

What kind of challenges did this project provide and which locations were the most challenging, problematic, memorable, and fun to work on? Which locations were the hardest to get permission to film at and were there any places you wanted to film but weren't allowed to? You originally planned to film at El Camino College instead of Los Angeles Memorial Coliseum for instance.

That's a big multi-question to answer. Here's what readily comes to mind. First off, CGI was still in its infancy and, although there was a lot of it in the film [and personally I think some of it hurts the film], we still filmed many practical elements. For instance, I'm told that *Escape From New York* was primarily filmed in St. Louis in a bombed out abandoned section of town where they could "hit a switch" and turn off blocks of a grid at a time.

The same night we shot the L.A. Theatre scene, we shot a big scene on 7th Street in downtown L.A. [Hollywood Boulevard/Alley]. It is a scene with all the shanty town huts in the middle of the street, not the chase scene with shanty town huts. In the film, there is a high overhead establishing shot of the place. We had a hard closure on 7th Street between Hill Street and Broadway. A hard closure means that we "own" the road for our shoot. I always like to say that we are "leasing" the road, not owning it. Sometimes when crews hear we "own" something they don't always treat it with respect hence why I like to say, lease. Our permit required that we reopen the street at 6 AM. Buses start at 6 AM and the public needs to have access. Typically, if you have a hard closure and a ton of equipment and dressing on the street, you stop shooting about an hour before so that you have an hour to clean everything off the street. 5 AM hit and we still had a lot to shoot left. These are the kind of moments that put a location manager in a sticky situation. Meaning, we work for the company and are tasked with providing what the company needs. We are also tasked with getting all the necessary permits and keeping the company legal. In this situation, we needed to complete the work. There is no way we could come back another night to finish the work but we also have to make sure we open up the street when scheduled. If we go past 6 AM, there could be serious consequences to be had.

This night, I was the most concerned through the course of the entire shoot. My lead LAPD officer, Don Stanley, was with me this night. I remember asking Don what he thought. He said, "Let's give them another half hour or so." 5:30 AM came and still we had a lot of work to do. I went to the first AD [Assistant Director] and reminded him that we had to be off the street at 6 AM. Not stop shooting at 6 AM, but OFF THE STREET with everything. ALL the dressing had to be off the streets as well. A ton of set decorating crew was standing by for hours waiting till wrap in order to clear the street when we wrapped. Once we wrapped, in addition to clearing the street of the set pieces, we needed to clear the street of equipment as well. Don and I stood by the 1st AD. 5:40 AM came, 5:45 AM, 5:50 AM. STILL we were shooting. "DON" I said!!!! "We are never going to make it!!!" Don's reply to me, "We'll make it. Let's give them another minute or two."

5:55 AM, "THAT'S A WRAP" rang out over the radio. "LET'S GO!" Everyone jumped into action. Everyone moved items, even stuff that was not theirs. Equipment that does not belong to your department, one does not touch. It's an unwritten rule in production, but everyone was chipping in. Even Don himself was dragging full set pieces off the street. At 6 AM on the dot, we were off the street. Holy shit, was I relieved! Now the street was cleared, but stuff was scattered all over the sidewalk and in the alley. In reality we should have been off those areas as well, but technically we did open the street right at 6 AM. It was Don who I credit with getting stuff off the street and helping us to get the shot by waiting till 5:55 AM. A different police gaffer would have demanded that the filming company stop shooting no later than 5:30 AM to clear the street. Don was right. We did it! That morning was probably the most nervous I have ever been as a location manager. I don't get nervous, but I did that morning. Remember, it was my first gig as a LM and would have been my ass if we were late opening the street.

All the scenes we shot in Carson, [Sunset Boulevard/Beverly Hills Hotel Exterior/Santa Monica Freeway] Jim McCabe secured that location. It was shot on a landfill [Former Cal Compact Landfill], so there were VERY strict restrictions on where we could place dressing and where we could stage.

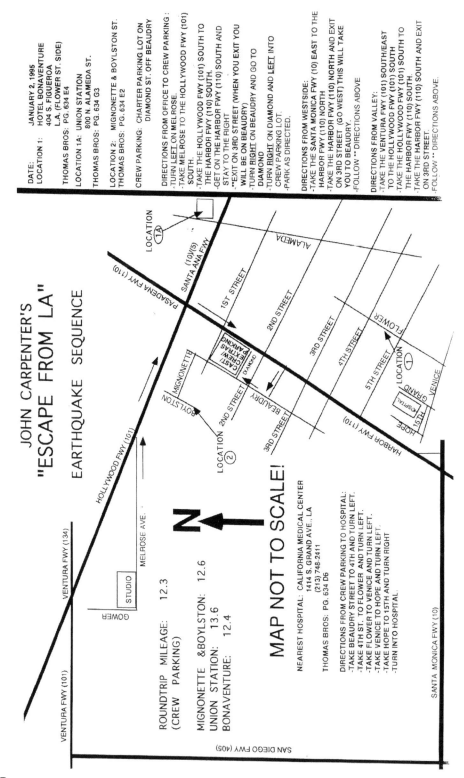

Location Map [Earthquake Sequence]
(Map Courtesy Gregory H. Alpert)

"The map is our standard crew map. Nowadays maps are digitally built but prior to the 2000's they were hand drawn and the directions handwritten. Ken Lavet was remarkable in the fact that he could take a straightedge [like a ruler] and with a PEN in 20 minutes draw out a map. One shot. He never had to ever redo it. Very early on when Ken and I started working together in 1991 we revolutionized crew maps. For the first time ever I would type the directions and then cut and paste them onto the map. I know it does not sound like anything special but trust me this was a HUGE thing and crews loved them. Remember, there was no GPS [Global Positioning System] or computer built maps. Crews depended on the maps provided by the location department to get to location/set. Being able to clearly read the directions was huge. It's not widely known but it was Ken and I who started this revolution in crew maps! It was a very big deal back in the day. We changed an industry." - Gregory H. Alpert

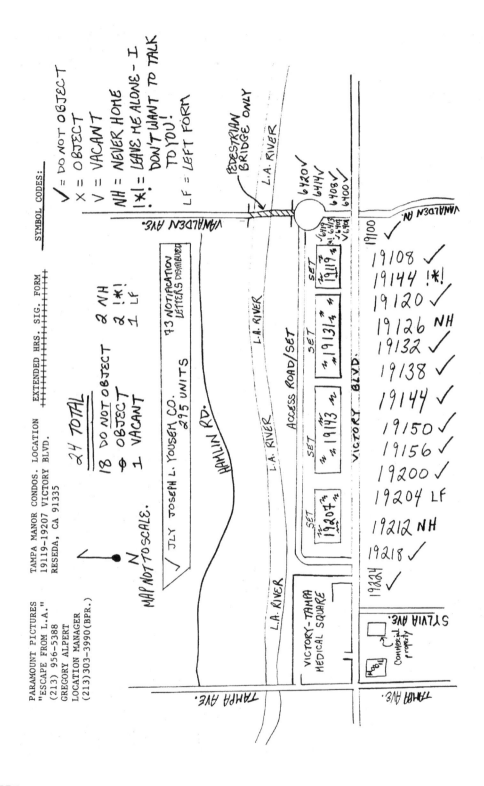

Signature Map [Devastated Streets]
(Map Courtesy Gregory H. Alpert)

"When acquiring a permit for filming in a residential neighborhood after hours [in this case all night], in addition to handing out a letter explaining what we as the company plan to do as well as "collecting" signature from those affected, once you compiled all that information you make a map of the location and add a key code to explain to the film office where you stand with approvals. Based on the number of approvals to the whole and # of dissenters that determines if the permit is issued or not." - Gregory H. Alpert

In some places, we were required to place something on the ground as a buffer prior to placing anything down. That buffer material would be disposed of afterwards. There were a number of off-limits sections. Those action scenes were very cool to watch while filming. The area was located across the 405 fwy [freeway] from roughly where the Goodyear blimp takes off from.

We shot at the Terminal Subway Building [Beverly Hills Sewer]. That was a VERY unique and interesting location and VERY difficult to work in. I believe no one shot it before or after us. I have never seen it depicted in any films or TV shows. I could be wrong but it takes a tremendous amount of work and commitment to make it functionable for a company to work that far underground. That fact alone takes it out of contention as a feasible location for most projects, but we were *Escape From L.A.* Hell yeah, we were going to shoot there! It was the ideal location for our show! We shot deep in the subterrain area of the building that used to house the old red line turn around. It was very difficult to access. Because there was no ventilation down there, it was quite the puzzle to figure out how to pump air down into the set. It was a very long way down that the air needed to travel so the AC company added air handlers every few hundred feet in order to push the air down. Also, there was no electricity down there, so each time we scouted it, it was by flashlights. Crazy, right?! The electric department had to rig lights just so the crew could work there long before the shoot and even before lighting the set. For the scene, we constructed a giant set piece in there. All our building materials and equipment for the prep and shoot needed to be hand carried down. In the end, I think it was absolutely worth it. If we were to explore that as an option to shoot nowadays, I guarantee you that no studio would ever allow it.

There was a scene in DTLA [downtown Los Angeles] we shot where we drove through several city blocks in a single shot. That meant that we had to work with several different city agencies to have traffic lights and streetlights turned off, then have major reroutes for traffic diversion. On some nights, we would have thirty plus LAPD officers working. We would also have thirty plus site reps in buildings with radios. If we saw a light on in an office, be it on the ground floor or twelve stories up, we would call the site rep on the phone and direct him where we see the light on. Then they would follow our directions and turn it off. Sometimes it was simply a light on a desk that had to be turned off.

Happy Kingdom [by the Sea] [Universal Studios Lot, Courthouse Square], that was a blast. LONG nights and painstaking setups but it was fun to shoot and I think looks really amazing in the film.

For the final scene of the movie where the helicopter crashes and blows up. We did not wind up shooting that scene until very late in the night/very early in the AM. The FX guys made sure that the whole crew was staged far away for safety reasons, but even at a safe distance when the helicopter blew up, we ALL felt the heat put off by the flames. It was a giant blast of hot air that hit us like a ton of bricks. It was a tad frightening that we were so far away and yet felt the impact of the explosion. Ever since that day, whenever I have been on set for a giant explosion, I always stage myself much further away than where the FX guys say it is safe to be. I trust them, but I believe in the old adage, better safe than sorry.

The hardest, by far, was filming at the L.A. [Memorial] Coliseum. They repeatedly said no to us. You are correct. We were going to shoot at El Camino College. All the credit goes to Ken Lavet for securing the Coliseum. Ken always stated that the Coliseum is city owned and that they should do whatever they could to accommodate us. Ken made it happen. Scheduling worked out great for us. Once we secured the venue then we had a big task ahead of us. The giant set of bleachers at the east end of the field had to be removed. That was an enormous undertaking. The area they were removed from is where the basketball court was laid down for picture. Two other thoughts come to mind about working at the coliseum.

We had five thousand extras per night working there. It was NUTS! Many were secured through the unemployment agency, in addition to going through background agencies, because the BG [Background] agencies simply could not fill our ask. A few times, knives were pulled out by some of the extras getting into fights with each other. Additionally, each day our count would go down as no one wanted to work all night sitting in the cold and not making much money. Sometimes people would leave in the middle of the night. To combat the loss, we started raffling off big ticket items like large screen TVs so that people would stay the entire night. They had to be present at wrap [like at 6 AM] to be considered eligible to win a prize.

Because there were unruly and potentially dangerous people bringing knives and guns to set, I started placing uniformed and plain clothes police officers up in the crowd for safety reasons. I really wanted my "top cop" aka lead officer Don Stanley with me on the nights we "shot" [pun intended] at the Coliseum. Don, along with his wife Dee, ran the company Walker Locations, who would arrange for officers to work sets for safety reasons, traffic reasons, or driving work. I remember clearly as a bell Don telling me that he would love to help out, but that the Lakers were in the playoffs and he just couldn't miss watching the games. He was sorry but he was a big Lakers fan and that had to come first. I came up with what I thought was a can't miss plan. "Don, what if I put the game up on the jumbotron for you to watch? As long as we weren't looking in that direction [meaning the camera], I'll have the game on and the sound on softly, but during takes I'd have to cut the audio off, obviously." He replied, "YOU can do that? Then sure. I'll be there tomorrow night."

I was VERY pleased with my quick thinking, but then again. Could I do this? Is this even possible or will it be allowed by the Coliseum and production? I knew one thing. I WAS going to make it happen no matter what and that's exactly what I did. I got permission from the Coliseum and John Carpenter signed off because Kurt is a HUGE sports fan, so he along with the whole crew could watch. The next night, I sat up in the control booth and I would ride the sound, turning it up between setups and off during takes. I'll never forget. We were about to roll. I heard the first AD state over the radio, "Pictures up," which was my cue to turn down the sound, but the trailer for the Jackie Chan picture *Rumble in the Bronx* rolled. It was an awesome trailer and I saw the entire cast and crew look toward the jumbotron, so I turned UP the volume and we ALL watched the trailer screaming and laughing throughout it. It was an awesome action filled commercial. The very moment it ended, I turned off the sound and heard over the radio, "And we're rolling." It was a very cool moment shared by all.

Any issues getting permission to film and working at the Los Angeles Union Station, Los Angeles Theatre and Queen Mary?

No. There were no issues working at all three of those locations mentioned above. Union Station was a relatively small unit/crew that shot that scene. Part of it was practical and part of it was a VFX unit. It was shot on our only one day of shooting. If you look at Union Station today, it looks different than what you see in the film as dozens of palm trees were added to the front of the building since we shot there.

You also filmed a scene inside the Donald C. Tillman Water Reclamation Plant [Firebase 7 Exterior/Access Tunnel] where Snake Plissken is being led to the submarine. Any issues filming there? Was it hard finding that specific spot and did anything had to be additionally built for the scene for instance?

No issues. We built/added the hatch that Snake enters into on his way to the submarine where he fires his weapon once he steps into it.

How was your experience working with the cast and crew?

John was great to work with, very approachable and open to input. He truly loved making films and enjoyed being on set. We all felt honored and blessed to be working alongside him. We all felt like he was the general we were following into battle.

Debra too was great. She was tough as nails, but very kind at the same time. She died young at the age of fifty-four due to cancer. A huge loss to our industry. She was instrumental in giving a lot of people their start in the movie industry. She was fiercely protective of John and the work they did together. I once saw her "go at it" with a backlot executive at Universal when we were shooting the Happy Kingdom scene. She was one hundred percent in the right and went toe to toe with this person in front of the entire cast and crew. She was very protective of her entire crew. You NEVER would want to get into a fight with her. You would absolutely positively lose! Then again, why would you ever get into a disagreement with her?

As for Kurt, I did not have a lot of interaction with Kurt other than I, along with transport, was in charge of toting around a portable basketball hoop to every location we went to. This was done so that Kurt could practice and work on his game in anticipation of shooting the basketball scene. He is a huge sports fan and, when not working on set, he would watch hockey in his trailer. He was great to everyone and he WAS Snake Plissken!

It was a good cast and crew. Being a fan of *Escape From New York,* coming to work everyday with Snake Plisken was a HUGE treat! We were the biggest show in town at the time and there was a mystique about shooting another *Escape* movie. *The Brady Bunch Movie* was also filming at the same time. Who wanted to do a movie about Greg and Marcia when you could be on a journey with Snake Plisken in L.A.? Every day and every location was new and exciting. How can you not root for Snake?

The cast and crew screening was held on the Paramount lot in the brand-new theatre currently named the Sherry Lansing Theatre but originally named the Paramount Theatre. I believe our screening might have been the first screening held in the theatre, but I do not know this for a fact.

What's your favorite memory or memories of working on the movie?

Simply coming to work each day working alongside Snake Plissken. It does not get much better than that! Kurt made all those basketball shots himself. It was impressive. The fact that the entire film was shot at night [save one day] over several months was very unique unto itself. From time to time when shooting outside on cold night shoots, I still wear my crew jacket. Everywhere we shot were BIG set pieces and BIG locations. Shooting in the under belly of the Queen Mary where no one is allowed to go.

Working with big time actors such as Pam Grier [Hershe], Steve Buscemi, Stacy Keach [Malloy], Cliff Robertson [President], and Peter Fonda [Pipeline]. Come on!!! Working TWICE with John Carpenter. I also did *Body Bags* with John and worked as an extra in the segment "Eye."

On one of the nights, our terrific Universal backlot rep [Terri Farley] informed me that *Seinfeld* was going to be shooting some insert shots for a scene at the upright underwater tank on the lot. It was a scene for Season seven, episode eighteen entitled "The Friar's Club," which originally aired on March 7, 1996 and was the 128th episode in the series out of 180. It is a scene where Kramer gets thrown into the Hudson River wrapped in a sack because his mob girlfriend thinks he has died, so she has her mob friends dispose of his body. I was a HUGE fan of *Seinfeld*. HUGE. So I thought I'd go over to watch, which I did. It was a quick shoot. Maybe an hour tops once they got going as it was only about three or four setups. Terri introduced me as the location manager on *Escape From L.A.* and that we were shooting a hundred yards away or so on Courthouse Square. Best known to many as Mockingbird Square or the town center of the fictional town, Hill Valley and the Hill Valley Courthouse as seen in the *Back to the Future* films. I met Michael Richards who played Kramer and Jerry Seinfeld, who stopped by to watch the scene with Michael being shot.

Both Jerry and Michael went nuts when they heard that we were filming with Snake Plissken right around the corner. They both asked me if they could see the set. They were extremely excited at the possibility of seeing Snake Plissken and maybe watching some filming but knew that it was a closed set. I said, "Sure" as they had allowed me to watch their filming so allow me to reciprocate. I told them that I would personally escort them around the set and introduce them to some of the cast and crew. They were so darn excited but then again, so was I. I was Jerry and Kramer's personal Universal Studios tour guide!

L-R: Michael Richards [Set Visitor], Gregory Alpert [Location Manager],
Jerry Seinfeld [Set Visitor]
(Photo Courtesy Gregory H. Alpert)

What do you think of the movie personally?

I absolutely like the film, but I like the original better. It's very hard to top *Escape From New York. Escape From L.A.* is more campy and kitch than the first one. I think some of the CGI work in L.A. works well, but I also think that some of it could have been better. I was/am very proud to have played a part in it. I think Ken and I absolutely were able to bring something to it and put our mark on it. When I watch it from time to time, I get a kick out of it because I worked as a featured extra in it. I am in almost every interior scene at Firebase 7. Exterior shots were done at the [Donald C.] Tillman Water Reclamation Plant, but interior scenes were shot in a warehouse [Pacific Tube Stage].

What are you currently doing and what do you enjoy doing in your spare time?

I am currently not working. It is VERY slow in L.A. because the studios/companies are waiting to see how the IATSE and Teamsters contracts go. Come August 1, we will know more. My IMDb page is pretty up to date so you can see I do and like to work all the time. When not working I like to travel and be outside.

JOSEPH YUSS SIMON
Special Makeup Effects [Uncredited]

How did you end up being a makeup effects/storyboard artist?

I was working in New York as a freelance illustrator for about ten years when I decided to follow up on my dream to work in the film industry in the realm of animation and special effects. In college, many of my classmates and I were blown away by the films created by [Steven] Spielberg and [George] Lucas and we all wanted to be a part of that world. I went out to California with my portfolio and received positive feedback about my work, but did not get a job at the animation studios. I did get a call back from someone I interviewed with in L.A. who had worked with Stan Winston on many feature films. He was heading up a TV series called *Ultraman: The Ultimate Hero* with many creatures and a hero suit for the lead character. He offered me a job. It was a great opportunity to learn everything about special effects. I packed up two bags, returned to L.A., and worked on that project for six months. I met some amazing talented individuals and learned many new skills regarding special effects.

One of those individuals I worked with on that project asked that I apply for a position at Rick Baker [Special Makeup Effects] where he was working at the time. In 1996, Rick Baker and Bill Sturgeon [Special Makeup Effects] [Uncredited], the overall supervisor of the effects shop were handling three feature film productions that had makeup effects. The most challenging and complex was *The Nutty Professor* in which Eddie Murphy played himself as a very overweight professor and also his entire family. Mother, father, brother, grandmother. That film alone was difficult to handle the amount of appliances for all the scenes and days of shooting. In the end, *The Nutty Professor* won Best Makeup Effects that year at the Oscars. Rick was very happy with this impressive achievement and acknowledged his crew for its collaboration in the acceptance of the award.

How did you get the job of special makeup effects maker on *Escape From L.A.*?

At some point, Rick Baker also took on *Escape From L.A.* and *The Frighteners*. It was very busy, but we did keep up with everything we needed to do.

How did you, Rick Baker [Special Makeup Effects] and Bill Sturgeon [Special Makeup Effects] [Uncredited] prepare for this project and how did you collaborate?

Most of the makeup was presented to us as essential parts of the scenes. We did not have access to much of the storyline. There was a basic understanding of the scene and the context of the story and that was it. Most of the crew that produced the prosthetic makeup were not given too much information about the R&D [Research and Development] or the development of project. Rick was very selective of how he would create the makeup. He had individuals that he trusted to develop the right concept and execution of the fabrication of the makeup. There was makeup testing all the time until it was to Rick's satisfaction.

How was the prosthetic makeup created, what kind of challenges did this project provide, how many people were involved, and how long did they take to make?

When creating complex makeup prosthetics, the actors needed to have a life cast. It's a process whereby alginate and plaster bandages are applied to the face or body of the actor and released to create a detailed mold of their true likeness. Plaster is poured into the mold and released to create a positive copy of the actor's likeness. From that point, special clay is applied to the life cast and sculpted to produce the desired look of the makeup. A mold is made from the final sculpting, sometimes in different parts depending on how complex the makeup effect is in order to give more movement or articulation. Especially for the face appliances. Next, foam latex is injected into the molds and baked in an oven and then released from the mold. It then can be painted and applied to the actor with adhesive by a makeup artist. This process requires many highly experienced and talented individuals with expertise in one or all areas described. For *Escape From L.A.*, there may have been over twenty or thirty individuals to create the makeup for the film.

How was your experience working with the cast and crew?

For the filming of *Escape From L.A.*, I was not present on the set, so I do not have any information of what it was like. I was in the shop fabricating the prosthetics.

What's your favorite memory or memories of working on the movie?

It was fun to help create make the makeup and see it come alive. It also is very satisfying to see it up on the big screen and know you were a part of that movie.

What do you think of the movie personally?

I like the film. It has a fun and dark view of the world. It makes you laugh because it touches on some truths about how this world might end up given the realities of this distorted world we all live in and the leaders that rule it.

What are you currently doing and what do you enjoy doing in your spare time?

Presently I primarily work as a storyboard artist for film and television. It is very creative and rewarding working with directors by helping tell stories and by realizing their vision. It has also brought me back full circle to illustrating, which I am still very passionate about. I am also pursuing personal works in drawing, painting and sculpting fine art. I also enjoy spending time with my family, my wife and two girls who love doing art projects and going to movies.

BRIAN KEENEY
Visual Effects Coordinator

How did you end up being a visual effects coordinator?

I attended USC film school, which is a prominent film school in California. Many famous directors, producers, and such went there and had a successful experience. USC is the University of Southern California. I was involved in student filmmaking and doing special effects. This was before computer graphics were more prominent. I did hands on special effects, models, makeups, and such with several of my fellow students. We had a little special effects company and, from that experience, we learned a lot of tricks and techniques, the language of visual effects. That experience brought me to Lightstorm Entertainment, which was James Cameron's production company doing model restoration and PA work. I did that off and on through college and after college. That got me an opportunity over at Disney and, through that, I got a position at Buena Vista Visual Effects, which was a small boutique, visual effects division at Disney. Being on the lot, I was then hired as a PA [Production Assistant] for *Mortal Kombat* and worked on that film for about ten months. From there, I worked on small films for about four or five months helping out around the office. As a coordinator, you're working with a producer helping with day to day managing for the show.

How did Buena Vista Visual Effects get the job to do the visual effects on *Escape From L.A.*?

If I remember, at the time they bid out to a few other mid-sized visual effects companies. John Carpenter is not inclined to work with large visual effects facilities like ILM [Industrial Light & Magic] or Boss or any of those kinds of companies. Mainly because they're much more expensive and John usually likes to keep his budgets down and somewhat in control so that he keeps control over the overall film. The bigger the budget, the more the studio gets involved in the actual production. Having an independent background, John is used to having full control and not getting meddling from the studio. It was bid out to other boutique places at the time whose names I can't remember. He just liked some of the ideas we presented and particularly the budget. We hit a budget number that fit within the dollars that they had, so we got the award.

How did you, Michael Lessa [Visual Effects Supervisor], Kimberly K. Nelson [Visual Effects Supervisor], Denise Davis [Visual Effects Producer] and Harrison Ellenshaw [BVVE Executive Producer] prepare for this project and how did you collaborate?

After nine months being with Buena Vista Visual Effects, we were awarded *Escape From L.A.* The company was small. It was only about forty or fifty people, so I worked out a network with Denise Davis. I was partnering up with her to pretty much help her get the show up and running and plan out the shots, plan the miniatures, and get everything lined up. You go into what we call pre-production mode and you start to breakdown the sequences. We're doing storyboards that were provided by the main production's art department. Some sequences need matte paintings. Some need pyrotechnics. Some need miniatures. After you do that process for several weeks, you start to get a picture of how many miniatures and matte paintings you'll need.

Visual effects supervisor Mike Lessa and myself were going out based on information we were getting from production, which was where the locations were to be. We would go there and take photos and just go, "Can some of these be used for matte paintings?" Back in the day, a lot of matte painters would take photos and just doctor or Photoshop them up as a quick way to get a simple matte painting. I was going out and taking reference photos of highways and downtown. Then I went out to Palm Springs for reference photos for the "destroyed town" look that we were going for. Out of those photos, we were able to decide what's gonna be a matte painting. In the midground, is it going to a miniature from that location's study? Then we started to contact vendors for what they can provide. I brought in a couple of matte painters. They were freelance and they were advising us based on what we were looking for in a shot and, "I can do the matte painting." We were also doing a lot of 3D projections where you built simple CG geometry like a square and then you can project photos of buildings on it. It's sort of what we call two-and-a-half D matte painting. It gives you a little bit of a feel of dimension to it compared to a more traditional matte painting where it's somewhat flat. When we started looking for vendors, we ran into John Stirber, our main special effects miniature supervisor. He was advising us for the collapse of the freeway [The Four-Level Interchange]. We went out to the freeway and specked as much as we could. We took photos and saw how the columns were stood up and worked with him to decide how the thing was gonna fall apart. Through that information, we went back and forth to John Carpenter to advise, "Here's how we think we can do this, what the scale would be," and he would give notes and comment on how it would be great to see a car fall that way or this and we would do our best to plan that.

The surf sequence was the most involved for us. We worked with a location scout on it. He was able to find a sort of open ravine area up north of L.A., I think just south of Simi Valley. It wasn't an old quarry, but it was an old area that had scrapped a lot of the land away, so on the right side of the frame was an actual rock cliff we could utilize. The left side was all open and went out into a field, so we were able to shoot at an angle. They shot all the principles there in the dirt and mud. On the right you see some rock and dirt. When you go to a wide shot, there would be a matte painting and other CG enhancements to make it look like this canyon coming down Wilshire Boulevard. We did night shoots up there for about three or four days and got the shots of Peter [Fonda] [Pipeline] and Kurt Russell. There's mostly dialogue back and forth, and they jump on the boards briefly and stuff like that. Then the whole thing shifts to the shoot that we did in Texas. That was my main focus for almost a month.

I had prepped the entire shoot out in New Braunsfels where they had the Schlitterbahn Waterpark [& Resort], which I had found by just searching around and talking to people. We were looking for a perpetual wave that we could somewhat control. We first looked up how we could actually shoot it out in the ocean and we canned that idea within a day. Then we came up with this by seeing something that was on a cruise ship [FlowRider] and we found out that they had one over at Texas. So we pretty much organized a crew to go out there to do a shoot and figure out how we could angle the shots and the scale. It wasn't exactly blended in perfectly, but at least it gave us a controlled environment with two professional surfers/skateboarders to get in there, so we organized hotels and cameras. We were there for about five, six days. I think it was like two days of prep and we shot for like two nights.

We were able to land great talent with Tony [Hawk] [Stunt Player] [Uncredited]. He was tall enough. We had to find people that were capable of doing the actual wave surfing but also have a certain height because Peter Fonda was a good size taller than Kurt Russell. Tony could usefully be Peter. Then we found a friend of Tony's [Chris Miller] [Stunt Player] [Uncredited] that could hopefully mimic the scale of Kurt Russell and then, yeah, we went out to Texas and shot that. It was a relatively easy shoot. It was at night and in the cold, so it wasn't the most pleasant experience, but we were able to get shots that worked and we shot a lot of extra footage. Then it really came up to Mike Lessa working with John Carpenter and just figuring out which shot and plate to use and how we could sort of bundle it. It was sort of like putting a puzzle together with all these water shots from the park. Then we were putting in matte paintings and they were cutting between Kurt and Peter against a green screen and we were spraying water around. It took a while for them to edit something together that at least sort of made sense. Yeah, it was one of the most involved shoots because we went out of L.A. and did a location shoot in a waterpark for that. It was a very good experience. The quality as it turned out wasn't necessarily the best, but it was a great experience.

Harrison Ellenshaw wasn't really involved that much. He was managing the company at the time, but he was definitely operating at the executive level. Kimberly Nelson was absolutely the effects producer on the production side. She was great. At that time, she had been working in the industry for many years. I think she trusted our approach to a lot of the shots and what we were planning. She also understood the perimeters that we were working with, the budget and the schedule and stuff like that. Yeah, she was great. She would come over occasionally to Buena Vista and look at stuff with Mike and then she was there when we were doing stuff with John. She was very supportive and collaborative in the whole process.

How did you get Tony Hawk [Stunt Player] [Uncredited] involved?

I wasn't that much involved in that, but I heard no rumblings. We just said, "Hey, is Tony up for doing this?" I'm not sure if he was a fan of the movie. One day they just told us, "Oh, great. We can work with that," and the thing is, we did this in '95. There weren't that many people that could actually do this. We didn't want just any surfer. These boards were not real surfboards. These were specially made boards to look like the prop boards that Kurt Russell and Peter Fonda were on. The key thing is, a lot of people that do this at the theme park or on a cruise ship, they literally fall off usually in two or three seconds. We needed someone to stay on this thing for fifteen, twenty seconds and there were very few people that could do that. So when we were able to get Tony, that was a huge win and he knew other people that were able do it. I heard no issues with getting the talents for which we were lucky for.

Top: L-R/BG: Chris Miller [Stunt Player], Tony Hawk [Stunt Player], Unknown / FG: Denise Davis [Visual Effects Producer], Michael Lessa [Visual Effects Supervisor], Unknown, Brian Keeney [Visual Effects Coordinator]
Bottom: Chris Miller [Stunt Player]
(Photos Courtesy Brad Mathis)

Tony Hawk [Stunt Player]
(Photo Courtesy Brad Mathis)

How did you get permission to use the Schlitterbahn Waterpark & Resort?

The park was closed at the time, so that was the key thing. This was Texas somewhere in the late fall or winter, which in Texas, it gets pretty cold. With the park closed, we just went to them and said, "Here's what we're proposing. We just want to utilize the ride for three or four days." We weren't building any set around it. We just put black behind it. I think we had some blue screen too. There was no set construction, nothing that would interfere with their park or the ride or anything like that so, yeah, they were very amenable. We just contacted them and talked and negotiated a price and worked out some contracts. They had some staff, of course, on set operating the ride for us and they did a great job.

What challenges did this project provide and which effects, scenes or locations were the most challenging, problematic, memorable, and fun to work on?

Probably the most difficult thing was the earthquake sequence. That was probably the biggest challenge. We decided to build a few large-scale freeway miniatures. That absorbed a lot of time and planning. Also, just figuring out how to shoot it properly and the scales for everything to work at. Working with John Stirber, we had to find a location to actually shoot this at because we couldn't shoot it at a parking lot. We wanted to have pretty much a clear sky around it at most of the angles, so we didn't necessarily have to add in additional work on it. We were able to locate one area in north L.A. It's called Acton, California, which has been used for movies in the past. There are several other movie ranches up there and with the research we were doing we said, "Hey, this could potentially work." so we did a scout up there, myself, John Stirber, and a bunch of other people. Mike, of course. And it's one of the few areas somewhat near L.A. where you can stand on top of this large sort of hill and almost do a 360 degree without getting any other mountain in the shot. We were almost getting a 360 degree view of the sky. With that, we said, "That'll be our main place." It was also just a large good plateau of dirt, so there were no issues that we had to work with utilities or plumbing or sewage or anything like that. John then went to work designing miniatures and figuring out the scale. That was a several months build up there every day just getting the miniatures all ready and then there were just the shoot days. I think getting that all prepped and shot was a challenge.

The other one probably would have been the destruction of the [Westin] Bonaventure [Hotel & Suites] because that was done in CG, which was just coming into play in the early 90s, especially for the mid-level companies. The large companies like ILM and such, they already had like six, seven years of experience with CG, but the smaller companies that don't have much cash flow were not getting into doing sophisticated simulations, which is what that was. They can do creatures, cars, and explosions, but doing effects simulation, that usually was the larger companies that had the capability of doing that well. So we had to do a lot of research and we worked with the software that we had, but planning that out and getting it to look somewhat ok was a big challenge. Other companies may have been able to do it differently or better, but for us at the time, having to do those kinds of shots was definitely one of our bigger challenges.

The hang glider one was relatively straight forward. That was a few matte paintings. We did miniature hang gliders with little puppets on them and it sort of worked. In the end, obviously the film's not known for its visual effects. Some things worked ok and other things just didn't.

Why were scenes such as an army of terrifying figures climbing atop a mountain of debris and raising their weapons into the night sky in the ruins of L.A., the sub passing by King Kong at Universal Studios, Plissken on horseback chasing Cuervo Jones at Sunset Boulevard, a group of vagrants clustering around the edge of the twin towers of Century City and a brush-fire sweeping through the hills, a bracero family having dinner in a skyscraper during the hang glider flight, and a beautiful woman dancing on a narrow girder during the glider flight omitted or cancelled?

A lot of that stuff was just in the early storyboards and, I guess, in earlier scripts. I didn't read all the scripts, but that's a normal flow of production. As they get the boards and see them, they are starting to see how some of the sequences, especially the action type sequences, are gonna flow. They start saying, "How many times can the sub pass some theme park ride or how many times can we do like the horse sequence?" and stuff like that. If it's expending the movie out too much or they've already had three action sequences and they're all somewhat similar, they often just go, "Alright, let's cut that one out or that one really doesn't help the story. It's purely just an action sequence." That's a normal process when you see ideas in storyboard form. They never make it to production. I definitely remember the King Kong storyboards. I remember the horse sequence was much more involved. It's just a normal process of winding down shots and production time to stay on the effects budget and also within the main shooting budget.

Some visual effects in the movie have been criticized for being a little subpar. Is there anything in retrospect you would like to have done differently and did the short post-production schedule affect the effects in any way?

I've heard that criticism and it's a totally fair criticism. There are shots in there that are subpar. Some of the reasons for that, as I previously mentioned, are definitely budget. This production and the studio were not interested in necessarily going over budget on visual effects or adding more money to it towards the end. When you have that budget limitation, unfortunately, choices have to be made on techniques. Also, choices have to be made on iterations, which is a thing a lot people necessarily don't know. A lot of visual effects, especially the higher end visual effects, are higher in budgets, meaning each shot gets multiple iterations to improve it. It gets reviewed by the director multiple times and by the visual effects supervisor multiple times. Each time, they provide notes on shots hopefully being improved and made more dynamic, more vivid, and more real. On other movies where the budget is tight similar to *Escape From L.A.,* the number of iterations the artists can do and supervisors can review is limited, so that's where some of the subpar work comes in. As for what sequences to do different? Based on the budget, I think we did pretty good. Some of the matte paintings, I think because matte paintings usually aren't that expensive of a task. I think we could do a little bit better there because we did so many of them, but the schedule definitely was tight near the end. We were on a release date that had to happen, so that definitely influenced us. We didn't have much time and then the budget was important to hit and we get a result of that on the screen.

How was your experience working with the cast and crew?

I didn't interact with them too much. I was at the night shoots here and there and, obviously, in some of the production meetings and stuff like that. To answer your question, my experience was great. I think John Carpenter is a very relaxed, laid-back guy. On set, he has a family crew he very often works with. He's very amiable to ideas. From my distant view, he worked very well with Mike Lessa and they were definitely very collaborative on the effects. During the course of the production, we had really no big issues or blowouts with John or the production. I would be there for the approval, so I would go over with Mike and we would sit with John and the editor. Some shots he would actually say, "Hey, that looks great. Let's go with it and move on to your next shot so that we can keep on going." And, in some shots, he let us know what didn't work and what we could do. He'd sit there and talk for a bit and exchange ideas and we would go back to the shop and start working on that and show it to John again two days later. So the process of working with him was relatively smooth.

What's your favorite memory or memories of working on the movie?

One of them is just overall working with the crew at Buena Vista Visual Effects. It was a small team compared to other projects. Some people were in their twenties, others in their thirties. It was a relatively young group of people and then some senior people. Yeah, we had a good time on it. We had a good crew that was very laid-back and very excited about working on a John Carpenter film and also a sequel to a cult favorite that we all grew up on. We had days of working with the crew in the shop doing dailies and staying up late there and bringing food because we had to hit a deadline the next day. Everyone had a really good demeanor and positive attitude and just wanted to have a fun time working on a movie.

That's the kind of thing I seek out and would recommend to other people. If you can get on a film, regardless of the budget and such, with a lot of great people and have a good time doing it, I find it to be the most valuable experience or memory. A lot of the work we do, sometimes it goes out to the world and it doesn't really get seen. Some movies go out there and just bomb and no one gets to see the last year and a half of your work. Then, if you had a whole bad experience doing it, it just leaves a really bad memory. So that's what I seek out. And probably some of the funnier times we had were shooting all the miniatures up in the mountains. The night shoots were grueling, but you're going up there and blowing stuff up. That's always fun and, again, we had a great crew up there too. Even though the nights were cold, everyone was excited. We were blowing these huge miniatures and getting some really cool shots, so that was fun to do. Those are two of my more memorable ones and I'm sure there are others.

What do you think of the movie personally?

If you're into John Carpenter or a major fan of *Escape From New York,* you can probably watch it and have a little bit of fun. Especially because it's Kurt Russell playing Snake Plissken. It definitely doesn't have the coolness of *Escape From New York.* It's missing something that movie had or at least it's missing a combination of things that *Escape From New York* had, which is kind of disappointing. I haven't seen it in years. There are certain sequences that I find fun to watch and there are other ones that are like, "Wow, that really doesn't work at all." But I'm not embarrassed I worked on the movie. I'm proud that I worked on it. We had a great time doing it and it's part of the legacy of *Escape From New York* for good or bad. If you go with the whole subplot of the U.S. pretty much claiming marshal law and taking everything over and the president being Cliff Robertson and his attitude, that was about twenty-five years ahead of its time.

What are you currently doing and what do you enjoy doing in your spare time?

Right now, I've been doing consulting work for companies over in Europe on post-production and such. I went back to Sony Imageworks and worked on *Spider-Man: Into the Spider-Verse* and a few other projects. I finished that up last year and have been doing consulting stuff. That has been my main focus. In my free time, I see a lot of film. I spend a lot of time with family and friends, of course. Other things are NFL football and sports and such. That's a big part of it. Also, I do go back and look at a lot of the older visual effects films to sort of see how they've been aging over the years.

The other thing is, I've been getting more into streaming TV. I've had Netflix for years, but getting more into the streaming shows and seeing the quality of the work coming out of the visual effects community for the streaming broadcasts and TV shows. Obviously, a lot of the streaming services are doing *Game of Thrones* kind of stuff like HBO. The quality work there is just astounding for what they're doing. I started watching *Stranger Things 3* a few days ago because we're under quarantine here. It's amazing. The quality of work being done on those lower budgets is quite impressive.

LES BERNSTIEN
Visual Effects Director of Photography

How did you end up being a visual effects director of photography and motion control operator/supervisor?

I started in New York as a cartoon animator, quickly training on camera and eventually moving to California. I continued to work in commercials and graphics, but started working in films and television as a designer and motion control operator, moving up through the ranks to DP [Director of Photography] for visual effects on films and television. Basically, I stumbled into it. I always wanted to be a cartoon animator like in the old Warner Bros. and Disney short films. If you ask me, I got out of it just in time. Cartoon animation now sucks.

How did you get the job of visual effects director of photography on *Escape From L.A.*?

I was working at Disney in the effects and matte camera department with Harrison Ellenshaw [BVVE Executive Producer], Peter Montgomery, Mike Lessa [Visual Effects Supervisor], etcetera. I had already supervised a few commercials and shot matte camera on films like *Honey I Blew Up the Kid*, *Dave*, and some others when Mike Lessa asked me to shoot effects on a Disney cartoon called *Trail Mix-Up*. We struck up a great working relationship and one of his next projects was supervising the effects on *Escape From L.A.* He asked if I wanted to shoot the effects. I said, "Sounds fun." The rest was history.

How did you and Gary B. Kibbe [Director of Photography] prepare for this project and how did you collaborate?

I, basically, was the FX director of photography on all the shots through Disney [Buena Vista Visual Effects]. I handled all the miniature photography like the collapsing freeway [The Four-Level Interchange] and exploding Union Station in the opening, various element shots throughout and the notable surfing down Wilshire sequence. I didn't handle the first unit green screen with Kurt and Peter

L-R: Mac Condro [Visual Effects Camera Assistant],
Les Bernstien [Visual Effects Director of Photography]
(Photo Courtesy Joey "Deluxe" Enyart)

[Fonda] [Pipeline] [though I consulted], but did all the full body green screen shots. We shot everything VistaVision and it was one of the first digital comp projects Buena Vista Visual Effects handled.

How were the miniatures shot?

We shot the big miniatures at the Acton Movie Ranch [Polsa Rosa Ranch]. It's in the middle of nowhere, so loud noises wouldn't bug anyone. Incidentally, near there at the airport, I shot the exploding miniatures for *Fight Club*. Also, for both projects [*Escape* and *Fight Club*] the miniatures were 1/4 scale, built and rigged by John Stirber [Miniature Effects Supervisor]. Stirber had to use a Gradall [Excavator] to level the area and pour a concrete slab for the Union Station miniature as there were gas explosions, fireballs, etcetera. There was also a water tank there, though I believe it's now gone. I shot some other stuff for *Contact* there later when I was at Sony. The Union Station miniature had to match lighting at the real station exactly, so I supervised the plate shooting in downtown L.A., then told John the direction to build the miniature so the sun angle would match. The freeway and station miniatures were the only ones we shot out there. Also, for the freeway miniature, there were hydraulic movers that "shook" the plaster construction apart. I had five or seven cameras on it, most [encased in] in crash housings. Film speeds ranged from 72 FPS to 96 FPS. Proper scale speed was 48 FPS [square root of the inverse of scale x 24], but tests told us 72 and 96 looked better.

The flying miniatures [helicopter, hang-glider] were shot on the Disney insert stage. There was a motion control system that had a two or three axis model mover. The flying miniatures were mounted on this and the camera was programmed to fly toward and over to make it look like they were flying toward the camera or vice versa. I lit the miniatures for night, I believe, and filmed a "beauty" pass against black. Sometimes there would be two or three passes for lighting exposures as we always had to maintain a very deep depth of field to make them look to scale. So, one pass could be, say an F16 at one second per frame exposure for one type of lighting [moonlight] while another would be F16 at 1/2 or 1/4 second per frame for fill or backlight, etcetera. All while the moves are repeated exactly so the passes line up in opticals. Then we would set up cards painted with fluorescent orange paint behind the model and all the lighting on the model is extinguished. UV [Ultraviolet] [blacklight] lamps and fluorescent lamps are placed around the cards so they illuminate evenly [very easy with UV-flos].

For model rods or supports, we would cut pieces of foamcore painted in the same paint and place them to camera so, when illuminated by another UV-flo, they would glow orange to match the background matte. The model is then a perfect silhouette and the optical department can pull B+W contrast mattes from that piece of film matching the move from all the other passes. This would hold out the ship against the city or landscape or whatever the background was. The advantage over other matte pass lighting techniques is that the UV light would only excite the orange phosphors in the paint. You could place the UV-flos close to the model to get a good position for lighting the orange cards and not worry about spill on the model.

It was only blacklight and the model would appear black. It was very fast and efficient. Silhouette mattes have been used since the original 1933 *King*

L-R: Steve Humphrey [Electronics],
John K. Stirber [Miniature Effects Supervisor], Unknown
(Photo Courtesy Les Bernstien)

Kong. We just updated it with psychedelic paint and blacklights. The orange paint phosphor backlit matte technique was developed by the late Gary Hutzel when I was shooting miniatures at Image G for *Star Trek: TNG* [*The Next Generation*] in the 80s. It was a hybrid of stuff from Apogee's UV matting except over there we would spray a clear lacquer with an embedded UV phosphor over the model and hit it with UV lamps to make the model glow. It was uneven due to contours in model ships and would cause the matte to "bloom" or get larger than the beauty pass element. This would cause matte lines and less than perfect mattes.

We also shot a bunch of 1/4 scale water backgrounds and elements at Castaic Lake [Cahuenga Pass Shoreline]. We shot a number of angles of the sub at Castaic Lake. I used a Chapman Titan crane to get several high camera angles quickly. Also, I remember using a mini Ritter fan to "chop" the water as I think we were shooting 1/4 scale and water is very hard to look convincing at that scale. Just look at old Hollywood miniature shoots of ships at sea or older Godzilla movies. When you try to get "white caps" on the water or create a lot of movement in water, it helps sell the scale.

What kind of challenges did this project provide and which visual effects, scenes or locations were the most challenging, problematic, memorable, and fun to work on?

Shooting the Union Station miniature was challenging. I had to plan the exact location of the miniature, facing the same direction, time of day, etcetera as the actual train station plate photography. John Stirber and his crew had to pour a concrete pad out at the Acton Ranch because of the scale of the gas explosion we were filming. I had given him the compass heading and coordinates of its placement ahead of time. There was an error in communication and they poured the pad facing the wrong way. They had to rip it up and do it again. Harrison and I decided natural sunlight was the best way to match the location, obviously, because of the shadows. "Parallel rays" was our mantra, meaning that sunlight creates shadows of the same scale in miniatures as in full-scale structures. But on the day of shooting, clouds started to move in and I had my gaffer Mark Cane rig an 18K to match sun angle. We got it damn close, but you could see diverging shadows because the lamp was a lot closer than the sun! Harrison and I were a little disappointed, but decided it would have to do. We couldn't reschedule the shoot. At the last minute, the sun came out and we got our parallel rays! Technically, the scale frame rate was 48 FPS, but I did tests at 72 and 96 FPS and I think the highest frame rate won. The formula for calculating scale frame rate works as a starting point for gravity effects, but more modern explosions use higher velocity pyro charges and higher frame rates tend to be more believable.

How was the "Surfing Down Wilshire" sequence shot?

These were done at a standing wave "surf park" [Schlitterbahn Waterpark & Resort] in New Braunfels, Texas called a "Wave Loc." [FlowRider]. One of the surfing stand-ins [for Peter I believe] was none other than Tony Hawk [Stunt Player] [Uncredited]! This was because the standing wave surf boards had no fins, so it was more like skateboarding in water. I had to fly a 20" x 30" green screen behind the wave machine. It was crazy.

What's your favorite memory or memories of working on the movie?

When we were filming the surf sequences in Texas and Tony Hawk was one of the surfers! I remember he had the flu and a 102 degree fever while we were shooting! There was a hot tub next to the Wave Loc [FlowRider] and he spent all the time in the hot tub.

What do you think of the movie personally?

I think it's not as good as the first one in New York but, hey, it was fun to work with all those guys and be part of a Carpenter movie. I haven't seen it in a while, though. I should watch it again. I'm assuming it's got quite a cult following.

What are you currently doing and what do you enjoy doing in your spare time?

Teaching workshops, writing movies [fairly non-FX oriented] and trying to push ahead with a couple documentary films. One I am planning is on my generation of effects veterans focusing on photographic effects, non-digital effects.

SHYAM "TOAST" YADAV
Visual Effects Production Assistant

How did you end up being a visual effects data wrangler?

When I was hired by Buena Vista Visual Effects, it was as a VFX production assistant who would also go on set as a data wrangler. To my knowledge, the title "data wrangler" did not exist yet and it was grouped in with production assistant. Working on *Escape From L.A.* was my first time wrangling and I had no idea what I was doing or why I was doing it. Since the job was in its infancy, there wasn't really anyone to bounce questions off of. From the beginning, my goals have been to work with the writers and directors that influenced my childhood. John Carpenter along with George Miller and David Lynch are my top three. So when the chance to work on set and watch John work came to me, I leapt at it.

How did you get the job to be visual effects production assistant on *Escape From L.A.*?

Up to that point, I had only worked on two films, *Congo* and *Twister,* in what would now be called the video playback department. Before those films, I had interned at James Cameron's company Lightstorm when *True Lies* was being made. I quickly became good friends with Geoff Burdick, who had been working for Lightstorm since *Terminator 2: Judgment Day.* Geoff recommended me to Brian Keeney [Visual Effects Coordinator] of BVVE [Buena Vista Visual Effects] and I was brought in for an interview.

The day before the interview, I had my wisdom teeth removed and so, when I went in to the interview, I was taking Vicodin pain pills. I was told later that I got the job because of how relaxed I was during the interview and they felt I would be able to handle the stress of being on set. They had no idea I was relaxed because of those pills!!! Being on set can be a high stress environment compared to being in an office, along with having long hours out in the elements. But for me, it was always about watching and learning how movies are made, something I felt I couldn't get in an office.

L-R: Shyam V. Yadev [Visual Effects Production Assistant], John Leonetti [Visual Effects Production Assistant], Denise Davis [Visual Effects Producer], Brian Keeney [Visual Effects Coordinator], Michael Lessa [Visual Effects Supervisor] (Photo Courtesy Shyam "Toast" Yadav)

How did you, Joshua Arsenault [Visual Effects Production Assistant] and Mark Soper [Visual Effects Production Assistant] prepare for this project and how did you collaborate?

Of the three of us, I was the only one that was to go on set, so we didn't really collaborate for the show. *Escape From L.A.* was my first job in visual effects. My job back then was a hybrid of a VFX production assistant on the days when I was not on set and a VFX data wrangler when I was. Back in those days VFX on set were confined to pre-chosen shots, so I didn't have to be on set every day. Back then, people in VFX actively did NOT want to go to set, so getting the assignment to go on set was far easier than it is today. I was thrilled to be there as John Carpenter's films have hugely influenced me and my life. One of my first days on the job before we began shooting, I was running some documents to the production office trailer on the Paramount lot. When I entered the trailer, there weren't any signs on where to go and so I was forced to choose either going left or right. I went left and who turns the corner and walks up to me but Kurt Russell wearing his ORIGINAL Snake Plissken costume from *Escape From New York*! [I think he kept it as a memento from the shoot]. I'm the first person he sees and he walks quickly up to me and says, "Can you believe it! It still fits!" I was shocked. Here I was standing face to face with Snake Plissken! What an amazing start to one of my most unforgettable jobs.

What kind of challenges did this project provide and which visual effects, scenes or locations were the most challenging, problematic, memorable, and fun to work on?

I found the entire shoot memorable and fun because I was just happy to be there. In some ways, it was a blessing to have no idea what I was doing as a data wrangler because I had no idea how many mistakes I was making! The crew at BVVE knew how huge a fan I was of John's and were open to my not always subtle suggestions to their work. I was too green to understand that they could have been insulted about my ideas as I was the lowest rung on the ladder, but instead it got some of them even more excited about the project. One of my ideas was that when Snake piloted the submarine through the waters around Universal Studios and the *Jaws* shark that he would spot the rusted cab of the Pork Chop Express from *Big Trouble in Little China*! I thought it would be incredible for the sub to rush past it and we would see the front grill of the truck which read "Haulin' ass" with the silhouette of a girl on it. The artists began to design the art intending to surprise John with it and then see if it could be approved. Sadly, they were unable to finish it in time and it was never shown. I don't have any copies of the art but remember it and it was incredible.

One day on set, we were shooting the scene of Snake being brought into a room to be interrogated by the President [Cliff Robertson]. Originally, the scene was blocked out that Brazen [Michelle Forbes] and Malloy [Stacy Keach] opened the door to let Snake into the room and we later learn that they are holograms. As I watched the blocking rehearsal, I realized that the Brazen and Malloy holograms couldn't open the doors, but since we hadn't blocked that moment, it had yet to be realized. I told my amazing VFX supervisor Michael Lessa about the problem because I certainly didn't have the courage to mention it to John. Michael walked over to John and I could see him explain the situation.

John immediately corrected the issue before the scene was shot by having two extras playing police open the doors. He then thanked Michael who pointed to me way in the background and gave me the credit for noticing the potential gaff. John then turned to me and gave me a quick round of applause. Having just entered the movie business only two years before, I was shocked and deeply touched to not only work with one of my heroes, but to also have him thank me. As the years have passed, I've realized how rare it is for a director or actor to acknowledge and appreciate someone on their crew and it explains the loyalty and love John's crew has for him. For that same sequence, I was allowed to be cast as an extra as Snake walks down that hallway. I was on my knees in front of a priest waiting for my execution.

Near the end of the shoot, we were shooting the helicopter escape from the Happy Kingdom [by the Sea]. We had the helicopter cabin on a raised gimbal above the stage floor and the crew inside were to react to an incoming rocket shot by Cuervo Jones [George Corraface]. By this point, I'd become good friends with Jeff Imada, a longtime collaborator and stunt coordinator of John's. Jeff was also playing the Saigon Shadow who dies when the rocket hits the helicopter cabin. Earlier that day, I went up to Jeff. Again, I was too green to not know to do this and suggested that the second before John gave the cue for the actors to react to being hit by the rocket, that he would put up his hand and form his fingers in the "L" shape the good guys did in *Big Trouble in Little China*. So Jeff, always a good guy kept doing it take after take. Finally John calls up to him and asks what the hell he's doing. Jeff points to me and says he asked me to do it. I quickly faded into the background and Jeff wisely stopped listening to me.

How was your experience working with the cast and crew?

John's crew, like the best directors I've worked with, are a family. I found it the same working with George Miller and Clint Eastwood. I couldn't have asked for a better family to join on my first VFX project.

What do you think of the movie personally?

When the movie came out, I saw it multiple times in the theater. I was just so excited to be part of a John Carpenter and Snake Plissken film. One time as I was entering the theater, two young guys were leaving having just seen the movie. "Leave! Don't go it's horrible!" They yelled to me as a warning, not knowing I had already seen it multiple times. When I saw it with my young eyes, I loved the opening and closing of the film. The dark cynical quality that I love in all of John's films, that Snake would prefer to shut down the world than compromise. I recently watched the film again and found that I loved even more aspects that I just didn't get back when we made it. How John mocked the shallowness of Hollywood as well as Snake's response to Pam Grier's Hershe character about how she wanted him to identify her as. Snake is an antihero and he's not going to say or do anything he doesn't mean. I'm proud to have been on this film and that it's part of my life story. A lot has been said about the poor quality of the VFX work on *Escape From L.A.* and I understand where people are coming from. But now, having been in VFX for over twenty-five years, I have worked on projects that have won the Oscar only to work with the exact same VFX team on another show and have cheesy subpar VFX. There are many factors in creating quality VFX, but the three most important are time, money, and if the director and VFX supervisor are a united front in how the effects are shot on set. On *Escape From L.A.*, I found John supportive of the VFX department just as he is with the rest of his crew. But BVVE was attempting to do work that was technically and financially out of our grasp.

What are you currently doing and what do you enjoy doing in your spare time?

Last year, I was fortunate to work in Australia on George Miller's *Furiosa*. I worked on *Mad Max: Fury Road* in 2012 and it was one of the greatest experiences of my life. I also am a co-founder of FTX, the French Toast and Hugs Gang that hands out free french toast and hugs around the world. Covid has slowed us down, but I look forward to resuming it soon.

JEFF PYLE
Car Model Crew Chief

How did you end up being a model maker?

I had a long history around age seven and up building plastic kits and clay sculpting. That moved into playing around with clay and taking figure modeling courses. Originally, my dream was to make creatures and work in that world, but my first offers spun off of each other year after year and that was in the miniatures world, which worked out better that way, ironically. Competition in special makeup FX is tight.

How did you get the job of car model crew chief on *Escape From L.A.*?

I had worked with John Stirber [Miniature Effects Supervisor] on *Waterworld* and we really connected well. I really, really liked the guy a lot. He was in charge of a big, big job there. He met me there and I went along with him when he started his own shop, Stirber Visual Network. The assignment for the cars, that was our first job there. I had the most experience with carving foam and building things at the time, in his opinion, I assume.

How did you, Sandy Stewart [Car Model Crew Chief] and John K. Stirber [Miniature Effects Supervisor] prepare for this project and how did you collaborate?

I know that the production company had specific ones that we had to have for them. I think we had some freedom on the truck. We might have had some freedom on some of the cars. I'm not sure. It was me and Sandy that were to take care of all the cars. The Cadillac had to be scratch built and Joey Enyart [Modeler], another great model maker there at the time, took care of another scratch build. Gosh, I can't remember which car it was. So we had three scratch builds and three shelves that we were able to get in that scale for background cars. Yeah, that was a great team.

Top and Bottom: Jeff Pyle [Car Model Crew Chief]
(Photos Courtesy Jeff Pyle)

How were the models constructed such as Cuervo Jones' [George Corraface] Cadillac for instance, what kind of challenges did this project provide, and how long did they take to make?

The reference material could be found online for the regular cars. The truck I found down the street. I found a grey semitruck. I just took all the measurements directly from that truck and could just go down the street and look at it for details at any time, so that worked out great. The Cadillac was all the same. I photographed it and took every single measurement I could. I had to go to the studio lot to do that, so I wasn't able to go and see the car all the time, but I had all the measurements. I bunched it to, I believe it was 1/5 scale on that particular shot [Wilshire Canyon], which was a bit silly obviously. Also, the construction. They were all fiberglass shelves. They were done in foam. Hard-coated, sanded urethane or a RTV silicone [Room-Temperature-Vulcanizing silicone] with a fiberglass jacket.

That was the way we did almost all our scratch build vehicles. Then you pull a copy out of the mold. We can do different things with that and make parts of it crunchable. That's how you get a nice hard shelved body that you can work with. The 59 Caddy 1/5 scale was done in six-pound urethane foam. Rigid urethane foam, I believe, and started with a block of that. If you have a large enough band saw that can cut the profiles of anything, it helps immensely. At least you can get the top and side profiles done. The band saw he had, had a really big throat. You could fit a giant piece of foam in there. That helped immensely. Otherwise, you had to carve all those. As far as building the real ones, they were real 59s. We had three of them down at the lot that they were using, so I could get reference of those.

Is it true that you sculpted the body of the submarine as well?

Joey Enyart and I both sculpted the submarine model that you don't really see in the film. That was also out of, I believe, six-pound foam. We usually use six-pound foam and get pretty tight detail and then you hard cut that, then molding and casting. A shelve comes back and there's more sanding. It's a long process.

How was your experience working with the Stirber Visual Network team?

Working for John for Stirber Network, that was a blast. Watching pyro going off on miniatures and setting up flying models on high-wires from cranes on fire. There's always that danger factor, too. Always there. Great place to be. I just got lucky that we hit it off well and had quite a few years. He's hard. He's tough, but he was great. We really happened to hit the best time of the last days of models, so we got lucky.

What's your favorite memory or memories of working on the movie?

Besides the massive destruction of the freeway, which was a nail-biter, the best memories were probably out on set. The car explosion in front of Union Station turned out to be a beautiful shot. The pyro guys did a great job and the model was flawless, even down to the luggage carts. Those fooled a lot of people. The memories of being out there doing radio control while that mammoth of freeway was collapsing and coming apart was really fun to see and be involved with.

What happened to the models after the movie was finished?

I know that the Cadillac model was saved. John put that in his office. He had it in a glass cage in his office, so that looked nice. The truck ended up in the shop. It was saved. Years later, I believe it was sold when the shop was closed down. The other ones ended up, I believe, in a landfill because they didn't have a lot of structure. They weren't made to stand up, so they were trashed. We could have pulled some of the RC stuff out of them, but their bodies, they were gone.

What do you think of the movie personally?

You know, it was ok. The movie was what it was. Snake Plissken takes on the world. It got a big following. That's great.

What are you currently doing and what do you enjoy doing in your spare time?

After the battle of models and CGI, I was offered work at Stan Winston's Creature Shop [later Legacy Effects] [RIP Stan] and stayed for years. From *Iron Man* and *Avatar* to steady commercials, I was brought in there to be a model maker and do a lot of sanding, something I was used to. I felt very grateful to the owners and am super proud of being noticed and invited. I do my own stuff at home. I like sculpting a lot. I've really been trying to get back to do the sculpting thing.

JOEY "DELUXE" ENYART
Modeler

How did you end up being a model maker?

I grew up building models for as long as I can remember. I was always building something, whether it was an RC plane, models, slot cars or a building, etcetera. Then I went through art school and studied industrial design/architecture in college. Then I was a hotel designer. I eventually became a full-time professional model maker for a company in Newport Beach, CA. That's how I made the connection to John Stirber [Miniature Effects Supervisor].

How did you get the job of model maker on *Escape From L.A.*?

That was the new project starting up when I was hired by John Stirber, just a few weeks before. It was my first movie. [I was a rookie]. It took me six years to finally get a break in Hollywood. You have to know the right people.

How did you and model makers Isaac Cohen, Duke Dixon, Richard Lea and John K. Stirber [Miniature Effects Supervisor] prepare for this project and how did you collaborate?

As I recall, my first day was John Stirber asking me to design/draw-up a futuristic sub for the movie. I almost shit myself! I remember that I immediately broke into a cold sweat as I was the new guy at his company and was hoping I could pull this off without anyone noticing how nervous I really was. Needless to say, I didn't sleep much the first week. He showed me a picture that the studio gave him as a kind of reference, but it was like a Jules Vern looking thing that they did not like. They wanted something more stealthy. I had no idea what I was going to draw. To this day, it's one of my best creative accomplishments, especially when I was told how much John Carpenter liked my sub design. Later on, after renderings were signed off on, I would build the sub tunnel doors, then RC cars and burnt up buildings. I didn't know anyone, so I had not yet met Isaac or Richard. I know Isaac worked on the plaster molds for the freeway [The Four-

L-R: Paul Vigil [Special Effects], Joey "Deluxe" Enyart [Modeler]
Bottom: Joey "Deluxe" Enyart
(Photos Courtesy Joey "Deluxe" Enyart)

Level Interchange] and Richard worked on some of the buildings. Both were very talented. I'm not sure if Duke worked on *Escape From L.A.* I first met Duke when we got on the project for the movie *Volcano*.

Did you collaborate with Tim Lawrence [Illustrator] in any way, who also did drawings of the submarine?

I never met Tim Lawrence. I didn't know about any other drawings except for my own renderings. I wasn't at the meeting when my renderings were presented to John Carpenter. All I got was a B&W Xerox that had the basic body shape with a rounder nose and more panels/rivets. Sometimes, studios will only give you limited info so they can see what you can come up with and design. It happened on another movie where all I got was a front view concept on a Xerox and had to build a prototype model from it. It took forever, a ton of back and forth. Anyway, I remember they wanted to keep the sliding canopy, so I moved the center point more forward, widened the outriggers to look more like a mini-batwing and took out the panels, lines, and rivets to make it stealthier. I also remember how much I really liked the rear stabilizer and exhaust, so didn't want to change that at all. After seeing Tim's renderings after twenty-four plus years, I now realize that my sub is only a revised version of what Tim designed. Tim's renderings are AWESOME!!! I would never want to take credit for somebody else's creation or design. That's just not me.

How were the models constructed, what kind of challenges did this project provide, and how long did they take to make?

Model construction varies, but we used pretty much any and all materials available. Example: The freeway was a huge, welded metal skeleton with elbow joints and hydraulics, covered with plaster pillars, fiberglass, plastic parts, etcetera. The plaster areas would crack and chip away as the frame shook. That made it look like the concrete was crumbling in an earthquake. The buildings were mostly wood framed, then skinned with thin material, Plexiglas windows, plaster, then painted and aged to look burnt, warped, distressed, and destroyed. RC cars/semitrucks were usually metal frames, motors, electronics, fiberglass, foam, etcetera. Example: The red Cadillac was also a custom size, so we had our sculptor Jeff [Pyle] [Car Model Crew Chief] shape it out of a big foam block. Then a mold was made. Then a fiberglass body was laid up and painted to spec. Jeff had sculpted the body for the sub too. LOTZ-O-WORK!

I think we were constructing for approx. six to eight months before filming on location. The problems were figured out through testing. This was a daily process as pretty much EVERYTHING was scratch built to scale. Sometimes you just grab stuff and start hacking it up, gluing it up or welding it up, etcetera. Then go from there with electronics, finish, and paint. I don't remember how many were built, but there were a lot. Working on location was a combination of long hours and cold days. For me, it was great because this was my first time on set. I got to see how the shots were set up and filmed. Secondly, I got to see the pyro explosions. AWESOME!!! There's a lot of down time between scenes, but overall, very cool to experience. Also, I was there when that sub landing footage was shot. It was at Castaic Lake [Cahuenga Pass Shoreline]. I believe we were filming from 9:00 PM till approx. 3:30 AM. Long day and night.

I'm pretty sure the footage of surfers was deleted. I remember that the guy saying the lines [Breckin Meyer] [Surfer] didn't sound good and he was having trouble sitting on that surfboard! I quietly told my boss that I could do a better job because I was a real surfer and could say the lines better. I think he got a big kick outta that! [I didn't have a SAG card anyway.] Oh well. We were second unit SFX, so we had to be there to set up the miniature sub pad so they could shoot it. We only had part of the crew at Castaic Lake for that shoot. The platform had a concrete looking hinged front section that would drop down so it looked like the sub slid backwards into the water. The sub moved forward [to look like it landed], then got pulled backwards. I think we had the sub on a cable system. After that, they added in the first unit footage with Kurt Russell trying to hold on to the sub to keep it from sliding back off the platform and into the water.

Were you disappointed that the miniature submarine was mostly deleted and only used briefly in the movie? It was only visible when it breaks the house foundation it lands on and falls into the water. The rest was done with CG.

Yes, I was very disappointed that they cut out a lot of footage with the sub. It looks hokey in the movie, which was too bad because the sub really looked cool with all the LED's and paint color when you saw it in person and the CG of my sub was terrible! But that was at a time when the movie industry thought it was a good idea to use all CG. It doesn't work! You have to use both models and CG together as they complement one another. That's what screwed up the SFX movies! It took them about a decade to realize that you CAN-NOT use all CG. A lot of great model builders lost jobs because of that mentality and arrogance.

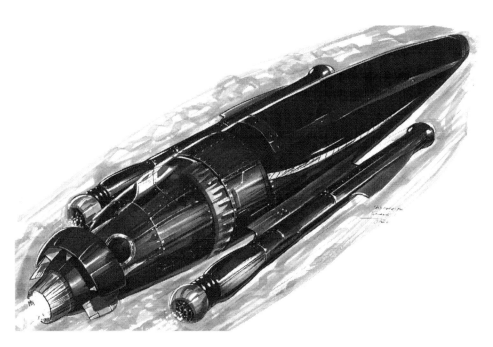

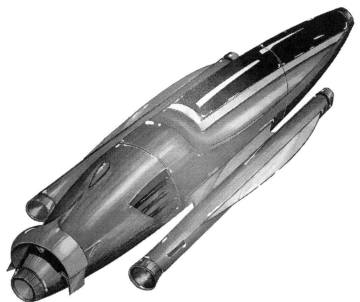

Top: Fireball Tim's Concept Art [Submarine]
Bottom: Joey "Deluxe" Enyart's Concept Art [Submarine]
(Art Courtesy Fireball Tim / *FireballTim.com* and Joey "Deluxe" Enyart)

Top: Submarine Miniature Model
Bottom: Los Angeles Union Station/Beverly Hills Hotel Miniature Models
(Photos Courtesy Joey "Deluxe" Enyart)

How was your experience working with the Stirber Visual Network team?

Well, I have worked in several major fields in my lifetime, so I can honestly say that working for Stirber Visual Network was one of the BEST companies I've ever experienced and for many reasons. John was ALWAYS encouraging people to push the envelope to maximize their talents and, let me tell you, there was MAJOR TALENT in that group. It was truly inspiring to be around. If you got stuck on something, there was ALWAYS someone that would offer up help or suggestions and, for that reason, it seemed like anything was possible when it came to design, function, and fabrication. There was no doubt that we were "one-hell-of-a-team!" It just seemed like everyone got along. That's saying a lot considering how many creative temperaments there were. I've not experienced that amount of talent ever since.

Here's an example of John Stirber's kindness, just one of many. I had only been working there for about five weeks and was heavy into the project when I received bad news about my father, who had suffered a massive stroke. I was devastated and had to fly to Florida fast. I was there for several days and spoke with John on the phone regularly to give him updates and on when I was returning to L.A. Before I came back to California, I asked John to not let anyone else work on my project as I wanted to finish it myself when I returned. Without hesitation, he said it would be fine as long as I felt that I was emotionally up to finishing the task myself. He took a chance on me and, yes, I did finish it! I was working on the doors that opened when the submarine came out. As you probably already know, Hollywood waits for NO ONE, so the fact that this man would extend this favor to me at a most tragic time and as a new employee is something that I'll NEVER FORGET!

What's your favorite memory or memories of working on the movie?

Seeing my work on the big screen for the first time with my friends. Working my dream job! Not everyone has that opportunity. I'm very blessed! Getting paid very good money to build models, then getting to wreck them and blow them up. That was CHOICE!!! My sense of accomplishment and the camaraderie. Getting my first crew jacket that has *Escape From L.A.* embroidered on it.

What happened to the models after the movie was finished?

I don't know how many props were actually kept or where they are stored. It's unfortunate, but a lot of movie models get trashed. Not sure, but I think John Carpenter may still have the one-man sub. We had built two of them.

What do you think of the movie personally?

I love it!!! It's the typical over the top sci-fi movie with great SFX. Yes, it's quirky, but that's what it's supposed to be. It's entertaining. Personally for me, I wasn't real fond of the basketball part, but I thoroughly enjoyed the rest of it. I am still a fan of *Escape From New York* and *Escape From L.A.*

What are you currently doing and what do you enjoy doing in your spare time?

I am currently trying to set up my website through Squarespace. It's not real good yet because I really suck at setting it up! Yes, I am still building high-end scale models of all types, mostly for myself, along with my millwork design and learning to weld. I'm not doing any client work until I get a new studio set up. I just need to have more space for my machines and airbrushing. I'm surfing as much as possible! It's what keeps me grounded and creative and it's still my one love, my passion. It has always been what my life has revolved around since 1966.

LARRY JOLLY
Miniature Helicopter

How did you end up being a model maker and how come you mostly build helicopters and such?

I grew up watching features from the World War II era that featured some extraordinary miniature work for the time. My family came from a performance model aircraft background. I started entering flying contests at age seven. A friend recalled that, when I was a high school senior, I told him I was going to fly model helicopters in the movies. I got my first chance in the pilot for *Airwolf*. The miniature Hughes 500 that blew up in that pilot was the first scale machine I had ever built and was the first of over 300 cinematic pyro demolitions. I was quickly educated in Hollywood miniatures requirements and the very real differences between professional miniatures and hobbyist models. I opened a shop and developed my crew and the skill set to produce high-quality in-house camera match flying vehicles for cinematic work.

How did you get the job of miniature helicopter maker on *Escape From L.A.*?

Around Christmas time 1995, I got a call from Debra Hill [Producer/Co-Writer] to come up to Disney and have a meeting with John Carpenter to discuss a miniature for a possible upcoming project. We looked over his [story] boards and discussed the possible methods we could use to get what he needed. I got a call a couple of weeks later and got the go on the project.

How did you, Steve Addis [Miniature Helicopter], Robert Eickenhorst [Miniature Helicopter] and Producers Air Force who did the full-size mock-up prepare for this project and how did you collaborate?

We used the same drawings that the art department used for the full-size mock-up. We spent a Saturday morning going over their mock-up looking for deviations from the drawings. We took our own photos and measurements to make sure everything matched.

Top: Miniature Helicopter Model
Bottom: Full-Size Mock-Up [Producers Air Force]
(Photos Courtesy Larry Jolly)

How were the models constructed, what kind of challenges did this project provide, and how long did they take to make?

We had four or five weeks to produce the miniature. We were doing two other features at the time, and I set three of my advanced guys loose on the project as I supervised the other projects that had to film first. The helicopter had fairly low mechanical requirements from a creation viewpoint. It had to be a faithful reproduction and had to have lights and working counter rotating main blades, but we had developed methods to cope with those details before. Steve Addis was our lead modeler on this project and he did a great job.

Since the shot was motion control, we decided to use a stepper motor-controlled transmission power drive unit that could be removed from the main body of the helicopter. Giving a director options is a sure way to get on his good side. Helicopters are prone to vibration with everything spinning. They are a true thing of joy when everything is spinning in harmony. Since the shot was on a computer-controlled model mover against a green screen, I designed the machine so that we could do a pass with the body of the helicopter and then film a pass separately with the blades power unit and then join them in post. This would keep any vibration isolated to the blades power unit and keep the body stable and steady simulating a larger object with good damping. We finished the machine on time and the shooting schedule was pretty low key being a total second unit ordeal.

What's your favorite memory or memories of working on the movie?

It was great meeting John and getting the chance to witness his creative process.

What happened to the model after the movie was finished?

The miniature was retained by the company. I kept the molds. I don't release those.

What do you think of the movie personally?

It was great being able to participate in the making of *Escape From L.A.* I am happy with the contributions and look of our miniature.

What are you currently doing and what do you enjoy doing in your spare time?

The last feature we did was *Interstellar*. We produced and operated the thirty-three percent [scale] Predator drones for the film. I still fly and compete. I currently design and produce agricultural surveying UAVs [Unmanned Aerial Vehicle] for DreamHammer, a San Diego based digital information company.

RICK LAZZARINI
Hang Glider Puppets [Uncredited]

How did you end up being a creature effects/animatronics designer as well as the head of The Character Shop?

I created my first illusion in first grade. I was six and playing Jesus in a school play, so I created my first prosthetics out of binder paper. I drew the wounds of Jesus. The stigmata for his hands, feet, and his side, and I taped them to my feet and hands and side. They told me I had to wear socks and I thought, "Jesus wouldn't wear socks!" Of course, the teachers didn't let me use my prosthetics, but that was my first illusion. There was a magazine I discovered as a kid called *Famous Monsters of Filmland*. My grandma bought me my first copy and I just ate it up. I'd research new monsters, new movies. I loved the Hammer horror and melodramas on TV and would watch them all the time. In seventh grade, I had a date with the hottest girl in school, but I found out that the original *King Kong* was going to be on TV that night, so I cancelled the date. That's how I knew I really loved this stuff!

In 1968, *Planet of the Apes* came out and an older friend and her boyfriend took me to see it and I was like GAGA! I absolutely loved apes and chimps. I went nuts for the behind the scenes stuff where they showed how the effects were made. I sculpted in Play-Doh and clay and went to the library to read up on stage makeup. In high school, I got the reputation as the guy who could make cool stuff. I airbrushed backdrops for plays and cool props for music videos. I made masks and sold them in costume shops in San Jose.

After that, I gravitated towards doing stage makeup for school productions, making Super 8 films with monsters in them and phoning Dick Smith WAAAAAY too late at night. I went down to Rick Baker's [Special Makeup Effects] house and hung out until he got sick of me. I got jobs working for rock bands [The Tubes, KISS] and then started doing music videos and low budget slasher movies. I got a job at Makeup Effects Labs and worked on such kickass films as *Evilspeak* and *Slumber Party Massacre*. Once you're there, you start to meet like-minded and talented people in the same field and you recommend each other for jobs. Eventually, I got hired at Stan Winston Studios where I set up his mechanical department and worked on *Invaders from Mars* and *Aliens*.

On *Aliens,* I became an independent contractor and was chiefly involved in designing the animatronics for the Queen Alien, running facehugger, and the opening egg. After Stan's, I worked at Boss Films, Apogee, and out of my garage shop on more music videos, commercials, and films like *Spaceballs.* I got offered a huge commercial job turning people into office workers with animal heads and spent all of that money on opening up a new shop in Van Nuys. It was the first of several. Over the years I've built a reputation as an extremely resourceful guy who cares a LOT about the quality of my FX and I come up with solutions that are very out of left field. It means I'm tenacious, passionate, a problem solver, and I think a damn good puppeteer, so I would just often get very difficult jobs because people knew I was the guy to solve people's X challenges.

How did you get the job of hang glider puppets maker of Kurt Russell, Pam Grier [Hershe], and Steve Buscemi [Map to the Stars Eddie] on *Escape From L.A.*?

I had worked previously with Peter Montgomery and Carolyn Soper making miniature likeness puppets for films such as *Wild Hearts Can't be Broken, The Phantom.* This was before CGI was de rigueur, so we would make these exquisitely detailed puppets practically. We did similar work on *Hocus Pocus* creating miniature flying witches for Bette Midler, Kathy Najimy and Sarah Jessica Parker.

How did you and hang glider puppets makers Jim Belohovek, Hiroshi Katagiri and Tom Killeen prepare for this project and how did you collaborate?

We first of all visited set and took many pictures and measurements of Kurt Russell, Steve Buscemi, and Pam Grier. Then we wanted to stay and take more pictures and measurements of Pam Grier, but maybe we got too creepy about it, so she kicked us out. [I'm just joking!]

How were the models constructed, how many worked on them, what kind of challenges did this movie provide, and how long did they take to make?

Sculptors, moldmakers, lab folk, painters, wardrobe folks, mechanics, model makers. Probably fourteen people in all and they took four weeks to make. Once we had detailed appearance and anatomical information, we created armatures, then sculptures very close likenesses of the three actors. We made jointed internal armatures and foam latex skins and then detailed and created things like their hair, wardrobe, and accoutrements [hats, eye patches, etcetera]. We then hired James Belahovek to create the miniature hang gliders. He and I had worked on *Aliens,* albeit in different departments. His miniature hang gliders were works of genius. Exquisite and accurate in detail made of bent and soldered brass tubing, tiny cables, turnbuckles, and ballistic nylon fabric.

Were you involved during the filming of the models?

Absolutely! We always take our creations to set and bring them to life.

How was your experience working with Buena Vista Visual Effects?

The experience and collaboration with Buena Vista Visual FX was easy and comfortable. Having worked with them before, we knew the style and approach to shooting that they liked to take. Carolyn Soper is the most pleasant and wonderful VFX producer and Peter Montgomery is whip-smart and witty, so everything went extremely easily shooting the puppets against green screen.

According to Bryan Sides [Uncredited], Jay Leno showed up behind the scenes and took the Map to the Stars Eddie puppet out of the box and ran around with it on set goofing around. Do you have any recollection of this?

I do remember Jay Leno being by craft service while we were showing off the puppets. I don't remember specifically him running around set with it, but that could have happened while I jumped into his Ferrari and did donuts in the lot!

What's your favorite memory or memories of working on the movie?

Meeting and hanging out with Kurt Russell and Steve Buscemi. Chatting with and measuring Pam Grier. Working with an incredibly talented team of artists and craftspeople. Being close to Pam Grier. Shooting the puppets with Peter making wisecracks. Did I mention I really liked being around Pam Grier?

What happened to the models after the movie was finished?

I had them in my display room for a very long time. Then one year, around 2000 or so, I held an auction and someone bought them. I don't remember who!

Kurt Russell [Snake Plissken/Producer/Co-Writer]
(Photo Courtesy Rick Lazzarini)

Top: Hang Glider Puppets
Bottom: Snake Plissken Puppet
(Photos Courtesy Rick Lazzarini)

What do you think of the movie personally?

Honestly, surfing a lava wave was kind of jump-the-sharky for me, so that took me out of it. But I'll watch anything with Pam Grier and that Kurt guy, what's-his-name.

What are you currently doing and what do you enjoy doing in your spare time?

Celebrating the release of the *Ghostbusters* reboot and our work on it wherein we created an animatronic puppet/costume of Slimer and his girlfriend. Working on commercials for Geico, Bank of America, and others. Creating installations for the Skirball Museum. Teaching students at the Animatronics Institute and looking for the next paying gig! When I'm not working, I enjoy relaxing and catching up on great TV series, watching UFC fights, and heading out to the desert or the mountains for off-road riding and camping.

KARL FORNANDER
Gunfire Animation and Compositing

How did you end up being a digital effects artist?

I had studied traditional character animation at CalArts starting in 1990. By my second year, I was already accepted into the CG animation lab. I was eager to get into computer animation as I thought it would become popular and I wanted to create something new and different. The CG animation department at the time was very small. Only four students, including me, had been accepted into the program.

How did you get the job of gunfire animation maker on *Escape From L.A.*?

The owner of the small boutique VFX post house, Available Light, hired me to take over the VFX animation. He was a master of hand-drawn VFX such as the electricity crawling over R2-D2 in a film called *Star Wars*. He mentored me a bit and I combined that with what I learned at CalArts. It was one of my first gigs after graduating from CalArts film/animation program. He asked me to take over all hand-drawn effects for many films. *The Craft*, *Bordello of Blood*, etcetera. I became the head of rotoscope and VFX animation at Available Light and created many hand-drawn effects for many feature films.

How were the effects accomplished, what kind of challenges did this project provide, and how long did they take to make?

I was mostly in a small dark room projecting the practical film plate onto the registered animation paper so I could draw muzzle flashes or whatever effect they needed onto the paper. You draw one frame at a time, ink it, and then shoot it on the Oxberry camera, which you then give to the optical printer compositor. I could crank out probably five to ten shots a day. It was kind of at the crossover time when VFX became more digital. This was an old way of working. It was a great experience to see how difficult it used to be creating VFX with optical printers and burning it all onto film. Now I can really appreciate all the tools we have on the computer.

How was your experience working with Available Light?

The really frustrating part is, I had an extensive background in computer animation as well as hand-drawn animation. I had already been doing computer animation for years, but because I was so good at the old school hand-drawn effects, my reward was to be sequestered to a small dark room slaving away at this old way of doing things. Having me excel at it meant the owner could oversee the studio better and work on practical VFX on set and deal with directors and clients. I was never given the chance to grow or work in the new digital department they tried to start, which they desperately needed help with.

So after a couple of years helping Available Light, I had to move on to computer animation and CG VFX. Available Light folded and shut down shortly after I left. The owner had to close the small VFX shop as he just could not compete. He underpaid his employees and treated them pretty badly. I am happy I only stayed there a year before moving on to more progressive studios. The old way of doing optical printing effects was cool to experience, but was labor intensive and took too much time. It was a good first gig but, unfortunately, no room for growth as they were slow to adopt digital new technologies. I can at least appreciate that I was able to improve some skill there and experience old school process and making practical effects.

What's your favorite memory or memories of working on the movie?

Just the fact that I loved *Escape From New York*. Some parts of that film were shot at my college, CalArts. I am a fan of *Big Trouble in Little China*, Kurt Russell and his partner Goldie Hawn. I have met both at classical Indian concerts in L.A.

What are you currently doing and what do you enjoy doing in your spare time?

I still work on feature films, TV, and commercials, mostly as a pre-visualization supervisor, CG supervisor or VFX supervisor. Mostly in Los Angeles, California but I work abroad every couple of years because I love to travel and other cultures. Some of the latest films I have worked on are *Godzilla vs Kong*, *The Jungle Book, Pacific Rim 2,* and *Trollhunters: Rise of the Titans.* My spare time is spent traveling, playing music, and training martial arts. I study and incorporate music from Africa, India, Middle East, Brazil, and Indonesia. I train and coach Wing Tsun [and southern Chinese martial arts] and Kali [Filipino martial arts].

PAUL TAGLIANETTI
Video Supervisor

How did you end up being a visual effects coordinator/producer?

I was hired by Robert Grasmere, who was also a veteran of John Carpenter films, to work on a film called *Demolition Man,* coordinating the film's extensive video and computer graphics. He supervised the computer effects on *Prince of Darkness* and played Frank Wyndham, the man who is covered in bugs in that film. The company I worked for was called Video Image and one of its founders and lead supervisors was John Wash [Video Image], one of John Carpenter's film school associates from USC. John did a lot of the effects and animations on *Dark Star* as well as computer graphics on *The Thing* and *Halloween III.*

How did you get the job of video supervisor on *Escape From L.A.*?

I stayed at Video Image for several years supervising video effects and playback for films including *Se7eN, Executive Decision, Jade,* and *Down Periscope.* While working for John Wash, we received a call from Paramount that Carpenter wanted John Wash to work on the sequel to *Escape From New York* because John did the graphics for that film. When the script came over, he was busy supervising several projects. He knew I was a HUGE fan of the original film and asked me if I would supervise the show. I was one of John Wash's producers at Video Image. John still oversaw everything and was very supportive.

How did you, Patti Cerami [Screen Graphics Coordinator], and Video Image colleagues Rhonda Gunner, Richard E. Hollander, Gregory L. McMurry and John C. Wash prepare for this project and how has the technology changed since John Wash's pre-computer work on *Escape From New York*?

The first thing I did was meet with John [Carpenter] and his producer Debra Hill over at Paramount Studios. It was one of the quickest meetings I've ever been in. John simply asked me if I saw the first film. He said to make the computer graphics look like the simulations in the first film. I think he was looking for visual symmetry with the first film. The graphics for *Escape From L.A.* were all done on Mac computers and transferred to 3/4" video tapes for on set playback. Wash's effects on *Escape From New York* were done by putting scotch lite tape on black miniature cutouts and then using motion-controlled cameras to shoot the resultant effect. This was done simply because they didn't have the money, time and tech to create vector graphics. In *Escape From L.A.,* we used computers and an apple graphics program called Elastic Reality to create the 3D vector simulations.

How did you come up with the graphic displays, how were they accomplished, and how long did they take to make?

Before principal photography, I met with production designer Lawrence Paull, who is well known in the industry as having been the production designer on *Blade Runner*. We discussed the look of the control room and what he wanted on the monitors. We had production designs and blueprints of Universal Studios and the surrounding area for the submarine schematic on the computer monitor. This was supposed to depict the area around Universal Studios submerged by the earthquake/tidal wave. We also had production design drawings for reference in creating the computer map in Stacy Keach's [Malloy] control center from production designer Lawrence Paull's artists. The graphics were all created by the digital artists at Video Image. I would bring the graphics to the set on a small playback monitor and JC [John Carpenter] would make comments/changes, etcetera. They were made over the course of a month or two.

In addition, we shot close-ups of the plutoxin countdown and Cliff Robertson [President] talking to the camera on hi-res monitors at Video Image in Marina Del Rey. These shots were cut in at the beginning of the film during the narration/prologue. Most of the other shots - the submarine interior, the control room at Firebase 7, the finger scanner, the laptop at the landing site at the climax - were all shot live on set by my Video Playback engineer Larry Potoker [Video Image Crew]. They were fed into the monitors from pre-made video tapes that are run through a time base correction system. We used 3/4" video playback decks that are synced to the cameras so that the visible roll bar caused by the discrepancy in frames per seconds from video to film doesn't occur. Back then, plasma and flat screens weren't as widely used yet. We were still using cathode-ray tube monitors which have 30 frame refresh rates. Without the special video equipment and sync boxes you would see the rolling bar on the monitors. The satellite demonstration by Leland Orser [Test Tube] was composited in post-production.

What kind of challenges did this project provide and which video effects were the most challenging, problematic, memorable, and fun to work on?

The EMP [Electromagnetic Pulse] satellite simulation that Test Tube shows on the small monitor was probably the most time consuming. It took a long time because it was texture mapped 3D when 3D was relatively new, so render times took a while. So, we were not able to shoot that on set through the small plasma screen, but instead had to feed a green screen signal into the monitor. Later Buena Vista VFX composited the shot together. The vector graphic simulation of Universal Studios probably took the longest. Most of this was overseen by my coordinator Patricia Cerami.

Were any video effects discarded or not used?

To the best of my knowledge, they cut in everything we made. There was more video footage of Plissken entering the Firebase station on the newsfeed, but that was cut down. There was also the Cuervo Jones [George Corraface] video to the President listing his demands, which might have been cut down a bit. As far as the computer graphics, I'm pretty sure they used all of it.

What's your favorite memory or memories of working on the movie?

It was watching John direct and Debra produce. Ms. Hill was one of the most professional filmmakers I'd ever seen. I was totally in awe of her. When I hear the word "producer" I think of her and rate everyone who wears that mantle against her. Not too many are up to her standards. I was really sad when I heard of her passing. John was so no-nonsense. No Drama. No BS. John is the closest thing my generation got to having our own Howard Hawks. I love all his movies and I was so glad I got to work on one of them.

What do you think of the movie personally?

I have always loved John's political and social commentary and *Escape From L.A.* is filled with sly and witty observations of government and society. John doesn't get enough credit for his films' insights. I prefer *Escape From New York*'s dark edginess to *Escape From L.A.*'s almost comic book-like visual tone, but it's still a fun film and I'm proud of my team's work on it.

What are you currently doing and what do you enjoy doing in your spare time?

I work in education teaching digital media and graphic design. In my free time, I do anything but think of computers, media, or work!

NINA SAXON
Title Designer

How did you end up being a title designer?

I wanted to work in film production and my mentor got me a job in the post-production of special effects, which I had studied at UCLA. The job was working in an optical house animating the red bullets for *Star Wars*. I had a good sense of "timing," leading to jobs on commercials with effect techniques.

How did you get the job of title designer on *Escape From L.A.*?

I was hired on *Escape From L.A.* by its producer, Debra Hill.

How did you and John Carpenter prepare/collaborate for this project?

I produce, budget, and art direct all main and end titles, logos, and animated corporate logos, working alongside the producers and directors who hire me along with the editors. I partner with designers as well as animators and typesetter, depending on the project's needs.

How did you come up with the title design, how many were involved in making it, what kind of challenges did this project provide, and how long did it take to make?

I would say that it is by conceptual instinct and watching a lot films, as well as seeing other designer's work [Saul Bass in particular], that inspire me. It is an art form, a "moving introduction," like a book cover that introduces a film. John Carpenter had no requests other than I follow my instincts to reflect the theme of the film. An action film would be entirely different than a romantic film in the design of its logo, titles, or title sequence. There were two of us designing the main titles for *Escape From L.A.*, myself and my typesetter, who supplied me with various samples for me to choose and show on paper. It took approximately three weeks. Designing an entire title sequence for a film, either at the head or the tail, takes much longer starting with storyboards, animating samples, and finishing.

Was the classic Albertus font used in most John Carpenter movies such as *Escape From New York* always the first choice?

No. We showed many [options] and they chose it anyway.

Did you have any input on the sounds used in the title sequence?

Editors, directors, and producers have their own opinions.

What do you think of the movie personally?

I thought that the film *Escape From L.A.* was well-executed and predictable as an action film featuring a major star at the time.

What's your favorite movie title or titles so far?

I am most proud of *Romancing the Stone* and *Back to the Future* as well as supervising the feather and designing the type for *Forrest Gump* as well as the recent *Salt*.

What are you currently doing and what do you enjoy doing in your spare time?

I just finished the titles for Phillip Noyce's *Above Suspicion*. In my spare time, I love daily intense exercise, taking Emeritus classes, procuring art with my husband, enjoying living in Santa Monica near the ocean, going to "foodie" restaurants as well as quality time at home with my husband, Elliott [an insurance expert witness], and our English mini golden doodle Gracie.

KEVIN J. GORMAN
Director: The Making of Escape From L.A.

How did you end up directing special content such as featurettes, promo spots and EPKs [electronic press kits] for Paramount?

After graduating from USC film school, I started working in the Paramount marketing department and, for over twenty years, produced and directed BTS [behind the scenes] specials, promo spots and EPKs. All these elements were shot to promote our films and support additional products like DVDs. We had a great team of editors, sound mixers, and DVD producers working there as well.

How did you get the job of director of *The Making of Escape From L.A. - Snake is Back* as well as the EPK and how did you prepare for this project?

Escape From L.A. was picked as one of our projects because we knew *Escape From New York* was a popular movie, John Carpenter had a built-in-fanbase, and that Kurt Russell and the visual effects would be fun selling points. We mainly concentrated on the biggest films for that particular year and, as the on-set producer, I worked with my boss to figure out what aspects of production we wanted to emphasize, what days to cover with a camera crew, and who to interview to support our footage. The final shows we produced for HBO and Showtime were often thirty minutes in length. Today's audience has no patience for that kind of length, but it gave us a chance to really explore different parts of the production challenges for each movie.

How do you work on set to get the footage you want?

When shooting behind the scenes material on set, we always try to be as unobtrusive as possible. We don't generally ever stand in an actor's eyeline, place ourselves in the way of a dolly or tracking shot, and otherwise ignore the crew around us. That's because we know the most important thing happening on that set is getting the movie made. At the same time, to get great shots with camera references at the beginning or end of a shot, we need to work our way into positions where the crew and actors know we are there. We don't want to surprise the actors or filmmakers and thereby ruin a shot, but standing miles away across the street isn't going to get the material we need. Some people say shooting on set is ninety percent politics and ten percent shooting. You need to convince the producer, director, studio, actors, and crew that you will show due consideration for what they are trying to do while also shooting great BTS material.

A lot of that is accomplished by working out a plan before we arrive with the first AD [Assistant Director] about the ground rules for actors and the plan for that day of shooting. We don't seek to surprise people or shoot them in unexpected places. And the interviews are generally coordinated through an on-set publicist who serves as a liaison between the film and any crews visiting for publicity purposes. As far as the director and major star of the movie, we often interview them later when we have a better idea of how the movie plays and what sequences we want to emphasize in our conversation.

How often were you on set, what kind of challenges did this project provide, and how much footage did you film?

By the time we had completed all interviews, after production and special second unit shoots [like the miniature freeway collapse] [The Four-Level Interchange] as well as first unit coverage, we probably shot somewhere in the range of twenty-five to thirty days. I don't remember the number exactly as it was twenty-three years ago.

Do you still have the footage or does Paramount own it?

Paramount owns all the footage, which is probably in their deep mine vault somewhere in Pennsylvania. At least that's where we used to send material to be archived. We shot everything on tape for a project like this, not film or digital, and while the final BTS show is available to view on the internet, I don't know if the tapes themselves are still viewable or even still in existence. I didn't keep copies myself, so that's a question for the Paramount archives.

How was your experience working with the cast and crew?

I do remember the interview with Kurt Russell took place on set around 2 AM in the morning and the John Carpenter interview took place much later at Paramount during post-production. We usually do the directors last in the interview process as they have the most to tell. I was a big JC [John Carpenter] fan, so it was great fun to see him work on a set. He was always prepared, a little cantankerous, had a great dynamic with Kurt Russell due to their long-standing collaboration and was always a total pro who knew exactly what he needed to shoot. That was especially important as this movie shot for something like seventy nights and that is really hard on any crew. Luckily, JC was often ready to wrap by two or three AM because he was so efficient in getting his day completed. One sign of a less experienced director is being there to watch the sun come up. You can get away with it for a few days, but when you have seventy nights in a row, you have to get through as quickly as you can. As with the actors, maintaining the energy of the crew is an important factor in getting your movie made.

What's your favorite memory or memories of working on the movie?

Kurt Russell is one of the coolest cats ever on set and it was just fun to watch him work through this latest genre movie. The rest of the cast was fun too, especially Bruce Campbell [Surgeon General of Beverly Hills]. Also great to watch JC at work and see his dark and sinister spin applied to a studio feature film. The broad swagger and hatred of authority that define Snake Plissken are clearly present in John Carpenter himself. No surprise as he is the creator of the character.

I have always loved working on movies where miniatures were incorporated into a bigger visual FX plan as it is amazing to see what the craftspeople can create. In my opinion, this is one of the greatest losses in the transition to digital filmmaking where CGI is used to create everything. Just not the same.

Last, but by no means least, it was great to have the pleasure to sit down and ask John and Kurt all about the movie they made. I was also a big fan of Debra Hill [Producer/Co-Writer] who worked with JC starting with *Halloween*. She's no longer with us but was a great producer for JC and the production team.

What do you think of the movie personally?

It's a blast to watch. It's bold and fun. A full-on popcorn movie. Silly, dark, and dystopian. JC's send up of a future none of us ever really want to see. It's not quite as dark as *Escape From New York,* but still has some uniquely JC sequences like surfing the tidal wave, etcetera. And Snake Plissken is such a great character

I wouldn't be surprised if he makes an appearance someday again. I also have a great admiration for filmmakers like John Carpenter who have worked for decades to get their creative vision on film. That's so hard to do for so many reasons and takes real tenacity, vision, and most of all. TALENT. Personally, my all-time favorite JC is probably *The Thing*, a remake of the Howard Hawks movie from the 1950s also starring Kurt Russell. I am also a big fan of the first *Halloween* movie, *Escape From New York*, *Starman*, and *Big Trouble in Little China*. This guy has done it all, so do yourself a favor and seek out some of the movies he's directed on Netflix, Amazon, or at your local library. Don't forget. Beyond writing and directing these movies, in many cases, he was also the COMPOSER. An amazing range of talents.

What are you currently doing and what do you enjoy doing in your spare time?

I'm currently working as a freelance producer [I'm available!], raising my teenage son along with my wife and enjoying living in Southern California. I still love movies, still love watching behind the scenes featurettes and TV shows, and just wish I had been able to work on a Stanley Kubrick movie or two or maybe even a Billy Wilder movie! You get the idea. At the end of the day, the true goal is to make a great movie. Being on a lot of sets taught me how difficult that can be. I hope I was able to give you some insights into what it was like watching this movie get made. Thank you for your interest.

GREG GORMAN
Portrait Photographer

How did you end up being a portrait photographer?

I borrowed a friend's camera in 1968 to shoot a Jimi Hendrix concert in Kansas City. Then I was so fascinated when we processed the pictures that I enrolled in a photojournalism class at the University of Kansas where I majored in photography and photojournalism. Then I finished college at the University of Southern California in film and decided I was much more interested in doing stills, so I stayed with the stills but ended up being in the movie business.

How did you get the job of portrait photographer of Kurt Russell as Snake Plissken on *Escape From L.A.*?

How that happened is, I worked for Tony Seiniger, who ran the production house that specializes in doing motion picture campaigns. It also happened that Kurt Russell was a good friend of mine. It was a perfect situation. You know, they asked me to shoot the pictures and Kurt and I were friends.

How did you prepare for this project?

Basically, the comps [comprehensive layout] for the advertising campaign were given to me. They were drawings of what they wanted to create for the advertising campaign. They were supplied by the graphic arts house and, when Kurt came in and we finished hair and makeup, he saw the comps and then we were just kind of going through the different poses for the main character.

How was your experience working with Kurt Russell?

Well, Kurt's great. I mean, we were pals. We're both big wine drinking buddies. We both made wine together. I talk to Kurt all the time. We had fun. We drank some wine. We shot pictures. We hung out. It was a pretty amenable situation as friends, so it was quite easy.

Where were the photos taken, how long did it take to do the shoot, how many photos did you take, and what kind of challenges did this project provide?

They were shot in my studio in L.A., not on a movie set. The shoot probably took four hours, something like that. That was in the day of film, so I probably took a thousand pictures. It was all medium format, so big negatives. It was a pretty straight-forward shoot. Primarily, it was him in the foreground and a little bit of action going on in the background, which was just stuff that came from post-production and pictures that they took while the film was actually being shot.

What's your favorite photo or photos?

We shot different concepts for the poster. I love some of the stuff where he's on that motorcycle. It was a great prop, but there are other pictures that were just as good.

What's your favorite memory or memories of working on the movie?

I had just come back from Africa and my assistant came to visit. He had contracted a disease. He'd gotten bit by a tick when we were hiking in Africa. He came in for the shoot and was quite ill. I remember that. He could barely function, but he was my first assistant, so of course he came in to the shoot.

What do you think of the movie personally?

It's been so many years since I saw it, but it was a fun movie. It was a good action movie. Kurt's always been a great action hero on so many projects. Always fun to watch on the big screen.

What are you currently doing and what do you enjoy doing in your spare time?

In my spare time, I love to go fishing. I'm actually getting ready to leave. Tomorrow I'm shooting a documentary on me here. I'm not shooting it, but for a television show called *Spectrum*. In terms of current work, you know, with covid and everything, I actually have been working where I'm not shooting people. I've been basically photographing a bunch of my African art. I have a big collection of voodoo and fetish dolls. I'm finishing up a big book project on African case studies. That's what I've been working on pretty much and shooting. I just finished an album cover for Elton John. Things like that.

Designing Escapes:
An Interview with Lawrence G. Paull
by Marc Shapiro

When *Blade Runner* production designer Lawrence G. Paull signed on to ravage the City of Angels for John Carpenter's super-sequel *Escape From L.A.*, one of his most daunting tasks was to turn Los Angeles itself into an island. It wasn't as easy as you might think.

"I hung this map in my production office during the early stages of pre-production and I would walk in every day and see this thing glaring down at me," recalls Paull. "I was stuck. I didn't know how to do it. One day I walked in, picked up a grease pencil and carved out a line near the edge of a mountain range where I knew, in my head, that Los Angeles would break away. For the next week, I worked my way south. In my mind, the San Fernando Valley became the San Fernando Sea. Basically, what I did was pull Los Angeles away from the rest of the United States."

Once Paull accomplished this act of God, he saw the big *Escape* challenge as being how to depict an earthquake-wracked Los Angeles. "The script showed L.A. as being very dismal, bleak and totally trashed. The damage was totally encompassing," he says.

To get a feel for just what kind of damage earthquakes do, Paull turned to footage from actual earthquakes, in particular the massive quakes in Los Angeles and Kobe, Japan. "The one that had the most impact on me was the Kobe earthquake. In some areas, there was such utter devastation that it was not to be believed. I ended up designing a series of beats when Snake Plissken first comes into Los Angeles in which we show scenes of partial damage. While he's walking or driving through Hollywood, we see large piles of rubble, buildings boarded up and graffiti all over everything. When he leaves Hollywood Boulevard and goes over to Sunset Boulevard, it simply does not exist. All we see is a six-lane street with mounds of rubble lining both sides of the street."

Paull concedes that "it was the people concept of all this that really hooked me." And once again he turned to real life - his extensive travels in Egypt and the Far East - as the jumping-off point for life in Island L.A.

L-R/BG: William Hiney [Assistant Art Director], Carol Kiefer [Art Department Coordinator], Lawrence G. Paull [Production Designer], Patrick M. Sullivan Jr. [Set Designer], Nathan Crowley [Set Designer], Darrell L. Wight [Set Designer]/FG: Bruce Crone [Art Director] (Photo Courtesy Carol Kiefer)

"In those parts of the world, it's not uncommon for people to live in cardboard boxes in the streets or even in cemeteries. In Thailand, night marketplaces are very common. I ended up creating a multi-layered, textured visual style for the movie. I made this Los Angeles a night world with vendors selling food and drugs on the street and people living in shacks amidst all the rubble. There's very little power, so a lot of life is carried out in darkness. If *Escape From L.A.* really happened, what we've come up with is a pretty good conceptualization of how normal people would live under those circumstances."

Paull also took another look at *Escape From New York*. But, with the exception of some slight modifications of uniforms and vehicles, he took nothing away from that film. "They did New York and we're doing Los Angeles. The look was *always* going to be different. We also decided early on that this was going to be more of an adventure film than a futuristic one, so the technology we see is only slightly advanced. Most of what we see people is using is rooted in the not-too-distant future. This movie is probably closer to *Mad Max* than anything else."

Top: Concept Art [Downtown L.A.]
Middle: Concept Art [Firebase 7]
Bottom: Concept Art [Wilshire Canyon]
(Art Courtesy Fireball Tim / *FireballTim.com*)

The production designer - who also damaged a very Disneyland-like Happy Kingdom by the Sea with a major transformation of the Universal Studios lot - claims that the true impact of what we did to turn Los Angeles upside-down came during the sequence shot on the Sunset Boulevard location. "When people came out to the location, they were silent. There was a quality about what we had done that really scared them. Suddenly, the realization hit home that, 'My God! This could happen and we could end up living like this.'"

But the stark reality of his *Escape From L.A.* work is ultimately replaced by a childlike sense of accomplishment. "It has been wonderful," chuckles Lawrence Paull. "I've had a lot of fun trashing Los Angeles."

[*This article first appeared in* Starlog, *(Issue 230, Sep, 1996). It appears here courtesy of Tara Ansley at* Fangoria.]

Escape Artists:
An Interview with Gary B. Kibbe
by Michael X. Ferraro

When it comes to big gambles, you can forget about Las Vegas: Los Angeles is the home of the ultimate game of change - a geological crapshoot in which the dice bounce off the Santa Monica Mountains and the Hollywood Freeway serves as the Don't Pass line. Yes, we're talking about the ever-present threat of the ultimate disaster: a cataclysmic earthquake, aka The Big One.

Although Los Angeles is nestled near an active line that could do with a world-class face lift, it remains an irresistible lure to the world's big dreamers, for whom the risks of relocating are always outweighed by the potential rewards. As Christopher Rand opined in his 1967 book *Los Angeles: The Ultimate City*, "There are other cities on the West Coast, but... none so imbued with the Northern willfulness in battling nature." Now, some fifteen years after his bleak, Manhattan-based actioner *Escape From New York*, director John Carpenter, which offers a cocktail party-premise come true: What if Los Angeles were chipped off the edge of the continent and became an island?

"We'd been talking about a sequel since 1985, but never came up with the right story for L.A.," Carpenter admits. The director credits the star of both films and his longtime friend, Kurt Russell [producer and co-writer on the new *Escape*, along with writer/producer Debra Hill], for reviving the dormant idea and helping to create another adventure for his cinematic alter ego, scruffy anti-hero Snake Plissken. "We thought about what L.A. has been through in the 90s: earthquakes, mud slides, fires, riots, drive-by shootings. Basically, it's pretty fruitful material. A lot of people living here are in denial. It's such a beautiful place, but we all live on the edge of this incredible earthquake fault and we never leave. From that premise, we worked our way into the story."

Although *Escape From L.A.* is not without its political and satirical sides, Carpenter notes that "the action part is the action part. Like Ulysses, [Snake] has to go through several adventures to get back home again and save his life, and those are the things that compel you through the film."

L-F/FG: John Carpenter [Director/Co-Writer/Co-Composer], Erica Pearce
[Production Assistant], Gary B. Kibbe [Director of Photography]
(Photo Courtesy Erica Pearce)

While writing the post-quake, "nihilistic cowboy noir movie" Carpenter and his
co-writers simply surveyed a map of Los Angeles and began to plot Plissken's
perils. Says the director, "We just sat down and said, 'Okay, he starts here.' He
goes under the 'San Fernando Sea' and through the various areas of Los Angeles.
We then decided the kinds of things we wanted him to encounter - earthquakes,
fires, etcetera. We then worked them into the story. It was a little bit like pins on
a map, if you know what I mean."

The story is set in 2013, years after a massive quake has turned Los
Angeles into an island. The rest of the country has become a militant theocracy,
and the ocean-encircled City of Los Angeles serves as a deportation center for
the "morally guilty," which Carpenter defines as "people like abortion doctors,
prostitutes, atheists - anybody who doesn't fit into this new, moral America."

As it turns out, the President's rebellious daughter [A.J. Langer] has
stolen a doomsday device and delivered it to Cuervo Jones [George Corraface],
the charismatic leader of a Peruvian gang who is unifying Third World countries

for an attack on the U.S. "They want theirs before everything is used up," Carpenter explains. "They want power, and everything else we have here in the United States."

Snake's mission, of course, is to get this doomsday device back and prevent further catastrophe. As the story begins, we learn that Plissken has been gunfighting for profit in New Vegas, Thailand ["Doesn't that sound like a happy place?" Carpenter asks]. He is soon enlisted, against his will, to save the world.

Carpenter's task was quite the opposite, as he was forced to trash the place he's called home for the past twenty-eight years. "I love it here," the Kentucky native-turned-Angeleno says with a sheepish grin. "I love the environment, I love the city, I love the architecture. But I wanted to do to L.A. what we did to New York [in the first film], which was to have a great time with it in a cynical, sarcastic way, and point out some of the things that L.A. has become - at least in this dark future of ours. So, it's a mixed, love/hate kind of deal."

Carpenter exhibits no such ambivalence in his professional relationship with cinematographer Gary Kibbe, who has now worked on eight of the director's films [six as cinematographer]. The partnership began in the mid-80s, at Carpenter's behest.

"John has been instrumental in my career from the beginning," says Kibbe, who was working as a camera operator before their paths crossed. After having lit and shot one set for the director's longtime cameraman, Dean Cundey, ASC, on *Big Trouble in Little China* [Cundey had previously photographed Carpenter's *Halloween*, *The Fog*, *Escape From New York*, and *The Thing*], Kibbe recalls that he "got a phone call [from a third party] who told me that John wanted to have lunch with me at Tiny Naylor's on Sunset. I went down and he introduced himself and said, 'I'd like you to do my next two pictures - as a cinematographer.' I was floored by all this. He told me what all his needs were from a cameraman, and asked me if I wanted to do it. Naturally, I was more than happy to."

The duo's first theatrical projects were *Prince of Darkness* and *They Live*, followed by the Showtime anthology project *Body Bags*, *In the Mouth of Madness*, and a remake of *Village of the Damned*.

Prior to his stroke of good fortune, Kibbe was no stranger to movie sets - the Studio City native was a regular studio baby. "My interest in camerawork started when I was nine years old, at Hal Roach Studios," Kibbe recalls. "My dad was involved in special photographic effects for years at Republic Pictures, RKO, and then wound up at Hal Roach. He used to take me to the set. I think the day that opened my eyes to the film world, other than what I did with my box camera [an old-fashioned Brownie that he carried religiously], was the day he put me on the back of the camera at *The Gale Storm Show* - a TV series in the 50s. As soon as I grabbed the wheels of the camera, it just set off a spark. Of course, "he chuckles," it was also nice to look at a pretty face. That had an influence, too."

At eighteen, Kibbe began an invaluable eleven-year employment at Warner Bros. that allowed him to cut his teeth and learn from the masters of the cinematographic craft. After stints in the mailroom, accounting and casting departments, Kibbe made the transition to the camera department, where his heart had always been. "But back then," he says, "you really had to be the son of a cameraman to get work." Starting out as a film-loader, he began the slow climb up the industry ladder, spending twelve years as an operator. "I worked with a lot of cameramen and directors," he says, ticking off a "dream team" list of mentors that includes such ASC luminaries as Cundey, Sven Nykvist, Lazlo Kovacs, William Fraker, Owen Roizman, and Andrew Laszlo.

Kibbe proudly recalls that his first job came under the guidance of two-time Academy Award winner Burnett Guffy, ASC on *Suppose They Gave a War and Nobody Came?* [1970].

All of this education paid off when Carpenter came calling. "Gary's been around a long time, he's a terrific operator, and I felt he deserved the chance," says Carpenter. "He has an enormous ability inside of him that you can't really quantify. He can really light scenes. The old cliché is, 'like a painter.' That Gary truly is. There are a number of really brilliant cameramen out there, and I've worked with a few of them - including Dean Cundey, Bill Fraker, and Gary - who have a vision and a sense of how light should fall on a performer and objects. And as a director, that's what I need: a cinematographer, if you know what I'm saying. My contribution to the look of a movie is the lenses, the movement - I can do all of that. But the lighting, the cinematography of the movie, is extremely important, and it has to be done with both professionalism and an artist's touch. And that's what I get [with Gary]."

Kibbe's artistic practicality does seem to be a nice fit for Carpenter's often epic projects, which are frequently shot on less-than-epic budgets. At fifty million, *Escape From L.A.* is the most expensive film of Carpenter's career [more than seven times costlier than *Escape From New York*], but it's a comparative bargain when compared to similarly scaled summer action films.

According to Kibbe, the key to keeping costs down [especially when shooting in the more light-hungry anamorphic 2:35:1 format, as Carpenter always does] is extensive preproduction preparation, and a thorough knowledge of the equipment at hand. The cinematographer marvels at the director's all-around filmmaking attack, noting, "John does the music, the writing, and the directing, which really helps. Perhaps that's why he's able to pull these pictures off in such an incredibly short time. He also gives me a lot of freedom which is nice.

"Certainly, there are times when you can only do certain things under the given conditions. Time is an issue. How long does it take to get your equipment in and out, and get the work done for the day? Sure, you'd love to have a Musco [for every big exterior], but we don't have the budget for that, so we have to come up with new ideas. Sometimes simplicity is better than [using] a lot of exotic pieces of equipment. Sometimes just one source and a little fill light is all you need.

"Overkill is quite prevalent in the business today," Kibbe continues, "and the budgets show it. A lot of shows go on without sitting down and asking, 'How much is this [piece of equipment] going to cost us to carry on the whole picture - for fifteen to sixteen weeks at $1,000 a week - when we only need to use it two or three times?' In my experience with John, we've never been in a situation where we've had carte blanche. For one reason or another, we've always been restricted, but that's fine."

Even armed with the arsenal a fifty million budget can provide, and the unlimited potential of a 21st-century Los Angeles tableaux, Carpenter chose not to make a wildly futuristic, effects-laden tale. Set almost exactly as far in the future as its predecessor [*Escape From New York* was released in 1981 and set in 1997; the sequel comes out in '96, and is set in 2013], *Escape From L.A.* is not so much sci-fi as it is an adventure which happens to be set in the next century.

Explains Carpenter, "It's just the day after tomorrow in the future. It's not like *Star Wars* or *Star Trek*, where things are so advanced. We don't have spaceships zooming around in this movie. The world is still very familiar to us, but the action takes place after the earthquake, so what we had to do was create a destroyed Los Angeles."

Prior to the initial location scout, the director figured that Los Angeles would offer plenty of pre-existing urban blight in the city to help guide the production, but he was a bit surprised by the scarcity of such areas. He recalls, "We looked around L.A. at night and discovered that, even in the most devastated areas, it looks pretty nice. There are palm trees, and so on. It's really hard to make that look devastated. So, for the most part, we figured that we had to create that feeling ourselves."

A driving force in this process was production designer Lawrence Paull [*Blade Runner*], who had previously worked with Carpenter on *Memoirs of an Invisible Man*. Together, they attempted to simultaneously build and crumble down the "instant island" that Los Angeles has become in the film.

"This was much different than *Blade Runner*," says Paull. "The challenge was portraying L.A. as an earthquake-ridden island in a realistic, yet stylized way. I've done a lot of traveling, and when I read the script, I thought of areas in Egypt and China, where you see the lifestyles of people hanging on by their fingernails, literally living on the edge of existence. That was how I wanted to depict this L.A. - people living in hovels, with black markets selling food, weapons, clothing, all at night. John wanted to make it realistic enough to bring home [to audiences] a feeling of 'This could really happen here.'"

Toward that end, research provided recent photos chronicling the aftermath of huge temblors in Kobe, Japan, and India. "Let me tell you, we just don't realize the kind of damage that was done [over there]," Carpenter reports with a low, respectful whistle.

Of course, Angelenos know a thing or two about earthquakes, and Paull drew on a few not-too-distant memories to add to the film's authenticity. "What stuck in my head from the 1994 quake were these huge piles of rubble that sat on the sides of the road, and became almost mountains," Paull recalls. "So we constructed fifty to sixty piles and put them on wood rollers."

Since the cinematic upheaval has rendered L.A. an island, the massive pileups on the freeway, long abandoned, have evolved into makeshift shantytowns. Snake has to sneak into the city via submarine ["Jules Verne-style," says Paull] through the "San Fernando Sea." En route, his one-man craft passes many famous landmarks, including the Hollywood sign and the Capitol Records building, which are now underwater. Much visual trickery went into pulling off this and many other sequences in the film, which employed over 140 CGI shots, as well as extensive green screen, miniatures, and matte work.

Having shot before and during Hollywood's special effects revolution, Kibbe is an unabashed proponent of modern CGI wizardry. "I have great admiration for the people in the opticals and effects [departments]," he says. "They make a lot of movies what they are. The basic bottom line doesn't change, it's just the applications, and the tools facilitate that."

In addition to the film's CGI work, Kibbe says, "We have some miniature shots - cars falling off multiple levels [of the freeway] during an earthquake - that I defy you to pick out. It's incredible what [effects experts] can do."

Mixing up the approaches worked both creatively and financially for the filmmakers. "All of these different [visual] contributions from different areas makes the film, as a whole, much more believable," states Kibbe. The sentiment is echoed by Paull, who concentrated on "building a texture of humanity." The designer contends that "there are a rash of films now exclusively using CGI, and it seems very obvious."

Carpenter explains that when it comes to "effects shots, what we do first is to ask ourselves, 'Okay, what's the best way to tell the story? How many shots is it going to require, and what's the money going to be like?' We compare that to what money we have and then make a compromise. We'll combine shots together so there aren't four shots here, there's one. But in the end, everything is predicated on storytelling."

Once the film's intricate sequences were plotted out, it was up to Kibbe, and his crew [along with Paull's department and the effects team] to execute them. Shooting in anamorphic - the rule on Carpenter pictures - Kibbe went multi-camera with his Panavision packages. He always had at least two operators on hand to shoot a given scene, "and sometimes as many as eight," he relates.

"We had a Panaglide that we used every day," Kibbe continues. "John is one of the pioneers of using the Panaglide; he loves it. All that camera motion in *Halloween* was great stuff."

Kibbe initially wanted to shoot the film on Kodak's 5287 stock, "but it was something like fifty cents a foot more, so I went to ninety-six, which is a wonderful film." The production used 5247 for the few daylight scenes, and ninety-three for all of the green screen needs.

Kibbe's entire crew, including A-camera operator Jud Kehl, Steadicam operator Chris Squires, gaffer Norm Glasser, key grip Charles Saldana and first assistant Steve Peterson, as well as stunt coordinator Jeff Imada - earned high praise from Carpenter and the cinematographer for their work, especially taking into account a nocturnal schedule that encompassed almost seventy nights.

"Everything had to be lit," Kibbe relates. "We didn't have the sun there to back us up. That was a challenge, but it also gave us the ability to create a look and enhance it, and make it as pretty as we wanted - and with less light, because all we were doing was adding light to darkness. So that in itself presents a lot of interesting moods, depending on where you are and what you're actually lighting - sets, alleys or open fields."

Indeed, there was no escaping L.A. for the crew, who shot in all corners of the metropolitan area - from the Sepulveda Basin's Water Reclamation Plant to the famous Courthouse Square on Universal's backlot, "which we turned to rubble," Kibbe says with a smile. "We had a great deal of variety, but we also had to keep everything on schedule."

While *Escape From L.A.* is similar in tone to its predecessor, the filmmakers chose to eschew the almost all-blue lighting scheme of the original - a look which Carpenter says has become, in the years since, "an action-movie cliché."

According to Kibbe, the West Coast setting also dictated a wider palette of light, including some ambers and oranges. He details, "We went for a little bit more reality. I thought about a combination of both [color approaches], and John totally agreed. We thought about using a backlight with a blue cast, or decreasing the intensity [of the blue look]. We'd use a blue with incandescents, but you can still feel it. There are also a lot of bonfires and torches [in the film], which make the [warmer lighting] more realistic. For all the night exteriors, I'd use a blue 12K, and throw on a half CTO. I generally shot at around twenty footcandles - on 5296, that comes to an f2.8."

Even though he had a Musco on all the large outdoor sets, and "a tremendous rigging crew" that tackled a huge job with almost 10,000 feet of cable [as well as five generators going at the vast Sunset Boulevard set in Carson City], Kibbe submits that he is often hesitant to use complex lighting rigs or to light too brightly. "What are you really saying by doing that?" he poses rhetorically. "Often, it decreases the audience's imagination. The darker the tunnel, the scarier it gets."

This less-is-more style of cinematography jibes well with Carpenter. While the director intricately storyboards for his effects shots, he points out that "a lot the visualization for a movie comes from instinct, from inside. It's based on how to tell the story, and how you want the audience to see it. And that particular part of filmmaking is 'directing.' If you don't direct the visuals, you're not directing at all.

"There are a lot of things that you can line up [beforehand]," Carpenter continues. "But I really don't know everything until I'm actually on the set, looking at it and saying, 'Okay, let's try this...' There are a lot of last-minute adjustments. What you thought was going to work sometimes doesn't, so you have to turn the camera around and try it another way. That's just part of the business.

In many ways, Carpenter is using this new production to finally realize his original vision for *Escape From New York*. "Essentially, this film's structure closely resembles that of the original," he says. "It's just a chance to do it in a bigger way. It's like George Lucas said after making *The Return of the Jedi*: 'That's the movie I wanted to make.' He finally had some money."

For his part, Kibbe is glad that his travels with Carpenter have continued. "From a cinematic standpoint, I think doing these types of pictures gives you the ability to do a lot of things that you wouldn't be able to on other types of stories," he says. "You get into a lot of fantasy, in terms of creating really bizarre moods and environments. There are a lot of situations in *Escape* that just don't present themselves in a conventional movie. I'm happy doing what I'm doing."

[*This article first appeared in* American Cinematographer *(Vol 77, Issue 9, Sep, 1996). It appears here courtesy David Williams.*]

Escape From L.A.:
An Interview with Shirley Walker
by Daniel Schweiger

In 1997, an antihero named Snake Plissken took us on an unrelenting tour of a penitentiary called Manhattan. Guiding him through this future hell was the music of director/composer John Carpenter, a self-taught synthesist who'd been playing his own scores since *Dark Star, Assault on Precinct 13* and *Halloween*. His eerie music for *Escape From New York*, written in association with Alan Howarth, turned the decaying Big Apple into a haunted jailhouse. It was a spare electronic atmosphere that would become the soundtrack for many Orwellian action fantasies to come.

Cut to 2013. This time the asylum is post-apocalyptic Los Angeles, a new place for our fascist government to send its exiles. And once again, Snake Plissken is back in urban hell, at the bidding of an even slimier President [Cliff Robertson]. Synth music once again guides Snake, but this time it's fuller, weirder - more fun. There's a different vibe going on here, one that tells John Carpenter's fans that Shirley Walker is along for the ride. Together, they've expanded the musical style of *Escape From New York* into a unique fusion of computer samples and ethnic instruments, all topped off with the blast of a full orchestra.

Scoring Hollywood action pictures had been a guy's playground until Shirley Walker got into the testosterone game. An instrumentalist who worked her way up through the system, Walker would gain recognition for her orchestrating and conducting work with such star composers as Brad Fiedel [*True Lies*], Hans Zimmer [*Backdraft*] and Danny Elfman [*Batman*]. Before she would score such TV shows as *Space: Above & Beyond* and *Batman: The Animated Series*, Walker was given her cinematic break by John Carpenter on *Memoirs of an Invisible Man*. This successful, symphonic collaboration made her the ideal composer to help Carpenter redefine the sound for Snake's greatest *Escape*.

L-R/FG: Shirley Walker [Co-Composer/Conductor],
John Carpenter [Director/Co-Writer/Co-Composer]
(Photo Courtesy Dana Ross)

John, how did you begin collaborating with Shirley Walker?

John Carpenter: It was a leap of faith for me to use another composer on *Memoirs of an Invisible Man*, and I was amazingly rewarded by Shirley Walker. She wrote sketches of the themes, sent them to me on cassette, and they turned out great. It's a director's dream to have a score like that dropped in your lap. I wanted a large orchestral feel for *Escape From L.A.* Because that kind of sound isn't my strong point, I wanted to team up with a composer who had the symphonic experience. Shirley was the first person I thought of, and she said, "Why not? Let's do it!"

Shirley Walker: *Escape From L.A.* was fun for me because I knew the score that John and Alan Howarth had composed for *Escape From New York*. This sequel was an opportunity to go away from the big orchestral stuff that everybody in town knows that I can do. *Escape From L.A.* gave me the opportunity to make a bridge to another style, starting with an homage to John Carpenter. His music is very direct, minimalist, and synthy. At our first meeting, we talked about retaining that quality for *Escape From L.A.*, while bringing in a symphonic element. Though it's there throughout the score, the orchestra really becomes noticeable halfway through the film, and builds exponentially from there.

Did you sit together at a piano to come up with the score?

Carpenter: I'm not going to sit at the piano and tell Shirley what to do. She's a much more accomplished musician than I am. I'm kind of street musician. I don't read music; I improvise a lot. What we did was divide the score up into who was going to compose what. Then I sketched out various cues, and gave them to Shirley to fill out my ideas. It was a great process, because I didn't have to work!

Walker: John would send over a tape of his music, and my assistant, Kris Carter, would put those synth sketches against the film picture. Then I'd have an orchestrator transcribe the material, which let me see where John's music was going. I could re-write it, and pick up the tempo if I felt the scene needed more drive. I basically tailored John's material to fit the picture. We'd often write music away from the picture. I composed "Motorcycle Chase" when I was in Vermont for the weekend. I took my computer and one synth, and I guess it was all of those frogs on the beaver pond that drove me to that groove! I came back with fifteen minutes of music, and practically all of it became part of the score.

How did you come up with this new version of the *Escape From New York* theme?

Carpenter: It was written in 1981, when Alan and I were using Prophets and other old synthesizers. I wanted to reprise that motif for *Escape From L.A.* and bring its sound up to date with the latest musical technology. Tom Milano, our music editor, tracked the melody lines from the original film into the sequel's opening. Because the theme was a little slow, we re-sequenced it and sped up the tempo.

Walker: My challenge was to change the theme without distorting it. I did a demo version of it on my computer. When John heard it, he said, "This is always the way I wanted the theme to sound." When I went into the studio, I tried to give it more of an industrial vibe. But John preferred my first approach, so I peeled off the layers of what I'd added until we had it sounding right with a simpler synth sound and a guitar.

The electronic sound of *Escape From L.A.* is very close to the original.

Carpenter: The synthesists brought that industrial quality to the film. I write and perform my musical sketches on a Korg XR3, which doesn't have the power that these guys put out with their racks of synthesizers. They create these awesome, thick sounds.

Walker: We had Jamie Mulhoberac, who's Seal's music director. He's an atmosphere specialist, and had all of these unbelievable strange sounds. He loaded them into a keyboard, then manipulated the samples. You can really hear his work during the "Motorcycle Chase" cue. We also had Nyle Steiner on board. He's the creator of the electronic valve instrument, which works completely on breath control. It has a humanness that can't be duplicated by samples. Then we had Mike Fisher doing the electronic percussion. I wanted something different from the sounds he usually provides, and Mike tore his hair out until he figured out what I was looking for! He ended up doing great stuff. Our principal keyboard synthesist was Mike Watts, who had the difficult job of carrying over my sounds into his system. They're the heart and soul of my electronic music, so I wanted to keep them. Mike built his own sounds upon that foundation. These people were the real orchestrators of the electronic score.

John, the scores you've written, and have collaborated on, have always been electronic. Why did you want to go in a symphonic direction for *Escape From L.A.?*

Carpenter: Film scores have become really big, complicated, and vast. There's a Hollywood style that I've always stayed away from. Shirley describes me as a minimalist in terms of my music. I use a lot of repetitive lines, as opposed to the Max Steiner mickey-mousing that everybody does now. But when you're making a big Hollywood film like *Escape From L.A.*, you have to reach out to the audience. So I wanted to combine an orchestral feel, which I really don't have in my scores, with an electronic sound.

Walker: I usually respond automatically to what I'm seeing on the screen. I used to think, "If it's fast, it's loud. If it's a sunrise, then it's soft." But John's approach made me think about what would happen if my music didn't play everything. This score demanded a new discipline from me, and it was wonderful.

How did you combine the orchestral element with the synthesizers?

Carpenter: We decided early on that the score would be a combination of synthesizers and the orchestra. But after the first pass, we knew that more music was needed. Shirley said "no problem," and we both went out and wrote. It worked out well.

Walker: Combining the synthesizers and orchestral instruments required a lot of detailed thinking. John can't take that on when he's busy finishing the film. He needs the musical focus that a specialist like myself can provide. We didn't have to change our minds about where the symphonic music would happen. That was lucky, especially since we came back and added another thirteen minutes of score.

Tell me about Snake Plissken's new theme.

Walker: When it comes to heroes and film music, a lot of people want to hear this big orchestral "da da da da duhhh!" It's got to be big chords, big brass, big percussion and all of that stuff. John had written a great, new theme for Snake Plissken, and I was excited that he was willing to consider using the harmonica and hammer-dulcimer for it. When we put those instrumental colors together, John and I went "Yeah! This is a western, this guy's a gunfighter and an outlaw!" That was the most enjoyable part of the collaboration for me.

Carpenter: *Escape From L.A.* is cowboy noir.

Hearing the harmonica and dulcimer over Snake adds a lot of humor to the score.

Carpenter: Well, there's a lot of humor to the movie. *Escape From L.A.* is an adventure that keeps you riveted to the screen, but doesn't take itself too seriously. It's a dark, dark film, yet you find yourself laughing through it. I think that's what we brought to the music. It's not a happy, peppy score, but we're having a good time with it.

Walker: Thank God we have a similar sense of humor! I'd call it "head humor." It's this sly, sardonic wit, and you can hear it in the scene where Cuervo Jones drives into the Happy Kingdom with this Latin beat. It's fun, and rocking at the same time.

How did you want the music to take the audience on a journey through L.A.?

Walker: I think the audience already knows Snake's character and what he's gone through. This film puts Snake into a new environment, which is L.A. after the Earthquake. Snake's never been there, and I wanted the music to do something different every time he turns around. It's not just a different street he's on. It's a different universe. It's as if the music is playing Snake's thought process. It has to figure out what the ground rules are so he can get from Point A to Point B, and survive.

Top: L-R: John Carpenter [Director/Co-Writer/Co-Composer],
Shirley Walker [Co-Composer/Conductor]
Bottom: FG: Shirley Walker [Co-Composer/Conductor]
(Photos Courtesy Dana Ross)

Carpenter: *Escape From L.A.* uses the classic story of a character's odyssey. The hero has to go on a mission to a completely alien world, then bring back something that will transform society. But while that plot sounds like Joseph Campbell a hundred times over, the difference here is that our story stars a psychopath. Snake Plissken's a killer, the baddest guy in the world. But when you think about it, Snake's an innocent victim who's forced to assassinate the President's daughter. The movie was written and plotted along the map of Los Angeles, and the score pulls listeners into a new environment with every corner that Snake turns. He goes into a very dark and strange city, and we needed to bring the audience along with a dark and strange score.

At one point, there's an interesting "Gypsy" sound to the music.

Walker: That represents Sunset Boulevard. Snake blows away this pesky guy who's been following him, then walks over a hill and sees this bazaar. There are people trading things and cooking in the open. John had temped the scene with world music, which gave me the idea of Sunset Boulevard as a gathering place for the third world, the people who've been herded together by the government.

What other instrumental and character motifs does the score feature?

Walker: The primary theme uses a harmonica, a hammer-dulcimer, and guitars for Snake. But as the score went along, we expanded the grooves, and went pretty far out with the idea of using a Jew's harp. Then there's a "death chime," which signifies the moral police in America's future. I didn't use snare drums or a typical military sound, because I wanted to get across the idea of a fascist, religious majority that's taken over the country. Their sound isn't about war. It's about God. So in certain moments, that "death chime" just steps right in and slams you in the face. I also wrote a theme for Snake. While John's identified his character, mine could go in a different musical direction, which became "Snake's Challenge."

Carpenter: The music represents what Snake's up against, and I just loved it. It's my favorite theme in the film. We hear it for the first time when Snake gets into the submarine. It starts out as a little synth piece with a horn feel. But by the end, it's a full orchestral piece for the attack on the Happy Kingdom, with Snake flying above it.

John, as a director-musician, what's it like to watch someone else do the composing for your film?

Carpenter: It feels absolutely wonderful. The scores that I co-wrote for my last two films, *In the Mouth of Madness* and *Village of the Damned*, were very arduous. I described myself to Shirley as a "carpet guy." I lay down music to support scenes. I couldn't have pulled *Escape From L.A.* off, because this is a film that's more "muscular" and driving than anything I've composed for. I can hear my work in there, but at the same time, Shirley has made it bigger and better. I've never heard a score that's like this before.

Walker: This was a much more active collaboration for us than *Memoirs of an Invisible Man*. That was the traditional process of a director talking about the dramatic necessities, and the composer coming up with all of the music. *Escape From L.A.* allowed both of us to come up with and share ideas. There was a fluidity to our collaboration that I rarely experience as a composer. Traditionally we're overwhelmed with the process of finishing the movie. But on *Escape From L.A.*, John and I were having fun tooling around when we were supposed to be getting the movie done!

Will you continue working together in the future?

Carpenter: I'd love to work with Shirley again, but I don't think I'll get the chance. Everyone will be snatching her up after *Escape From L.A.*

Walker: I'll be doing *Turbulence* next, which is MGM's big Christmas film. It has a very attractive story to me as a woman. In one respect, *Turbulence* is a thriller set on an airplane. But the film's core idea is that females have a tendency to victimize themselves in their relationships with men. The story begins with the heroine breaking up with her boyfriend, and then she has to deal with a psychotic killer and save the day! I don't know what the rest of the future will hold for me after *Turbulence*, but if John calls and asks me to do another film, I'll certainly consider it. *Escape From L.A.* has allowed me to write music that's completely different from anything I've composed before.

[*This article first appeared in* Film Score Monthly *(Issue 72, Aug, 1996). It appears here courtesy Daniel Schweiger.*]

MEMORABILIA

Film Crew T-Shirt
(Courtesy Joe Diaz)

Location Manager Sweatshirt
(Courtesy Gregory H. Alpert)

Stirber Visual Network, Inc. Special Effects Crew Sweatshirt
(Courtesy Les Bernstien)

Film Crew Jacket
(Courtesy David Witz)

Visual Effects Crew Jacket
(Courtesy Joey "Deluxe" Enyart)

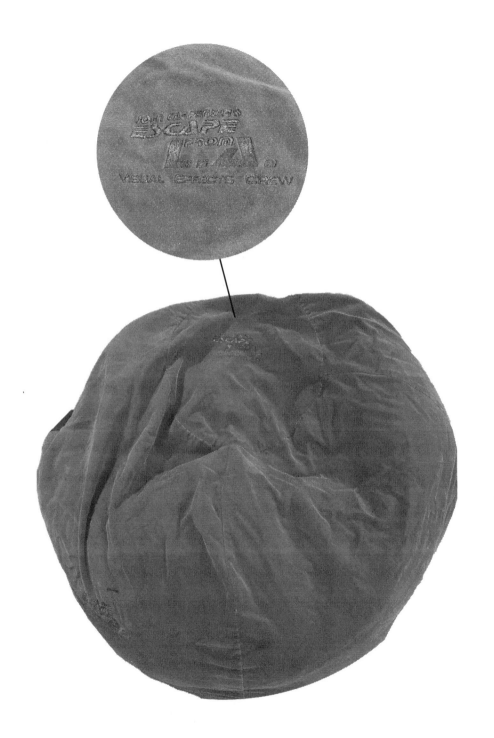

Visual Effects Crew Bean Bag
(Courtesy Brian Keeney)

Film Crew Backpack
(Courtesy Denise Davis)

Film Crew Cap
(Courtesy Jerome Fauci)

Gregory Alpert
Location Manager
"Escape From LA"

Paramount Pictures

Motion Picture Group

5555 Melrose Avenue
Hollywood, CA 90038-3197
213-956-5388 Fax 213-862-1200
Pager: 213-303-6365

Top: Film Crew Sticker (Courtesy Brian Keeney)
Bottom: Film Crew Business Card (Courtesy Gregory H. Alpert)

Film Crew Badge
(Courtesy Shyam "Toast" Yadav)

JOHN CARPENTER'S

ESCAPE FROM "ESCAPE FROM L.A."

AT THE...

WRAP PARTY

Sunday, March 24, 1996

8PM - Midnight

B.B. KING'S BLUES CLUB

1000 UNIVERSAL CENTER DRIVE.

2ND LEVEL CENTER COURT AT UNIVERSAL CITYWALK.

(818-622-5464)

 hors d'oeuvres 8 pm - 10 pm

 liquor, beer and wine 8 pm - midnight

 live music, dancing and schmoozing all night

By invitation only. One guest only please.

Parking Structure is 6 bucks (sorry, we couldn't make a deal!)

Valet parking is $3 for 2 hours with validation ($1.50 each additional 1/2 hour)

RSVP IS MANDATORY.

To add your name to the Guest List, please call 213-956-2500 by March 20.

DIRECTIONS TO B.B. KING'S BLUES CLUB

FROM HOLLYWOOD
1. 101 (Hollywood Fwy.) North
2. Exit Universal Center. Turn right.
3. Go through intersection at top of hill.
4. Turn left into parking structure.

FROM THE VALLEY / PASADENA
1. 101 (Hollywood Fwy) South
2. Exit Lankershim Blvd. Turn left.
3. Go to Universal Center Drive. Turn left.
4. Go through intersection at top of hill.
5. Turn left into parking structure.

5555 Melrose Avenue Trailer 9 Los Angeles California 90038 FAX 213-862-1200 TEL 213-956-5388

Wrap Party Invitation

(Courtesy Shyam "Toast" Yadav)

ESCAPE!

...to the Hollywood Hills
for BUENA VISTA VISUAL EFFECTS'
ESCAPE FROM LA wrap party

JULY 20, 1996
7pm-12am

WATTLES MANSION
1824 N. Curson Ave.

RSVP by July 16
818·560·2735

Bring a guest!   Watch the sunset!   Valet provided

Buena Vista Visual Effects Wrap Party Invitation Card
(Courtesy Shyam "Toast" Yadav)

Paramount Pictures
Cordially Invites You and a Guest
to the Cast & Crew Screening of

JOHN CARPENTER'S

Saturday, August 3, 1996
7:30 P.M.

Paramount Theatre
5555 Melrose Avenue
(enter Bronson gate)

R.S.V.P. to 213/956-2275
by Wednesday, July 31, 1996.

NON-TRANSFERABLE.

Paramount Pictures
Cordially Invites You and a Guest
to Attend The Premiere of

KURT RUSSELL

JOHN CARPENTER'S

Wednesday, August 7th
7:30 P.M.

Mann Chinese Theatre
6925 Hollywood Boulevard
Hollywood

A party to immediately follow the screening.

R.S.V.P. to 213/956-4880

Tickets of admission will be mailed to you.
This invitation is non-transferable.

Left: Cast/Crew Screening Invitation Folder (Courtesy William Luduena)
Right: Premiere Invitation Folder (Courtesy Alexander Büttner)

Mauritz Pavoni [Production Assistant]
(Photo Courtesy Mauritz Pavoni)

A NOTE ON SOURCES

The following original interviews were conducted by author Andreas Johansson between 2011 and 2024. The authors of any archival interviews in this book have been noted in the byline where the articles themselves appear.

Coleman Luck [Commissioned Script Writer] [2011/Email]

Peter Briggs [Speculative Script Writer] [2016/Email]

Stacy Keach [Malloy] [2018/Email]

Valeria Golino [Taslima] [2019/Phone]

Georges Corraface [Cuervo Jones] [2017/Phone]

Leland Orser [Test Tube] [2015/Email]

Edward A. Warschilka [Editor] [2020/Email]

Robin Michel Bush [Costume Designer] [2018/Email]

Peter Jason [Duty Sergeant] [2017/Phone]

Jordan Baker [Police Anchor] [2016/Email]

Robert Carradine [Skinhead] [2023/Phone]

Shelly Desai [Cloaked Figure] [2020/Phone]

William Luduena [Mescalito] [2018/Email]

Mark Thompson [Guard] [2022/Phone]

Michael Dawson [Extra] [2016/Email]

John Sencio [Extra/MTV Host] [2015/Email]

Johnny Torres [Extra] [2020/Email]

John Casino [Stunt Player] [2015/Phone]

James Lew [Stunt Player] [2023/Email]

David Witz [Unit Production Manager] [2017/Email]

Christian P. Della Penna [First Assistant Director] [2017/Phone]

Martin Jedlicka [Second Assistant Director] [2016/Email]

Jeffrey Berk [Production Coordinator] [2021/Phone]

Leo Napolitano [Camera Operator] [2020/Phone]

Jerome Fauci [Camera Operator] [2016/Email]

Mark J. Coyne [Second Assistant Photographer] [2021/Email]

Robert Zuckerman [Still Photographer] [2015/Phone]

Jason Roberts [Second Second Assistant Director] [2017/Email]

Patrick M. Sullivan Jr. [Set Designer] [2018/Email]

Carol Kiefer [Art Department Coordinator] [2017/Email]

Fireball Tim [Illustrator] [2015/Email]

Joseph Musso [Illustrator] [2021/Email]

Gina DeDomenico [Illustrator] [2016/Email]

Robert Zullo [Second Company Rigging Grip] [2021/Email]

Donald Flick [Sound Effects Editor] [2023/Email]

Ron Bartlett [Re-Recording Mixer] [2023/Email]

Karin Costa [Assistant to Director] [2016/Email]

Mauritz Pavoni [Production Assistant] [2016/In Person]

Ken Lavet [Location Manager] [2023/Email]

David Thornsberry [Location Manager] [2023/Email]

Gregory H. Alpert [Location Manager] [2024/Email]

Joseph Yuss Simon [Special Makeup Effects] [2017/Email]

Brian Keeney [Visual Effects Coordinator] [2020/Phone]

Les Bernstien [Visual Effects Director of Photography] [2016/Email]

Shyam "Toast" Yadav [Visual Effects Production Assistant] [2023/Email]

Jeff Pyle [Car Model Crew Chief] [2021/Email]

Joey "Deluxe" Enyart [Modeler] [2021/Email]

Larry Jolly [Miniature Helicopter] [2017/Email]

Rick Lazzarini [Hang Glider Puppets] [2016/Email]

Karl Fornander [Gunfire Animation and Compositing] [2021/Email]

Paul Taglianetti [Video Supervisor] [2018/Email]

Nina Saxon [Title Designer] [2017/Email]

Kevin J. Gorman [Director: "Making Of" Documentary] [2019/Email]

Greg Gorman [Portrait Photographer] [2021/Phone]

If you enjoyed this book, consider other titles from

HARKER PRESS
PUBLISHER OF SCARY GOOD BOOKS

THE SOUL OF WES CRAVEN

JOSEPH MADDREY

TRACE HALLOWEEN'S CINEMATIC JOURNEY FROM FIRST STAB TO FINAL CUT

TAKING SHAPE
DEVELOPING HALLOWEEN FROM SCRIPT TO SCREAM

Dustin McNeill
Travis Mullins

Learn more at

HarkerPress.com